INTERNATIONAL LAW
LEGAL RESEARCH

INTERNATIONAL LAW
LEGAL RESEARCH

Anthony S. Winer

Mary Ann E. Archer

Lyonette Louis-Jacques

CAROLINA ACADEMIC PRESS

Durham, North Carolina

Library of Congress Cataloging-in-Publication Data

Winer, Anthony S.
  International law legal research / Anthony S. Winer, Mary Ann E. Archer, and Lyonette Louis-Jacques.
    p. cm.
  Includes bibliographical references and index.
  ISBN 978-1-61163-068-8 (alk. paper)
  1. International law--Legal research. 2. International law--Legal research--Problems, exercises, etc. I. Archer, Mary Ann E. II. Louis-Jacques, Lyonette. III. Title.

  KZ1234.W565 2013
  341.072--dc23

2012038569

CAROLINA ACADEMIC PRESS
700 Kent Street
Durham, North Carolina 27701
Telephone (919) 489-7486
Fax (919) 493-5668
www.cap-press.com

Printed in the United States of America

Summary of Contents

Contents

Series Note

This groundbreaking book on *International Law Legal Research* launches a new legal research series for Carolina Academic Press, following a path similar to its acclaimed series of state legal research guides. Books in the Carolina Academic Press International Legal Research Series will include guides to researching international law generally, guides to common international research areas (such as treaties and other international agreements, or to specific topic areas such as international criminal law), guides to the work of international organizations and tribunals, and guides to researching foreign law of selected jurisdictions or regions (such as the law of Canada, the United Kingdom, or the European Union).

The inaugural volume in this series by Anthony S. Winer, Mary Ann E. Archer, and Lyonette Louis-Jacques is the culmination of years of study, work, and experience. Their collective effort has produced a book that will serve long-overlooked needs for materials focused on how to research international law. Professors teaching international law courses will find this book to be a useful supplemental text that will reinforce substantive international law principles but also empower students to put that knowledge to use in advocacy and scholarship. With this new book, many law schools can now offer formal classes on how to research international law. Students competing in international moot court competitions will treat this book as a secret weapon with the answers to many of their international legal research questions. Editors of international law journals and contributing authors will keep this book close at hand. And law librarians will find themselves recommending the book to patrons with international legal research questions.

This book will also serve private practitioners, in-house counsel, government attorneys, and attorneys at international organizations whose legal work may touch upon international law issues (such as determining the applicability of a treaty, or finding an elusive document from the United Nations). The book includes basic information essential for any professional researcher as well as a great many secrets of cost-effective international legal research. While providing a useful guide for a novice, there is also information here new to even the most experienced researchers. This is an invaluable guide to finding established and emerging rules of international law as well as to understanding the ongoing work of international organizations.

By helping researchers find international law, Anthony S. Winer, Mary Ann E. Archer, and Lyonette Louis-Jacques have also created a tool that may ultimately strengthen the field of international law and lead to more frequent application of its principles. Researchers who can confidently find rules of international law can cite them authoritatively and accurately to tribunals and legislative bodies whose work will be informed by international law. With more frequent citation to international law sources, international law itself becomes more firmly established. The authors of this inaugural volume in international law legal research have made a great start for this series.

Prof. Mark E. Wojcik
The John Marshall Law School—Chicago
Series Editor

Preface

We would like to welcome the reader to *International Law Legal Research*. We designed this book for several audiences, each of which can use it in distinctive ways.

- *For law students enrolled in a doctrinal course in public international law*, this book will provide additional knowledge and technical advice about how to conduct research in the field, to complement your doctrinal curriculum.
- *For law students who have never formally studied public international law*, this book will provide both background knowledge about public international law and practical advice about how to do research in the subject.
- *For competitors in international moot court competitions*, this book will provide advice that will assist your research and preparation.
- *For legal practitioners who are new to the area of public international law*, this book will help you learn how to do research in public international law, and provide the basic doctrinal points necessary to guide early research.

We believe this book is unique in its two-fold approach. First, it contains the essential introductory instruction on how to research public international law. However, it also provides a complete yet concise introduction to the substantive legal concepts underlying the subject area. The combination of these two features should make the book especially useful to each of its audiences.

We believe that this book will be most useful if we address a few important points before beginning the full discussion.

I. Generalized Search Methods: Non-Specific Electronic Search Tools and General Databases

We use the phrase, "non-specific electronic search tools," to refer to Google and other search engines that are not designed specifically for legal research. We use the phrase, "general databases," to refer to Wikipedia and other databases that may contain legally oriented material, but are not designed particularly for legal materials. We sometimes call the combined use of these two tools, "generalized search methods." In our daily lives, many of us use generalized search methods to find books, car repair services, airline flight times, and all manner of other goods, services, and information. The temptation can be to use them to find legal source material as well.

Sometimes that temptation need not be resisted, but in most significant contexts it should be. Generalized search methods can be used legitimately for introductory purposes, but should not be the basis of advice that needs to be relied upon by clients or colleagues.

A. An Example Demonstrating the Frequent Lack of Suitability of Generalized Search Methods

As one example, suppose a researcher needs to learn about the original international treaty limiting the liability of the owner of an ocean cargo ship when cargo is damaged during a violent ocean storm. Suppose that the researcher has no background in the area, but has heard something about "the law of the sea treaty." The researcher might not be sure what this treaty is. But the researcher would like to determine whether the "law of the sea treaty" addresses ship owner liability in any major way.

In such a case, generalized search methods could be used legitimately to get a preliminary view. The researcher might enter "law of the sea treaty" as a search term in a non-specific electronic search tool. Right away there would be at least a bit of confusion, because the researcher would probably discover that there are at least five different treaties that could be called "law of the sea treaties." Four are from 1958 and the fifth is from 1982.[1] A certain amount of background reading, and probably not all of it through generalized search methods, would be necessary to decide which treaty the researcher initially had in mind. The researcher would probably decide that the document envisioned was the 1982 United Nations Convention on the Law of the Sea.[2]

---

1. The five treaties are the 1958 Convention on the Territorial Sea and the Contiguous Zone, the 1958 Convention on the High Seas, the 1958 Convention on Fishing and Conservation of Living Resources, the 1958 Convention on the Continental Shelf, and the 1982 Convention on the Law of the Sea. *See, e.g.,* Malcolm N. Shaw, *International Law* 555 & n.5 (6th ed. 2008) (listing these conventions and indicating that all of them are considered "Conventions on the Law of the Sea").

2. Dec. 10, 1982, 1833 U.N.T.S. 3, 21 I.L.M. 1261 (entered into force Nov. 16, 1994). The United States is not yet a party to this convention.

However, a brief review of the material in any general database would convince the researcher that the 1982 convention does not have much to do with ship owners' liability. The convention chiefly demarcates the territorial sea, and various other regions within the oceans. It does this in order to define the rights of coastal states over the surface of, and the resources in and below, the waters in each type of region.[3] It has relatively little to do with the liabilities of ship owners or other private persons vis-à-vis one another. Linked information for the other four conventions would be similarly unavailing.

So in this example, using generalized search methods did not yield information that was directly useful in addressing the question. But at least the failure to turn up useful information would help narrow the field of subjects for further consultation; the researcher has learned that at least "the law of the sea treaty" does not involve ship owner liability.

Suppose the researcher gets more precise in composing search terms, and next searches "treaty for liability of ship owners for cargo damage." Here again the non-specific electronic search tool will turn up a set of links to material in databases. Some of these links presented now may be more on point than those presented through the first search. They may be headed by phrases like "Charterer's risk of liabilities," "Insurance for ship owner's cargo liability," or a U.S. domestic statute called the "Carriage of Goods by Sea Act." But once again, if the researcher does not have prior background, it will not be immediately clear if these concepts are relevant, which treaty is most directly involved, or how the information at these links might or might not relate to that treaty, whatever it is.

It turns out that, for most contexts involving U.S. nationals, the original international treaty most fundamentally relating to the limitation of ship owner liability is the 1924 International Convention for the Unification of Certain Rules Relating to Bills of Lading.[4] This is often called the "Brussels Convention on Bills of Lading."

And yet this convention would probably not turn up as a link even for the second, more refined, search using generalized search methods. The researcher, not being knowledgeable in the area, would not have searched "bills of lading" or "Brussels Convention," for example. And the link headings retrieved from the terms the researcher *did* search would be unlikely to reference the

---

3. Key provisions of the 1982 convention define and regulate the use of the territorial sea and contiguous zone, straits used for international navigation, the exclusive economic zone, the continental shelf and the high seas. *See id.* parts II, III, V, VI and VII.

4. Aug. 25, 1924, 51 Stat. 233, 120 L.N.T.S. 155, 2 Bevans 430 (entered into force June 2, 1931).

convention. Accordingly, reliance solely on generalized search methods would be problematic even with the more refined search terms. However, the 1924 convention would be more directly retrievable using the traditional and analytical techniques outlined in this book.

So, the main problem with relying only on generalized search methods is *suitability*. Although they can be legitimately used at the early stages of research, they often will not retrieve a useful and relevant final answer. This was the case in our ship owner example: using the most normal search terms and most typical links simply did not get the researcher to the treaty desired. However, even when generalized search methods *do* provide a useful and relevant answer, there are still three more problems with them.

B. Additional Concerns Regarding Generalized Search Methods

The first of these additional problems is *accuracy*. Many websites and general databases are not prepared by the most highly qualified authorities. The information they contain may simply be wrong (or at best inaccurate). Using the official international law sources described in this book will result in a greater assurance of accuracy.

The second problem is *currency*. Even if generalized search methods provide material that is useful, relevant and accurate, it may not be current. Many websites and databases are not updated as often as would be ideal. For example, a given treaty may be found at a website using generalized search methods, and the text of the treaty may have been accurate when it was first uploaded to the site. But the treaty may have since been amended, or denounced by relevant parties. It is quite possible that nothing at the website where the treaty was found, using generalized search methods, will indicate that the treaty has been altered. Again, using the research methods outlined in this book should help assure that the material obtained will be sufficiently current.

The third problem is *authenticity*. Most international treaties and conventions, and most international court decisions and arbitral awards, for example, are best located at particular "official" or "authoritative" sources. And yet many times they can also be found at unofficial, private, commercial or other non-standard sources. It is important to know which sources are official or authoritative for each kind of material. This is for several reasons. First, the official and authoritative sources are more likely to have accurate and current versions of the material. An unofficial source may have posted an earlier draft of a document rather than its final version.

But even beyond accuracy and currency, research is most productive when it uncovers authentic sources. This is because authentic sources are most useful when communicating the research results to others. Unofficial, private, or commercial versions of these materials (such as treaties or arbitral rulings, etc.) may not be readily retrievable to other parties in other places at other times. And certainly, if one is dealing with a particular court or governmental authority, one wants to reference versions that have been officially issued, produced, or catalogued by that court or authority rather than an unofficial, private, or non-standard version. Accordingly, authenticity is usually very important when researching international legal materials.

II. Electronic Versus Print Sources

Even within the realm of official and authoritative sources, material is often available in both electronic and print formats. For example, recent treaties to which the United States is a party can often be found at authoritative sources in both electronic and print formats. One electronic format would often be available through the *United Nations Treaty Collection* electronic database.[5] A print format would usually be available through the volumes of *United States Treaties and Other International Agreements* (usually called "UST").[6]

In this book, we make every effort to describe search and retrieval techniques for both electronic and print versions of source materials, whenever authoritative versions are available in both formats. When the official or authoritative version of a particular type of material is available in only one format (either electronic or print), then we emphasize that format. Depending on the importance of the material, we may also reference unofficial, but usually reliable, versions in the other format. One example involves resolutions by certain bodies of the United Nations (the "UN"). Resolutions of the UN General Assembly and the UN Security Council are authoritatively available at the UN website.[7] We accordingly emphasize working with, and citing from, resolutions at the UN website. However, we also

---

5. Usage of *The United Nations Treaty Collection* database is discussed in detail in part VIII.A of chapter 5 of this book.

6. Usage of UST is discussed in part VII.B.3 of chapter 5 of this book.

7. Usage of the UN website to retrieve General Assembly and Security Council resolutions is discussed in parts IV.B and IV.C of chapter 7 of this book.

discuss the availability of some resolutions at reliable but unofficial print sources, such as the print version of *International Legal Materials* (often called "ILM").[8]

For purposes of citation, it is still preferable to cite a print format first, whenever it is broadly available.[9] For some especially common sources, citation rules require reference to the print version, prohibiting the substitution of an electronic version. (For example, the citation of a treaty that appears in UST generally must include the UST reference, or at least a print reference to *Statutes at Large*.[10] As noted in part III of this prologue, we have adopted the *Bluebook* citation system for this book. The *Bluebook* rules would not permit exclusive citation to an electronic format when the UST text is available.)[11] Similar citation rules can require print texts in other cases as well.

These citation-based concerns are reason enough to be familiar with search-and-retrieval techniques for print materials. However, it is also desirable to be conversant with both print and electronic research techniques for practical reasons. Websites or electronic connections can be subject to disruption, whether through blockage at the site, problems with individual devices, or general service interruptions. Conversely, practical circumstances can sometimes limit access to print resources.

For all these reasons, we have a dual-track approach to research, and offer guidance on both print and electronic research.

III. The *Bluebook* Uniform System of Citation

We emphasize citation rules and practices more than most other books on this subject. This is due to our focus on practicality and usefulness by practitioners and others working in the field.

We have chosen to adhere to *The Bluebook: A Uniform System of Citation*,[12] as compiled by editors of four leading academic law reviews and journals in the

---

8. We also refer briefly to the ILM as a source of information regarding particular UN resolutions in part IV.D of chapter 7 of this book.

9. *E.g., The Bluebook: A Uniform System of Citation* r. 18.2, at 165 (Columbia Law Review Ass'n et al. eds., 19th ed. 2010) ("*The Bluebook* requires the use and citation of traditional printed sources when available, unless there is a digital copy of the source available that is authenticated, official, or an exact copy of the printed source . . . .").

10. *See id.* r. 21.4.5, at 189 (requiring the use of UST or *Statutes at Large* as treaty sources, when they are available).

11. *Id.*

12. *See supra* note 9.

United States. We are mindful that other citation systems can be chosen. However, there are basically three reasons for our choice of the *Bluebook*.

The first is that this citation manual is still frequently used not only in U.S. legal education but also by many international law journals around the world. It is a system familiar to U.S.-trained students and lawyers as well as law journal editors and scholars worldwide. Second, we believe that the *Bluebook* approach to international legal sources, while certainly not ideal, is somewhat more sophisticated than the approaches used in the other more prominent systems.[13] The *Bluebook* specifies the different types of international authorities in detail, and generally provides complete guidance for the citation of each.

Finally, the *Bluebook* also uses a complete and sophisticated approach to legal sources generally, such as domestic cases and statutes. The *Bluebook* is designed so that citation rules from the international context are compatible with, and complement, those in the domestic context.[14] There are still some coverage gaps, and we point these out where they are significant. However, we view the *Bluebook* as being (currently) at least marginally preferable for international law research over other prominent systems.

At press time, the nineteenth edition of the *Bluebook* is current. Citation rules may differ, of course, in the event another edition is consulted or brought into force.

IV. Library Guides

A large number of law libraries have made available electronic research guides on the subject of international law. These guides are generally of high quality and can be very useful. As a rule, we do not reference these guides in this book. This is not to disparage the guides themselves, but simply to recognize that the guides are not independent sources in their own right. They simply guide the way to other materials and sources that (for the most part) we discuss in this book directly. Many law library guides also highlight materials particular to each library, rather than providing an overall guide that could be used in any library.

---

13. As evidenced throughout this book, rule 21 of *The Bluebook* is devoted to "International Materials." It prescribes detailed and distinct treatment, for example, for treaties and conventions (rule 21.2), international law court cases (rule 21.5), international arbitral rulings (rule 21.6), UN materials (rule 21.7), and so on.

14. For example, the *Bluebook* prescriptions for the citation of books (rule 15) and for "Short Citation Forms" (rule 4) dovetail acceptably with normal usage for international materials.

These library guides exist on the public websites of many law libraries. We invite readers who would like to supplement their review of this book to investigate the online research guides prepared by law libraries.

This book does reference, in a few particular contexts, research guides published by certain international organizations and associations (such as the UN and the American Society of International Law, or the "ASIL").[15] We believe that these references are warranted because of the special prominence of these institutions. The UN is of course in a special position to advise on researching UN materials, and the ASIL (along with other national associations around the world) has a significant preeminence and experiential background that makes its observations on certain points especially noteworthy.

V. Authoritative Versus Less Authoritative Sources

In part I of this preface we explained that this book chiefly directs researchers to the most official and authoritative locations for materials involving international law. That discussion was to encourage deliberate searching for authoritative sources as against the use of non-specific electronic search tools and general databases.

We would now like to observe directly that there are many websites, databases, and other (now usually electronic) sources that can contain international legal information. These websites, databases, and other sources are often generated by private persons, groups, and non-governmental organizations ("NGO's") who are commendably committed to certain goals and causes. These websites and databases can be colorful, enjoyable, and dramatic in their presentation of the issues.

We do not want to discourage investigation of these sources, but again we caution readers against using less authoritative materials as the final basis for research. Private persons, groups, and NGO's have distinct interests. While not disparaging the integrity of any particular person, group, or organization, we point out that many of the materials generated in this way fulfill substan-

---

15. We encourage the use of UN research guides in various contexts, especially when researching UN ancillary bodies. *See infra* chapter 9 ("Other UN Materials"), part V. Similarly, we prominently include the ASIL's *"Electronic Resource Guide"* among useful electronic sites for working with treaties and conventions. *See infra* chapter 5 ("Treaties and Conventions"), part VIII.C.

tial public relations and advocacy purposes. They are not necessarily objective, and on occasion they can be incomplete or inaccurate.

At very least, researchers need to be aware that information presented with a view toward maintaining public relations and advocacy positions needs to be viewed with an appropriate degree of circumspection, and even skepticism where warranted. More generally, reliance on the traditional methods and sources outlined in this book will assure that legal source material retrieved is accurate, timely, and authoritative, with minimal danger of opportunistic taint.

VI. Certain Terminology and Usage Points

Finally, we note briefly that in a small number of instances, we have opted for every-day terminology at the expense of traditional usage employed in international legal discourse. We have made these decisions in view of the character of this book as introductory and as based in practical advice. For example, we usually refer to the laws of individual countries as their "domestic law," rather than their "municipal law." We have also made common-sense alterations to what the *Bluebook* would normally require in some situations, although we always point this out explicitly when doing so. For example, we encourage the use of unofficial treaty sources to a greater extent than that specified by the *Bluebook*, in view of the difficulties of access that can be associated with some of the "official" sources.[16]

We hope that readers will understand and appreciate these touches of informality, and wish all our readers a productive and fulfilling experience in the use of this book.

---

16. *See infra* chapter 5 ("Treaties and Conventions"), part XI.

Acknowledgments and Authors' Notes

We would like to thank Professor Mark E. Wojcik of The John Marshall Law School for his encouragement and assistance in reviewing drafts of this book, and Sarah Gibson, for her much appreciated contributions as research assistant. We furthermore thank our students, who have contributed so much to the effectiveness of our endeavors over the years. Finally, we thank the staff at Carolina Academic Press for their excellent work.

We would also like to provide the reader with a brief note of attribution regarding the different aspects of this book. Ms. Louis-Jacques contributed solely the "Additional Resources and General Bibliographic References" for each chapter. Ms. Archer contributed the general inspiration, guidance, and friendship she had provided to us over the years leading up to the preparation of this book. All other features of the preparation, composition, and review of the book were the responsibility of Professor Winer.

INTERNATIONAL LAW
LEGAL RESEARCH

Chapter 1

What Do We Mean When We Say "International Law"?

I. Several Distinct Subjects

Different people can mean different things when they say the phrase, "international law." Several distinct subject areas all masquerade as international law, at least in the minds of many people. When you're researching in this area, it's crucial to keep these different subject areas separate. Obviously, the research strategies and tools you use vary depending on which of these subject areas you are actually researching.

II. Public International Law

Researching public international law is the primary focus of this book. Traditionally, public international law was viewed as the set of legal rules applying to the relations of different countries as they acted among one another.[1] In public international law, what we call "countries" are referred to as "states."[2]

---

1. *E.g.,* James R. Fox, *Dictionary of International and Comparative Law* 267 (3d ed. 2003) (defining "Public International Law" as "law dealing with the relations between states"); *accord,* Rebecca M.M. Wallace & Olga Martin-Ortega, *International Law* 2 (6th ed. 2009) (referring to "the traditional definition of international law" as being "a body of rules governing the relations of independent states in times of peace and war").

2. The Montevideo Convention on the Rights and Duties of States effectively defines a "state" as an entity possessing "(a) a permanent population; (b) a defined territory; (c) government; and (d) capacity to enter into relations with other States." Convention on Rights and Duties of

Under the traditional definition, therefore, public international law involves such matters as: territorial disputes among states, the use of armed force among states, recognition of one state by another, the application of treaty terms to the behavior of states, and many other legal issues affecting states as such. It also involves judicial decisions by international courts, such as the so-called "World Court" in the Netherlands, and other judicial and arbitration bodies that hear disputes among states.[3]

The current view of public international law is somewhat broader than the traditional view. For example, most authorities now include within it issues and disputes involving international organizations.[4] Such international organizations would include the United Nations (the "UN"), the International Atomic Energy Agency, the World Trade Organization, and many other similar bodies. Now in the modern era, private companies and even individuals can sometimes also be subjects of public international law.[5] Instances involving private companies and individuals are still somewhat less common, however. For the most part, public international law still usually involves legal relations and disputes among states, among international organizations, or among states and international organizations.

Although it is most accurate to use the phrase "public international law" when describing legal rules affecting states and international organizations acting among one another, sometimes in this book we will be a bit imprecise. For ease of reading, we will sometimes use the simple phrase "international law" to describe public international law. This abbreviated usage is common in other authorities, as well.[6]

States, art. 1, Dec. 26, 1933, 49 Stat. 3097, 3 Bevans 145, 165 L.N.T.S. 19 (entered into force Dec. 26, 1934).

3. A detailed discussion of the World Court (technically, the "International Court of Justice," or the "ICJ") is included in chapter 6 of this book, on "Judicial and Arbitral Decisions." Introductory discussions of the ICJ also appear in chapters 3 and 4.

4. *E.g.,* Malcolm N. Shaw, *International Law* 2 (6th ed. 2008) ("Public International law covers relations between states in all their myriad forms, from war to satellites, and regulates the operations of the many international institutions.").

5. *E.g.,* Wallace & Martin-Ortega, *supra* note 1, at 2 ("Contemporary international law refers to those rules and norms that regulate the conduct of States and other entities which at any time are recognized as being endowed with international personality, e.g., international organizations and, to a certain extent, individuals, in their relations with each other.").

6. *E.g., id.* at 1 ("The term international law as used throughout the text refers . . . to public international law."); *accord,* Shaw, *supra* note 4, at 1 (stating that "public international law" is "usually just termed international law").

Since in earlier years, public international law related mostly to states and international organizations, the number of lawyers directly involved with it was limited. Most lawyers involved with public international law used to be employed by the foreign-relations offices of national governments. But that is changing now.

With increased globalization, it is becoming more necessary for lawyers who have not previously worked with public international law to become more able to work with it. This book is designed to help them, as well as students and government researchers who would like an introduction to researching in this area.

III. Private International Law as Conflict of Laws

Public international law can be distinguished from private international law. Since tradition viewed public international law as applying only to states, tradition also viewed "private international law" as applying to private persons acting across international borders. In today's world, individuals and companies engage in international activities in a variety of contexts. Examples include international business transactions; marriages in which the different marital partners reside in, or own property in, different states; adoptions by persons living in one state of children from a different state; and many other situations.

The meaning of the phrase "private international law" is a matter of interpretation. According to the traditional meaning, "private international law" is equivalent to "conflict of laws."[7] The phrase "conflict of laws" comes into play whenever a situation arises in which the law of more than one jurisdiction might reasonably be thought to apply.[8] Sometimes this is described as those situations in which a given legal situation contains a significant element foreign to the forum state.[9]

---

7. *E.g.,* Wallace & Martin-Ortega, *supra* note 1, at 1 ("private international law [is better described using] the correct term, conflict of laws"); *accord,* Shaw, *supra* note 4, at 1 (stating that "conflict of laws . . . is sometimes called . . . private international law").

8. *E.g.,* Fox, *supra* note 1, at 66 (defining "conflict of laws" as "rules to help determine whether the courts of a given state will apply their own municipal law or the law of another state in adjudicating a case somehow involving that other state").

9. *E.g., Cheshire, North & Fawcett: Private International Law* 3 (J.J. Fawcett, J.M. Carruthers & P.M. North eds., 14th ed. 2008) ("Private International Law comes into operation whenever the court is seised of a suit that contains a foreign element.").

A. A Hypothetical Illustration of Conflict of Laws Issues

Suppose a Spanish resident drives his car into France, picks up a Portuguese passenger in France, then drives with the passenger through Belgium into the Netherlands. On the way there is an accident in Belgium. At first the parties thought there were no injuries in the accident, but it turns out that after arrival in the Netherlands the passenger detects an injury resulting from the accident in Belgium. If the passenger wants to sue the driver of the car in a court in the Netherlands, which state's law should govern the passenger's relief action against the driver? This is a question of "conflict of laws." It is called this because the question potentially involves the legal systems of several different jurisdictions. (In this case, the legal rules potentially involved would come from Belgium, the Netherlands and (perhaps even) Spain and Portugal.) Deciding which jurisdiction's law should apply to the driver/passenger liability issue can be thought of as putting into "conflict" those legal systems. Such a "conflict" is then resolved by applying the legal rules of one of the jurisdictions to the issues in question.

Each state around the world enforces its own conflict of laws rules.[10] The courts of a state in the Netherlands' position in the example might enforce a rule applying the local law of the state where the injury occurred.[11] On the other hand, the courts of such a state might conceivably enforce a rule applying the law of the forum state when the injured party is located in the forum state and injury was not detected until the party appeared in the forum state. The courts of each state apply that state's conflict of laws rules, which may derive from statutory law, case law, or even treaty obligations,[12] depending on

---

10. Ulrich Drobnig, *Private International Law, in* 3 *Encyclopedia of Public International Law* 1115, 1115 § 1(a) (Rudolf Bernhardt ed., 1997) ("Since every State . . . has its own private international law, there are as many bodies of private international law as there are legal systems.").

11. This is the rule that authoritative sources believe would generally be applied in most U.S. courts. *See* Restatement (Second) of Conflict of Laws § 146 (1971) ("In an action for a personal injury, the local law of the state where the injury occurred determines the rights and liabilities of the parties . . . .").

12. For example, all the states in the above hypothetical are members of the European Union (the "EU"). They are all therefore subject to a regulation promulgated by the EU Parliament and Council, prescribing conflict of laws rules covering this kind of tort. Regulation 864/2007, of the European Parliament and of the Council of 11 July 2007 on the Law Applicable to Non-contractual Obligations (Rome II), 2007 O.J. (L 199) 40. This regulation would probably prescribe the law of Belgium for the example, since the damage occurred in Belgium, and the regulation requires application of "the law of the country in which the damage occurs." *See id.* art. 4(1), at 44.

the legal authorities in each state. It is the different conflict of laws rules such as these, applied by states around the world, that were traditionally called rules of "private international law."

B. Real-World Illustrations of Conflict of Laws Issues

We can find illustrations of international conflict of laws issues in "real world" U.S. case law, as well. In the U.S. Supreme Court, for instance, a 1993 decision featured antitrust claims brought by U.S. plaintiffs complaining about certain practices of defendant insurance companies in London.[13] (The plaintiffs were engaged in business with the London defendants, the plaintiffs said that the defendants' activities in London adversely affected them, and the London defendants did not contest that the U.S. courts had personal jurisdiction over them.[14])

The defendants argued that there was a conflict of laws issue, since (in their view) the U.S. antitrust laws and British law were in conflict.[15] They said that British law clearly permitted the defendants' practices, while the U.S. Sherman Antitrust Act prohibited them.[16] They contended that the Supreme Court should resolve the asserted conflict by heeding British law, rather than applying U.S. law.[17] The Supreme Court recognized that the defendants were asserting the existence of a conflict of laws problem,[18] but the Court's ultimate decision found the defendants' attempted assertion of British law unpersuasive.[19]

Another example would be a Federal Court of Appeals case from 1976.[20] In that case, a group of Hondurans sued a U.S. bank for personal injuries,

---

13. Hartford Fire Ins. Co. v. California, 509 U.S. 764 (1993).

14. *Id.* at 773–79 (detailing the claims by the plaintiffs against the defendants, and describing the allegedly negative consequences of the defendants' acts regarding the plaintiffs); *id.* at 812 (Scalia, J., dissenting) (noting that "personal jurisdiction is not contested").

15. *Id.* at 798 ("The London reinsurers contend that applying the [U.S. Sherman Antitrust] Act to their conduct would conflict significantly with British law . . . .").

16. *Id.* at 798–99 ("They assert that [the British] Parliament has established a comprehensive regulatory regime over the London reinsurance market and that the conduct alleged here was perfectly consistent with British law and policy.").

17. *Id.* at 799.

18. *Id.* at 798 ("The only substantial question in this litigation is whether 'there is in fact a true conflict between domestic and foreign law.'").

19. *Id.* at 799. The Court found that there was no genuine conflict between U.S. and British law. ("No conflict exists, for these purposes, 'where a person subject to regulation by two states can comply with the laws of both.'")(citation omitted).

20. Timberlane Lumber Co. v. Bank of Am., 549 F.2d 597 (9th Cir. 1976).

allegedly suffered at the hands of the bank's agents in Honduras.[21] The Court of Appeals noted implicitly that a conflict of laws issue would arise if the actions brought by the Hondurans were to proceed in the U.S. federal trial court.[22] The Court of Appeals stated its view that a U.S. trial court would need to apply Honduran law in such a case.[23]

It is also worth noting that conflict of laws questions arise domestically within the United States.[24] This can happen whenever a particular dispute concerns persons, things, or events that have meaningful contacts or relationships with more than one U.S. state.[25] The domestic study of conflict of laws within the United States is a separate subject, however, and outside the scope of this book.

C. General Observations

Observe that private international law, viewed as conflict of laws rules, is not a distinct set of substantive rules that directly affect private behavior.[26] Conflict of laws rules don't tell you what the legal rule is that addresses a given issue; they tell you only which state's law to consult in order to find the applicable legal rule. In this sense, private international law is simply a set of rules

---

21. *Id.* at 600–01 & 616.

22. *Id.* at 616 ("The alleged torts took place in Honduras. Most of the witnesses and evidence are apparently based there, as are two of the plaintiffs, and Honduran law would have to be applied.").

23. *Id.*

24. Indeed, the phrase "conflict of laws" might conjure in the minds of most U.S. lawyers primarily the idea of domestic application of conflict of laws rules within the United States. Section 3 of the *Second Restatement of Conflict of Laws* defines "State" as "a territorial unit with a distinct general body of law." Restatement (Second) of Conflict of Laws § 3 (1971). Comment a to this Section provides that "[e]ach State of the United States is a state under the definition. So too, for example, are the District of Columbia, the Commonwealth of Puerto Rico and the Territories of Guam and the Virgin Islands." Although foreign countries would clearly be included within this definition, none is included as an example in Comment a!

25. *See* Eugene F. Scoles, Peter Hay, Patrick J. Borchers & Symeon C. Symeonides, *Conflict of Laws* 1 (4th ed. 2004) ("The term 'Conflict of Laws' describes generally the body of law that aspires to provide solutions to international or interstate legal disputes between persons or entities other than countries or states *as such*. A dispute is considered international or interstate if one or more of its constituent elements is connected with more than one country or state.")(emphasis in original) (citation omitted).

26. *E.g., Cheshire, North & Fawcett: Private International Law, supra* note 9, at 8 ("It must be observed that the function of private international law is complete when it has chosen the appropriate system of law. Its rules do not furnish a direct solution of the dispute . . . .").

that courts and others can use to decide which of various legal systems that might be applicable is in fact applicable to a given legal situation.

Traditional research in conflict of laws rules is beyond the scope of this book. However, more modern notions of private international law have developed in recent years. The methods described in this book will be very useful in researching private international law, as that topic is understood in its more modern, expansive sense.

IV. Additional Modern Concepts of Private International Law

Some significant modern authorities expand on what is considered "private international law." For example, a more modern view of private international law considers it as all the treaties and other legal rules that pertain to the activities of private persons across national boundaries.[27] This modern view sees private international law as going beyond mere conflict of laws. Instead, it includes substantive principles and legal rules that actually regulate the international behavior of private parties.[28]

Different kinds of legal documents and authorities can be the sources of these kinds of rules regulating international behavior of private parties. They can come from treaties and conventions entered into by states, from the domestic legislation of states, and from other sources. Among these are an international organization called "The Hague Conference on Private International Law" and completely private organizations. Accordingly, when we look at private international law in the modern, expansive sense of the phrase, we find its content in many sources. We will look at some of them in turn.

---

27. Louise Tsang, *Private International Law*, American Society of International Law Electronic Resource Guide, www.asil.org/erg/?page=pil (last updated June 21, 2001) ("Private international law is the body of conventions, model laws, national laws, legal guides, and other documents and instruments that regulate private relationships across national borders.").

28. *E.g.*, David P. Stewart, *Private International Law: A Dynamic and Developing Field*, 30 U. Pa. J. Int'l L. 1121, 1123 (2009) ("[P]rivate international law instruments . . . regulate relationships between private parties, and provide . . . rules for the resolution of disputes arising from those relationships . . . .").

A. Treaties and Conventions that Apply Directly to Private Behavior

We noted earlier that under the traditional view, public international law involved only matters among states, or states and international organizations. We also said that in more recent years, rules of public international law sometimes now apply to private persons, like companies or individuals.

An example of this latter situation is a treaty or convention among states (thus a rule of public international law) that directly mandates certain behavior by private persons within the states that are parties to the treaty or convention. A treaty or convention that does this is both an example of public international law (since it is an agreement among states), and an example of private international law (to the extent it regulates the international conduct of private parties).

One example is the UN Convention on Contracts for the International Sale of Goods,[29] often called the "CISG Convention." This Convention provides rules for the enforcement of contracts that private parties enter into for the sale of goods across national borders. Any time a private person enters into a sales contract for goods with a buyer or seller in another state, and one or both states involved are parties to the CISG Convention, the Convention's rules may apply to the transaction, rather than the domestic law of either state.[30] In any such case, the CISG Convention will be directly affecting the rights and responsibilities of private parties, and in the modern expansive sense, will be a rule of private international law.

Treaties and conventions like this are not numerous, but they do exist and their number is growing. This is part of why it might be said that the distinction between public international law and private international law is weakening in the modern era.[31] But, once again, the number of such treaties is small, and most commentators and other authorities still make the fundamental distinction between public and private international law.

---

29. Apr. 11, 1980, 1489 U.N.T.S. 3, 19 I.L.M. 668 (entered into force Jan. 1, 1988).

30. *See id.* art. 1(1) (stating its applicability to contracts of sale of goods between parties whose places of business are in different states, when the states are contracting parties to the CISG Convention, or when "the rules of private international law lead to the application of the law" of a contracting party to the CISG Convention). Under a reservation entered into by the United States, the CISG Convention applies to contracts involving a U.S. party only when both parties to the contract are in states that are contracting states under the Convention.

31. Shaw, *supra* note 4, at 43–49 (discussing the expansion of the scope of modern public international law to include individuals, groups, and public and private organizations).

B. The Hague Conference on Private International Law

In 1955, fifteen European states and Japan entered into a convention that established a permanent organization called "The Hague Conference on Private International Law" (sometimes simply called the "Hague Conference").[32] Since that time, over 50 other states (including the United States) have become members of the Hague Conference.[33] The purpose of the organization is to "work for the progressive unification of the rules of private international law."[34] As we noted above, traditionally the authorities of each state developed that state's own conflict of laws rules. So, private international law, in the sense of being the same thing as conflict of laws, was different in each state.

The Hague Conference drafts conventions that prescribe the same conflict of laws rules, for particular legal topics, for every state party to each convention. (Each such state is called a "contracting party" to each such convention.) The goal is uniformity of conflict of laws rules among all the contracting parties to each convention the Hague Conference prepares.

For example, in 1970, the Hague Conference prepared a Convention on the Recognition of Divorces and Legal Separations.[35] Each contracting party to that convention agrees generally to recognize divorces and legal separations obtained in all other contracting parties, under specified conditions. As another example, the Hague Conference also prepared a 1973 Convention on the Law Applicable to Products Liability,[36] under which each contracting party, when its courts are considering the liability of manufacturers for damages caused by products, agrees to apply the law of the state of the place of injury.

Conventions prepared by the Hague Conference address issues of conflict of laws, and thus involve private international law in the traditional sense. However, as time goes on, Hague Conference conventions are also addressing the rights and responsibilities of private individuals directly.

One example is the 2000 Convention on the International Protection of Adults,[37] involving the protection of incapacitated and otherwise vulnerable

---

32. *See* Statute of the Hague Conference on Private International Law, Oct. 9–31, 1951, 220 U.N.T.S. 121 [hereinafter Hague Conference Statute] (entered into force July 15, 1955) (the preamble clauses indicate the original signatories).

33. *See Status Table*, Hague Conference on Private Int'l Law, http://www.hcch.net/index _en.php?act=conventions.status&cid=29 (last updated Nov. 18, 2011).

34. Hague Conference Statute, *supra* note 32, at art. 1.

35. June 1, 1970, 978 U.N.T.S. 393 (entered into force Aug. 24, 1975).

36. Oct. 2, 1973, 1056 U.N.T.S. 187 (entered into force Oct. 1, 1977).

37. Jan. 13, 2000, 39 I.L.M. 7 (2000) (entered into force Jan. 1, 2009).

adults in international contexts. Much of the Convention unifies conflict of laws rules. However, the Convention also gives potential effect to the written requests of individual adults who wish to be under the protection of a state other than the one in which they may be present. Thus, the Convention can directly affect the legal rights of private individuals, and is in that sense an example of the expanding nature of private international law.

The Hague Conference is thus both an important monitor and facilitator for the unification of conflict of laws rules (that is, traditional private international law), and one of the engines of the expansion of private international law into legal rules directly affecting private persons acting internationally.

C. Domestic Statutes

Many domestic statutes directly affect the behavior of private parties acting across borders. Under the more modern, expansive definition, these statutes would come within private international law as well. In the United States, a dramatic example is the Foreign Corrupt Practices Act (often referenced as the "FCPA").[38] Broadly speaking, the FCPA criminalizes the making of corrupt payments by any U.S. company or its representatives to any foreign government official for any corrupt purpose. The U.S. government takes FCPA violations very seriously, and the statute allows for fines of up to $2 million and imprisonment of individual violators for up to five years.[39]

The FCPA was originally passed in 1977, and was an indirect inspiration for several later international agreements addressing corruption.[40] It is a primary example of how domestic statutory laws can affect the international behavior of individuals. In this sense, it can be legitimate to refer to domestic statutes like the FCPA as examples of "private international law."[41]

---

38. Pub. L. No. 95-213, 91 Stat. 1494 (1977) (codified as amended principally at 15 U.S.C. §§ 78m(b), 78dd-1 to 78-dd3 & 78ff (2006 & Supp. 2009)).

39. *E.g.,* 15 U.S.C. § 78dd-2(g) (1998).

40. Among these are the Convention on Combating Bribery of Foreign Public Officials in International Business Transactions, Nov. 21, 1997, 37 I.L.M. 1 (1998) (entered into force Feb. 15, 1999), and the United Nations Convention Against Corruption, Oct. 21, 2003, 2349 U.N.T.S. 41 (entered into force Dec. 14, 2005).

41. The discussion in the text of domestic statutes as private international law focuses on a particular U.S. statute, the FCPA. The domestic statutes of other states can also affect, or even constitute, private international law. For example, if one is located in a particular non-U.S. state, that state's domestic law might prohibit or require individual behavior of a certain kind across its international boundaries with other states. Any such laws would at least affect, or perhaps constitute, private international law, conceived in its more expansive sense. For guidance on researching the domestic laws of non-U.S. states, see part

D. Private Sources

In a small number of contexts, groups that are completely private and non-governmental in character can have a significant role in creating private international law, in the more modern and expansive sense.

A significant example of such a group is the International Chamber of Commerce, located in Paris. Most prominently, it has published for many years the *Uniform Customs and Practice for Documentary Credits* (often called the "UCP").[42] This is a collection of rules for the interpretation and enforcement of letters of credit, a kind of international financial instrument issued by banks around the world.

The International Chamber of Commerce is a completely private organization, unaffiliated with any government, yet the UCP virtually has the effect of law. Its terms are incorporated by reference in a large majority of letters of credit issued by international banks. As such, the UCP's rules become contractual terms for the letters of credit, and have been regularly enforced by domestic courts. Since the UCP's rules thus become legally binding on the banks and their customers in many internatonal transactions, the UCP can readily be viewed as a set of private international law rules, at least in the modern, expansive sense of "private international law."

Another example of a private organization with substantial influence in formulating private international law is the Institut de droit international (or the "IDI," sometimes known by its English name, the "Institute of International Law").[43] The IDI is currently headquartered in Belgium. It regularly formulates proposed rules of international law, including private international law. We will have much more to say about the IDI in chapter 10 of this book.

E. Researching Private International Law

The best method of researching any area of private international law will depend on the type of source one is consulting. If one is consulting treaties

---

V of this chapter, and especially note 44, *infra*. Note also that researchers can contact the Law Library of the Library of Congress for assistance in locating official websites for national laws.

42. The current version of the UCP has the serial number "UCP 600," and was published in 2006, with revisions issued in 2007. *ICC Uniform Customs and Practice for Documentary Credits: UCP 600* (2006 ed. & 2007 rev.), *available at* http://www.iccbooks.com/Product/CategoryInfo.aspx?cid=95 (last visited June 7, 2013).

43. *Institut de droit international*, http://www.idi-iil.org/ (last updated Dec. 1, 2009).

or conventions, then the methods outlined in this book for researching treaties and conventions will be helpful. If one is consulting domestic statutes, one will need to use the research methods applicable to the particular domestic jurisdictions involved. Research regarding the Hague Conference, and private groups such as the IDI, will be addressed in chapter 10 of this book.

V. Foreign Law: Proceed with Caution!

Foreign law is the law of any jurisdiction which is not the home jurisdiction of the speaker or writer using the phrase. If you are a U.S. lawyer practicing law in the United States, the law of France would be "foreign law" to you. Conversely, if you were a French lawyer practicing only French law in France, the law of the United States would be "foreign law" to you.[44]

Note the distinction between public international law and foreign law. The first generally has to do with the law that operates externally on all states. The second is the domestic law of a particular jurisdiction, other than the home jurisdiction of the person using the phrase.

This distinction is sometimes lost on lawyers in the United States who, having experienced the first part of their careers only with U.S. clients, begin seeing clients or issues touching on foreign countries. Sometimes such lawyers can assume that, with a foreign person or foreign feature involved, public international law will become relevant. However, it is often true that the presence of the foreign client or foreign feature does not entail any issues of public international law, and that only issues of a particular foreign law are presented.

---

44. Many websites provide access to the statute and other written law of foreign jurisdictions. For the reasons indicated in the text, lawyers using these websites should exercise utmost caution. Among such websites are:

    (a) Yale Law School Country-by-Country Guide to Foreign Law Research, http://m-library.law.yale.edu/country_guide;

    (b) Harvard Law School Library Research Guide Web Resources for International, Foreign and Comparative Law; http://www.law.harvard.edu/library/research/guides/int_foreign/web-resources/foreign-law_a.html;

    (c) The World Law Guide, http://www.lexadin.nl/wlg;

    (d) World Legal Information Institute, http://www.worldlii.org/;

    (e) Globalex, maintained at New York University, http://www.nyulawglobal.org/Globalex/; and

    (f) Foreign Law Guide, http://www.foreignlawguide.com/.

Researchers can also contact the Law Library of the Library of Congress for assistance in locating official websites for national laws: http://www.loc.gov/law. *See* note 41, *supra*.

In such a circumstance, the rules of conflict of laws should first be consulted to determine whether U.S. law applies to the matter or some other law. If the conflict of laws rules point to U.S. law, it is possible that there is no international issue at all.

If the conflict of laws rules point to the law of a foreign jurisdiction, then the issue is still not really an international law issue; it is instead an issue of "foreign law." That is, since the conflict of laws rules point to the law of a foreign jurisdiction, the question becomes how that jurisdiction's law resolves the issue. This is a question of the domestic law of that jurisdiction, not a question of international law.

When it is clear that the laws of a foreign jurisdiction apply to all or part of a matter on which a U.S. lawyer is working, that U.S. lawyer must be very careful! Most lawyers who practice law in the United States are licensed to practice law only in the state in which they do most of their work. On occasion, a U.S. lawyer will be admitted to practice in more than one state. It is even rarer, however, for a U.S. lawyer to be licensed to practice both in the state of the lawyer's location and a foreign country. There are some people who do attain such combinations of qualifications, but not many.

Remember that it can be a violation of ethical standards, and even a violation of law, to hold one's self out as an expert on the law of a particular jurisdiction if one has not legally qualified to do so. U.S. lawyers should generally not formally give advice about the law of a foreign jurisdiction unless they are licensed to practice law in that jurisdiction.

The usual method of operation in such cases is that when a U.S. lawyer or law firm has a client whose matters begin to involve foreign law, the U.S. lawyer or law firm engages a licensed lawyer from that foreign jurisdiction to serve as co-counsel. This must be done with full explanation in advance to the client, and with the client's consent, of course, understanding that the use of the additional co-counsel can involve additional time and expense.

On the other hand, the mere observation that a particular issue is probably governed by the law of a particular foreign jurisdiction should not generally require the engagement of foreign co-counsel. Accordingly, assuming that issues of language and availability of sources do not present problems, a U.S. lawyer can sometimes permissibly do basic research in a foreign law simply to confirm that the foreign law would apply and that it would address the issues involved. But as soon as it becomes clear that the client's issues cannot be resolved without addressing substantive issues of foreign law, foreign co-counsel should usually be obtained.

By contrast, it is generally not required, as a matter of law or ethics, for a U.S. lawyer to obtain co-counsel if issues of public international law are raised.

As a practical matter, a U.S. lawyer may need to become more familiar with the international law issues involved to provide adequate representation. But in terms of formal ethical and legal requirements, this is normally assumed to be within the U.S. lawyer's area of capability.

VI. Comparative Law

Comparative law is not a separate body of law. Rather, it is the academic study of comparing different national legal systems, or parts of them, against each other.[45] For example, if a student or professor were to study the federal bankruptcy law of the United States, and compare it with the bankruptcy law of Japan, that would be an exercise in "comparative law." Similarly, a study of the federal antitrust law of the United States, which compares it to the "competition law" enforced by the European Union, would also be an exercise in comparative law.

If one is undertaking a comparative law project, one is generally not researching international law. Instead, one is researching the two (or more) national legal systems being compared. Doing research for a project in comparative law will generally involve the same techniques as researching foreign law, since presumably at least one of the legal systems involved is foreign. (And sometimes they all will be foreign to the person doing the research.)

Some studies in comparative law contrast differing national legal systems, or differing groups of national legal systems, as a whole. These studies can be called "macro-comparisons."[46] Other studies in comparative law contrast particular legal institutions or subject areas across national boundaries. These studies can be called "micro-comparisons."[47]

VII. Chapter Summary

Different people can mean very different things when they use the phrase, "international law." Sometimes the phrase is meant to refer to "public inter-

---

45. Jan Kropholler, *Comparative Law, Funtion and Methods*, *in* 1 *Encyclopedia of Public International Law* 702, 702 § 1 (Rudolf Bernhardt ed., 1992) ("Comparative law should be understood as the juxtapositioning and relating of entire legal systems or individual parts of them.").

46. *Id.*

47. *Id.*

national law." This is the law of states acting in the international arena vis-à-vis one another. In the modern world, it can also involve the activities of international organizations, acting either among themselves, or with states. It can involve territorial disputes among states, the use of armed force among states, recognition of one state by another, the application of treaty terms to the behavior of states, and any other legal issues affecting states as such. It can also involve decisions by judicial and arbitration bodies that hear disputes among states. Researching in this area is the major focus of this book. For ease of reading, this book will on occasion use the shorter term "international law" to refer to public international law, and this is a usage often followed by other authorities. However, the reader should keep in mind in these cases that the intended reference is to public international law.

Sometimes the phrase "international law" can include a reference to "private international law." This term, in turn, can have a variety of meanings. Under the traditional meaning, private international law is equivalent to "conflict of laws." Under a more modern and expansive view, private international law covers all legal rules that regulate private relationships across national borders. These rules are sometimes found in treaties or conventions. They can also be found in conventions prepared by the Hague Conference on Private International Law, in the domestic law of various states (such as the Foreign Corrupt Practices Act in the United States), and in certain rules prepared by private groups (such as the UCP for letters of credit, issued by the International Chamber of Commerce).

Sometimes people confuse international law, whether public or private, with "foreign law." When any person refers to "foreign law," what is meant is the law of a jurisdiction other than the home jurisdiction of the person speaking. Foreign law is simply the domestic law of a jurisdiction other than one's own. It is not "international law," per se, although it often becomes of interest to researchers when they are working internationally.

Finally, "comparative law" is a type of academic study that compares different areas of domestic law between different states. Some comparative studies contrast entire legal systems, and can be considered "macro-comparisons." Others contrast individual legal institutions or subject areas across borders, and can be considered "micro-comparisons."

VIII. Chapter Review Questions

1. What is meant by the phrase, "public international law"?
2. What is the traditional meaning of "private international law"?
3. In what type of situation might an issue involving "conflict of laws" come into play?
4. What are four kinds of legal authority that can be sources of "private international law" rules, in the modern sense of the term?
5. What is the difference between "foreign law" and "international law"?
6. Why do most researchers need to be careful when an issue of foreign law is presented?
7. What are two different major kinds of comparative law studies?

IX. Additional Resources and General Bibliographic References

Anthony Aust, *Handbook of International Law* (2d ed., Cambridge University Press 2010).

David J. Bederman, *International Law Frameworks* (3d ed., Foundation Press 2010)(Concepts and Insights Series).

Brierly's Law of Nations (Andrew Clapham ed., 7th ed., Oxford University Press 2012).

Brownlie's Principles of Public International Law (James Crawford ed., 8th ed., Oxford University Press 2012).

Thomas Buergenthal & Sean D. Murphy, *Public International Law in a Nutshell* (4th ed., West Group 2007).

Mark W. Janis, *International Law* (6th ed., Wolters Kluwer Law and Business 2012).

Robert Y. Jennings, *What Is International* Law *and How Do We Tell It When We See It?*, 37 Swiss Y.B. Int'l L. 59 (1981). This source is also commonly referred to by its German title: *Schweizerisches Jahrbuch für Internationales Recht*.

Robert Jennings & Arthur Watts, *Oppenheim's International Law* (9th ed., London: Longman's 1992).

Martti Koskenniemi, "What Is International Law For?," in *International Law* 89 (Malcolm D. Evans ed., 3d ed., Oxford University Press 2010).

Peter Malanczuk, *Akehurst's Modern Introduction to International Law* (7th rev.

ed., Routledge 1997).

Stephen C. McCaffrey, *Understanding International Law* (LexisNexis 2006).

Sean D. Murphy, *Principles of International Law* (Thomson/West 2006)(Concise Hornbook Series).

John M. Rogers, *International Law and United States Law* (Ashgate 1999).

Oscar Schachter, *International Law in Theory and Practice* (Martinus Nijhoff Publishers 1991).

Georg Schwarzenberger & E.D. Brown, *A Manual of International Law* (6th ed., F.B. Rothman 1976).

Malcolm N. Shaw, *International Law* (6th ed., Cambridge University Press 2008).

Max Sørensen, *Manual of Public International Law* (St. Martin's Press 1968).

J.G. Starke, *Introduction to International Law* (10th ed., Butterworths 1989)(*see also* I.A. Shearer, *Starke's International Law* (11th ed., Butterworths 1994)).

Phillip R. Trimble, *International Law: United States Foreign Relations Law* (Foundation Press 2002)(Turning Point Series).

Rebecca M.M. Wallace & Olga Martin-Ortega, *International Law* (6th ed., Sweet & Maxwell/Thomson Reuters 2009).

Rüdiger Wolfrum, *The Max Planck Encyclopedia of Public International Law* (Oxford University Press 2012)(10 volumes), *available at* http://www.mpepil.com/home.

Chapter 2

Historical Introduction

I. Reasons for Looking at History

In chapter 4, we will review the basic sources of modern international law. Each of these sources has deep historical roots. Understanding their historical background will help us appreciate these sources.

It is not so much that modern practitioners and commentators rely directly on the history of international law. (Although they sometimes do.) Rather, knowledge of the historical development of international law can guide practitioners to use its modern forms most effectively.

II. Classical Greece

During much of the classical period in Greece, the different city-states (such as Athens, Thebes, and Sparta) engaged in relations with each other that were sometimes peaceful and sometimes warlike. As a result, their mutual interactions included alliances, truces, and other arrangements. These arrangements can seem to modern eyes to be forerunners of today's international law.[1] And indeed, some activities in classical Greek history may have served as models

---

1. Wolfgang Preiser, *History of the Law of Nations: Ancient Times to 1648*, in 2 *Encyclopedia of Public International Law* 722, 724 § B.2 (Rudolf Bernhardt ed., 1995) ("International legal relations within the ancient Greek world existed . . . at the latest by the end of the seventh or the beginning of the sixth century B.C.").

for some later developments.[2] However, certain aspects of classical Greece prevent these activities from being exact precursors to the modern system.

For example, most of the formal agreements engaged in during this period were among the Greek city-states themselves,[3] rather than with other powers outside the Greek ambit. There was a strong cultural identification among the city-states, and on the whole the Greeks considered non-Greeks to be barbarians, designated by nature as inferior to the Greeks.[4] Agreements among different Greek city-states would thus not have been viewed as "international" in the modern sense. While there were agreements between Greek and non-Greek powers,[5] the range of foreign powers with whom binding agreements could be entered into was limited.[6]

Also, sometimes conflicts between the city-states resulted in arbitration.[7] But some authorities view such instances to have been tools of political maneuvering rather than genuine attempts to resolve legitimate differences between equal

---

2. *Id.* at 725 § B.2 (referencing the "importance" that the constitutions of the ancient Greek "amphictyonies [international associations among the Greek city-states] had on the development of the laws of war").

3. *Id.* ("The lively contacts between the Greek City-States . . . gave rise to a considerable number of institutions of international law."); *see also* Baron S.A. Korff, *An Introduction to the History of International Law*, 18 Am. J. Int'l L. 246, 250 (1924) ("The exchange of commercial goods and products was always intense among Greek cities. . . . This led to the establishment of all sorts of legal institutions for the protection of foreigners . . . .").

4. Arthur Nussbaum, *A Concise History of the Law of Nations* 5 (rev. ed. 1954). *See also* Marcellus Donald A.R. von Redlich, *The Law of Nations* 1, 1–2 (2d ed. 1937) ("There was a law regulating the mutual relations of the Greek City-States which did not govern the relations between Greeks and Barbarians. The Greeks did not work out any scientific system of International Law."); *id.* at 39 (to the same effect); Korff, *supra* note 3, at 248 ("Surrounded by 'barbarians,' neither Greece nor Rome could acknowledge the principle of equality . . . ."). Prieser is less extreme. Preiser, *supra* note 1, at 724–25 § B.2 (maintaining on the one hand that during the classical period the Greek city-states were "treating subjects of other Greek States in exactly the same way as non-Greeks," while on the other hand allowing that "the Greeks, because of their literary spokesmen, both philosophers and tragedians, were no longer prepared, after the Persian Wars at any rate, to regard barbarians (non-Greeks) as legal subjects of equal rank").

5. Preiser, *supra* note 1, at 725 § B.2 ("The number of peace treaties and alliances concluded between Greek and non-Greek powers is large.").

6. *Id.* at 724 § B.2 (referencing the "undeniably small scale of all the relationships").

7. *Id.* at 725 § B.2 (referencing arbitration as an "institution of international law" engaged in by the Greek city-states, and noting that "[m]ilitary conflict was, as a rule, preceded by an attempt to settle the dispute by arbitration"); Korff, *supra* note 3, at 251 ("With the idea of [Greek] federation there came a better understanding of another institution, that of arbitration.").

parties.[8] And during the conduct of armed conflict, forces of one city-state might show particular clemency or restraint to those of another. On the one hand, these were more acts of grace, rather than the application of anything considered a legal obligation.[9] On the other hand, there may have been a budding awareness of general moral obligations not to engage in certain behaviors in war.[10]

While behavior in classical Greece provided examples for later behaviors, the rules observed by the city-states did not exhibit an awareness of supranational relations in the modern sense. They stemmed at least partly from the desire for cultural and ethnic unity among Greeks, while still allowing for some relations with non-Greeks.[11]

III. Classical Rome

Roman law was one of the key features of Roman civilization. Its initial renown stemmed from the civil law, or *jus civile*, originally developed under the emperor Justinian.[12] This *jus civile*, however, only applied to legal issues that developed among Roman citizens.[13] Over time, more foreigners interacted with Rome and became part of communities in the Roman Empire.[14] The Roman authorities

---

8. Nussbaum, *supra* note 4, at 7 (detecting "scarcely half a dozen authentic instances of arbitration scattered over two centuries"); *id.* at 8 ("[A]rbitration was now a kind of administrative machinery in the hands of the . . . ruler—a form of statecraft concealing the use of what amounted to coercive authority.").

9. *Id.* at 9 ("[T]here are many reports on acts of restraint and clemency in inter-Greek armed contests. But it is difficult to discover lawlike rules of warfare.").

10. von Redlich, *supra* note 4, at 39 ("This law of the Hellenes to some extent regulated and mitigated the conduct of warfare between Greeks. . . . The Greeks appear to have had some very indefinite ideas to the effect that certain methods of warfare could not be employed, even in their conflicts against the Barbarians, since they were in conflict with 'the laws of all mankind.' ").

11. Nussbaum, *supra* note 4, at 9 ("In no way were . . . the rules observed in the relations among the ancient Greek states . . . related to a broad conception of a family of nations. They were simply the expression of racial and cultural unity."). *But see* Preiser, *supra* note 1, at 724 § B.2 (observing that the "Greeks never formed a single nation in the political sense" while acknowledging, and limiting the significance of, "their consciousness of their cultural unity").

12. Nussbaum, *supra* note 4, at 10 (characterizing Roman private law as "compiled and handed down to posterity by the *Corpus juris civilis* of the Byzantine emperor Justinian (A.D. 527–565)").

13. Peter Stein, *Roman Law in European History* 12 (1999) ("Where one or both of the parties was not a citizen, it was inappropriate to apply the traditional civil law to their disputes.").

14. *Id.* ("After the Roman victory over the Carthaginians in the Punic Wars of the third

developed the *jus gentium*, which they applied to disputes arising between a Roman and an alien, or between aliens.[15] The *jus gentium* was supposed to represent all the best common features of any legal system that could be reasonably devised by human societies, at least as the Roman authorities of the time might have conceived of such features.[16]

Gradually the *jus gentium* became more progressive and more desirable as a legal system than the *jus civile* itself.[17] Roman authorities began to apply elements of the *jus gentium* even to legal issues only involving Roman citizens. Ultimately, *jus gentium* became the primarily applicable Roman law.[18] With this development, the phrase *jus gentium* attained a fundamental ambiguity. On the one hand, it referred to the practical set of legal rules actually used to resolve legal issues between private parties in Rome.[19] On the other hand, it also could refer to the philosophical precepts underlying the process by which the rules were established. That is, it could still refer to the philosophical ideas underlying the "best common features of any legal system that could reasonably be devised by human societies."[20]

---

century, Roman rule extended over the whole of the western Mediterranean and the number of non-citizens . . . in daily contact with Romans increased to such an extent that they had to be brought expressly within the ambit of the law.").

15. von Redlich, *supra* note 4, at 40.

16. *Id.* (The *jus gentium* "was supposed to contain all that was common to, or best in, the various legal systems of the ancient world."). *Accord* Nussbaum, *supra* note 4, at 14 (the *jus gentium* could be viewed as "the law established among all men . . . by natural reason and observed as it were by all nations"). *See also Brierly's Law of Nations* 16 (Andrew Clapham ed., 7th ed. 2012) (the *jus gentium* "was believed or feigned to be of universal application; its principles being regarded as so simple and reasonable that they must be recognized everywhere and by everyone"); Stein, *supra* note 13, at 12–13 (referencing certain "institutions of Roman law . . . which were considered to be found in the laws of all civilized people," which "collectively formed what the Romans called the *ius gentium*").

17. *See Brierly's Law of Nations, supra* note 16, at 16 ("[T]he process of expansion and adaptation took the form of admitting, side by side with the *jus civile*, or original law peculiar to Rome, a more liberal and progressive element, the *jus gentium* . . . .").

18. Nussbaum, *supra* note 4, at 13–14 ("Gradually the new liberal body of rules was extended to litigation between Roman citizens and became, as the *jus gentium*—in contradistinction to the *jus civile* of old—the core of what we consider today as the classical Roman law."); *see also* Korff, *supra* note 3, at 254 ("The Roman *jus gentium* acquired . . . important general human elements, becoming more flexible and of wider scope than the rigid civil law.").

19. Nussbaum, *supra* note 4, at 14 (emphasizing the extent to which *jus gentium* "consists of private law"); *see also* von Redlich, *supra* note 4, at 40 (emphasizing the character of *jus gentium* as "a system of private law").

20. *See* Nussbaum, *supra* note 4, at 14 (But the *jus gentium* can also be viewed as "the

As a separate matter, the Roman legal framework also involved an idea of natural law, or *jus naturae*, a very broad concept relating to how the world worked as a matter of natural physical reality.[21] But for those to whom the philosophical *jus gentium* was especially meaningful, *jus gentium* could be seen as an aspect of the general law of nature, or *jus naturae*.[22] Indeed, over time, the philosophical interpretation of *jus gentium* came, at least in the minds of some, to be synonymous with natural law.[23]

This philosophical interpretation of *jus gentium*, sometimes conflated with ideas of natural law, later began to serve as the basis for the development of a "law of nations."[24] After all, as human societies became aware of larger and larger numbers of other societies existing, one way of addressing the need to deal with legal problems across societal boundaries was by trying to arrive at the "best common features of any legal system that could reasonably be devised by human societies."

IV. The Middle Ages

The Middle Ages saw the increasing development of certain aspects of international relations that had strong legal components. For example, there were ample quantities of formal written agreements between different polities,[25] arbitration continued in its evolutionary path,[26] and the practice of permanent diplomatic presence was being strongly developed.[27] At the same time, there

---

law established among all men . . . by natural reason and observed as it were by all nations.").

21. Nussbaum, *supra* note 4, at 15; *see also* Stein, *supra* note 13, at 13 (noting that the *jus gentium*, as a forerunner to the "law of nations," and the developing "natural law," were "similar").

22. *See id.* at 14 (stating that the philosophical *jus gentium*, since it was the set of rules that are "established among all men by natural reason and observed . . . by all nations," could be viewed as an element or aspect of *jus naturae*).

23. *Brierly's Law of Nations*, *supra* note 16, at 17. *Accord, id.* ("[F]or rules which were everywhere observed, i.e. *jus gentium*, must surely be rules which the rational nature of man prescribes to him, i.e. *jus naturale*, and vice versa.").

24. *Id.* at 22 ("The grandest [sic] function of the law of nature was discharged in giving birth to modern international law." (quoting Henry Maine, *Ancient Law* 99 (1920), who reads "greatest function")).

25. Korff, *supra* note 3, at 256, 257 (referencing maritime codes such as the "Tables of Amalfi" and the Venetian Code of 1255); Preiser, *supra* note 1, at 734 § D (asserting that the "law of international agreements of the period contained genuine international law").

26. *E.g.*, Preiser, *supra* note 1, at 737 § E (stating that, toward the latter part of the Middle Ages, "the use of arbitration [was] firmly established in wide areas of the law").

27. *Id.* at 737–78 § E (noting that "the 15th century saw the beginning of the practice of

were also major influences that tended to prevent these developments from creating a system truly similar to the current framework of international law.

For example, the Roman Catholic Church and the Papacy had extensive reach throughout what was then the Christian world,[28] and in many respects were able to exercise dominance over authorities who held political power.[29] The Church developed a unified and detailed system of canon law, applicable wherever the Church held authority.[30] Canon law was "supranational" in character, that is, "above" the concept of nations or polities.[31] So, even if cohesive nations or states (in the modern sense) had existed at the time, the canon law of the period would not have been the equivalent of modern international law.

But also to the point, cohesive autonomous and completely sovereign states, in the modern sense, did not really exist through much of the Middle Ages.[32] On the one hand, the Church and the Papacy had a significant role in assuring that regional political powers did not develop complete sovereignty on their own.[33] On the other hand, a similar constraining role was played by the dominant political authority of the time, the Holy Roman Empire.[34]

---

permanent diplomatic missions" and emphasizing their "almost revolutionary character"); *see also* Korff, *supra* note 3, at 258 ("[G]radually and imperceptibly there grew up in the Middle Ages an entirely new system of permanent diplomatic missions.").

28. Korff, *supra* note 3, at 255 (noting "the claim of the Popes to the right to depose the Emperors" and their claimed right "to absolve the subjects of their oath of allegiance to the Emperor, in case the latter was in opposition to the church").

29. *Id.* at 256 ("Toward the end of the [early Middle Ages], the supremacy of the Popes became unquestionable."). Some authorities view the Church as having been a strong impediment to the development of international law. *E.g.,* Nussbaum, *supra* note 4, at 22 (asserting that canon law was an influence that worked toward the counteracting of any evolution of international law). *See also Brierly's Law of Nations, supra* note 16, at 4 ("[One of the influences] which retarded the growth of states in the Middle Ages was the Church.").

30. Nussbaum, *supra* note 4, at 17 ("[T]he Church developed a comprehensive legal system, the canon law . . . codified during the late Middle Ages."). Preiser, *supra* note 1, at 736 § D ("The canon law theory of the prerequisites for a state of war and the rules for its conduct became important in the laws of war of this period.").

31. Nussbaum, *supra* note 4, at 17 ("Canon law was not 'national' or 'international'; it was 'supranational' and even universal . . . all over the Christian world.").

32. Preiser, *supra* note 1, at 733 § D ("The scope for the development of a system of international law based on the sovereign equality of its subjects was . . . relatively small [during the early Middle Ages, and] internal constitutional problems . . . outweighed the international aspects both in size and importance.").

33. *Id.* (noting the "tendency" of the Papacy to "seek to unify the West into a single whole").

34. *Id.* ("It was not until these two representatives of the universalist idea [the "Western Emperors" of the Holy Roman Empire and the Papacy] were decisively weakened toward the

The Holy Roman Empire was a medieval construct consisting of numerous principalities, dukedoms, fiefdoms, and other polities situated mostly in and around Central Europe.[35] Since the Empire was viewed chiefly as "one grand monarchy," there could not be international relations among its members.[36]

Another major influence that complicated the evolution of international law was the feudal system.[37] Feudal structures were hierarchical, but they were not based on nations or cities in the modern sense. They tended to be based on loyalties to particular persons, such as the Emperor, the Pope, or feudal kings.[38] Feudal ties were strong, but cut across what we today would think of as national frontiers.[39] The elements of the feudal system were so concentrated on personal hierarchies that they were inconsistent with the modern idea of a state.[40]

During the Middle Ages, major philosophers did develop concepts that later could be viewed as relating to what we now call international law. One of these was the "just war" doctrine, developed by St. Augustine and St. Thomas Aquinas.[41] For example, under the approach in Aquinas' *Summa theologica*, it was not a sin to wage war if the prince had authorized the war,

---

end of the High Middle Ages that the way was open for the formation of a system of nation States . . . .").

35. *Id.* ("[T]he Empire stood as a powerful block at the center of the West, occupying too dominating a position for a society of free States to be able to form and assert itself beside the Empire and against the Empire's claim—never completely abandoned—to world dominion.").

36. Nussbaum, *supra* note 4, at 21 (noting, of the Holy Roman Empire, that "as one grand monarchy, . . . there could not be 'international' relations among its members").

37. *Id.* at 22 (asserting that feudalism "worked in [the] direction" of counteracting the "evolution of international law").

38. Preiser, *supra* note 1, at 734 § D ("The stabilization of territorial boundaries and the exercise of sovereignty were long retarded by the tenacious survival of the feudal system of personal obligation."). *See also* Nussbaum, *supra* note 4, at 22 (Feudal hierarchies were not based on nations or cities, but were "often under the overlordship of Emperor, King or Pope.").

39. Preiser, *supra* note 1, at 734–35 § D ("The line between national and international law was fluid throughout the whole period."). *See also* Nussbaum, *supra* note 4, at 22 ("Feudal ties cut across national frontiers.").

40. *Brierly's Law of Nations, supra* note 16, at 3 ("[T]o speak of a feudal 'state' is almost a misuse of terms; in a sense the feudal organization of society was a substitute for its organization in a state . . . .") *See also* Preiser, *supra* note 1, at 735 § D ("[T]he principle of mutual personal obligation, which is the characteristic distinction between feudalism and all other social orders, knows no fixed territorial boundaries. It consequently impeded the consolidation of 'nation States' . . . .").

41. Nussbaum, *supra* note 4, at 35–38; Preiser, *supra* note 1, at 732 § C, 736 § D.

there was a just cause, and the belligerent intended to promote good or avoid evil.[42]

The concept of natural law continued in its development during the Middle Ages. Although related to the ancient Roman idea of natural law, the Middle Ages version varied from the earlier meaning. Under Aquinas, "natural law" was the "necessarily imperfect participation, willed by God, of human reason in the eternal law," which was the eternal plan of God's wisdom.[43] The express involvement of a deity had not been a feature of the Roman construction.

Concepts such as the just war doctrine were viewed as aspects of moral theology, rather than specifically legal concepts, much less concepts of what we would call international law.[44] Natural law was also an element of moral theology, and clearly viewed to be superior over law. If a mere law were shown to violate natural law, it would be considered invalid.[45]

While the inhabitants of the Middle Ages did not recognize anything they were saying or doing as being what we now call international law, their moral precepts serve as background for later developments. Clear parallels can be observed to more modern ideas of customary international law, general principles of law, and *jus cogens*, all developed in later chapters of this book.

V. The Spanish Scholastics

During the early Renaissance, two Spanish clerics introduced additional theological concepts that would add important background for the later development of international law. The first of these was Francisco Vitoria (1480–1546).[46] He is most remembered for examining moral issues associated with Spanish conquest and settlement in the New World.[47]

---

42. Nussbaum, *supra* note 4, at 36; Preiser, *supra* note 1, at 736 § D.

43. Nussbaum, *supra* note 4, at 38.

44. *Id.* at 37.

45. *Id.* at 39 ("In the dominant view of the Middle Ages, statutes, judgments, decrees, and, in general, all legal transactions were null and void if violative of natural law.").

46. *See* Preiser, *supra* note 1, at 741 § F (regarding the characterization of Vitoria's work as theological, "it was more the work of a theologian than of a lawyer—Vitoria himself emphasizes that questions of this kind are . . . for the priest who deals with matters of conscience").

47. *Brierly's Law of Nations*, *supra* note 16, at 24 (describing Vitoria's chief collections of published lectures); Nussbaum, *supra* note 4 (providing translated titles for these lectures as "The Indians Recently Discovered" and "The Law of War Made by the Spaniards on the Barbarians"); *see also* Preiser, *supra* note 1, at 740 § F ("His views on international law are known

For example, he considered whether certain wars by the Spaniards against Indians in the Americas were "just." While he did not decide that all the Spanish rationales for the wars were unjust, he determined that many were.[48] He also seemed to acknowledge the possibility that both sides in a war could legitimately consider their causes to be just, although his views on this point were not well-developed.[49] His idea of reciprocal justness was based on the qualification that one of the parties was operating out of justifiable ignorance that prevented that party from perceiving the justness of the other party's cause.[50] However rooted in his time and circumstance, his work is considered remarkable for the comparatively humane attitude that he showed toward the Native Americans, which was (unfortunately) unusual among published authors of that age.[51]

Most generally, in looking to the moral standards of Spanish forces in the New World, Vitoria demonstrated that the "just war" concepts could have applicability outside Europe, and could protect non-Christian peoples. His was the first body of work to make such a proposition so explicitly. It was a step toward a realization that concepts later called international law could have universal validity. This was the most important aspect of his contribution.[52]

The other Spanish cleric was Francisco Suárez (1548–1617). He was one of the earliest writers to emphasize at length the secular character of the state, as opposed to the religious character of the Church.[53] His work began to hint at

---

principally through his two lectures . . . on the legal position of the natives in the recently discovered West Indies and on the laws of war applicable to them . . . .").

48. Nussbaum, *supra* note 4, at 80.

49. Preiser, *supra* note 1, at 741 § F (noting that the "concept" that a "war . . . could be a just war for both sides" was "taken up and generalized by Vitoria"); *see also* Nussbaum, *supra* note 4, at 82 (Vitoria recognized "the fact that a war might be just on either side." But "he attributed the role of judge to the victorious prince, if his cause was 'just'—an objectionable theory.").

50. Preiser, *supra* note 1, at 741 § F (paraphrasing Vitoria as opining that "if the opponent of a party waging a just war is in a state of invincible error . . . concerning his own justification for waging war, so that there is no fault on his part, a justified 'punitive' war against him is not possible").

51. *Id.* 741 § F (praising the "logical clarity with which he develops the arguments" that were critical of the " 'conquistador ideology' " of the day); *see also* Nussbaum, *supra* note 4, at 80 (Vitoria "dismissed imperial claims to world supremacy" and "showed humaneness and intelligent understanding toward the Indians.").

52. *See generally Brierly's Law of Nations, supra* note 16, at 24 ("Vitoria's teaching marks an important step in the expansion of international law into a world system; for it meant that a law which had its rise among the few princes of European Christendom was not to be limited to them or to their relations with one another but was universally valid . . . .").

53. Nussbaum, *supra* note 4, at 85 (Among other similar statements, Nussbaum notes of Suárez: "[H]is theories of the secular character of the state and of popular sovereignty

the interdependence of secular states with one another.[54] He also revisited the Roman *jus gentium* idea, in a way that brought it closer to a modern notion of international law.[55]

VI. Secular Scholars on the Law of Nations During the Renaissance

At about the same time Suárez was working in Spain, a French legal theorist, Jean Bodin (1530–1596), was beginning to develop the modern idea of state sovereignty.[56] He published his major work, *De Republica*, in 1576.[57] He was motivated by the desire to help reduce the destructive impact within France of the many harmful conflicts then raging among different feudal and religious factions.[58] In developing the idea of sovereignty,[59] and attaching it to the idea of a unified French government, he was hoping to help assure French stability and domestic peace. He was convinced that within a strong state there must be one and only one authority that is the source of its laws, and that that authority needed to be the sovereign.[60] In his day, the position of sovereign was held by the monarch, but in more recent times the idea of sovereignty is often said to inhere in the state itself, or its people.

One of the main innovations of Bodin's approach was the explicit connection between the sovereign and the legislative capacity.[61] In the Middle Ages, the making of laws tended to be viewed as an interpretive act, either of divine will,

---

came to be widely acclaimed by Catholic and by later Protestant writers.").

54. *Id.* at 87–88.

55. Preiser, *supra* note 1, at 742 § F; Nussbaum, *supra* note 4, at 88–89.

56. *Brierly's Law of Nations*, *supra* note 16, at 7 (noting that the doctrine of sovereignty was "first explicitly formulated" in *De Republica*).

57. *Id.* at 7.

58. *Id.* at 8.

59. Preiser, *supra* note 1, at 740, § F (crediting Bodin with the origination of "the modern concept of sovereignty").

60. *Brierly's Law of Nations*, *supra* note 16, at 8.

61. *E.g.*, Geoffrey Butler & Simon Maccoby, *The Development of International Law* 8 (Lawbook Exch., Ltd., photo. reprint 2003) (1928) (These authors thus characterize Bodin's approach: "The sovereign Power possessed the right of making laws, waging war, naming officials, levying taxes, sitting in ultimate judgment, pardoning and receiving oaths of allegiance or obedience, though it might adopt fixed agencies, principles or methods for exercising any of these functions.").

or of the natural order, for example. With Bodin, the sovereign's act of law-making began to be viewed as a political process that could be legitimate in its own right.[62]

During this general period, two other secular authors made some of the most significant strides in the development of international law.

A. Alberico Gentili (1552–1608)

An Italian protestant academician who spent most of his professional years in England, Gentili published his *Law of War* in 1598.[63] His work is notable for a variety of reasons. First, the scope of his treatment is broad. It has been said to have covered "practically all the pertinent problems of the period."[64] He also broke new ground by positively declaring that a war could be just on both sides as an objective matter,[65] although he acknowledged that there could be different degrees of justness.[66]

Gentili has also been viewed as an originator of a purely secular approach to the ideas that would become part of international law.[67] It was especially clear that he viewed his work as being of a distinctly legal character, as opposed to being rooted in theology or ethics.[68]

---

62. *Brierly's Law of Nations, supra* note 16, at 9–10 ("Where Bodin broke away from the medieval tradition of law was in making his sovereign a legislator, for legislation was a function which that tradition did not readily admit; when a medieval ruler made new law, it was regarded as an act of interpreting . . . .").

63. *Id.* at 25.

64. Nussbaum, *supra* note 4, at 95.

65. *Id.* at 97 ("Gentili departs from the teachings of the scholastics by stating that a war may be just on both sides, and not only because of excusable ignorance, as Vitoria concedes, but objectively."). *See also* Wilhelm G. Grewe, *The Epochs of International Law* 211 (Michael Byers trans., 2000) ("Gentili went even further in his conclusions[, declaring] that it was possible that a war could objectively be just on both sides.").

66. Nussbaum, *supra* note 4, at 97 ("Gentili adds that [while a war may be objectively just on both sides]. there may be differences in the degree of justness.").

67. *E.g.,* Nussbaum, *supra* note 4, at 101 ("One may call him the originator of the secular school of thought in international law."). *Accord Brierly's Law of Nations, supra* note 16, at 25 (Brierly quotes Gentili as saying: "Let the theologians keep silence about a matter which is outside their province.").

68. *Brierly's Law of Nations, supra* note 16, at 25 (He "was perhaps the first writer to make a definite separation of international law from theology and ethics and to treat it as a branch of jurisprudence."). *See also* Grewe, *supra* note 65, at 220 ("Gentili . . . was always eager to disconnect the links which bound the law of nations to theology . . . .").

B. Hugo Grotius (1583–1645)

Hugo Grotius was a Dutch aristocrat who served as ambassador of Sweden to France during much of the Thirty Years' War. His most significant work was *De jure belli ac pacis* ("On the Law of War and Peace"), published in 1625.[69] Some authorities consider him to be the "founder" or "father" of modern international law,[70] although the opinion on this point is not unanimous.[71]

Like many of his predecessors, Grotius dealt with the concept of *jus gentium*.[72] However, with him it is explicit that *jus gentium* refers to the law between states, rather than a universal natural law or any set of private-law rules.[73] To his admirers, this was a major step towards the conception of modern international law.[74]

His discussion of just and unjust wars is a significant feature of *De jure belli ac pacis*.[75] He was notable in advocating restraint in the conduct of war, particularly vis-à-vis the treatment of prisoners and subject populations.[76] His

---

69. *See, e.g., Brierly's Law of Nations, supra* note 16, at 26 ("Few books have won so great a reputation as Grotius's *De jure belli ac pacis* . . . .").

70. Nussbaum, *supra* note 4, at 113 ("Rightly . . . Grotius has been considered as the 'founder' or 'father' of international law."); *accord* von Redlich, *supra* note 4, at 2 (maintaining that Grotius is "properly called 'the father of modern International Law' ").

71. *E.g., Brierly's Law of Nations, supra* note 16, at 26 ("[T]o regard its author [of *De jure belli ac pacis*] as the 'founder' of international law is to exaggerate its originality and to do less than justice to the writers who preceded him . . . ."). *See also* Grewe, *supra* note 65, at 195 ("However, as far as the law of nations is concerned, the legend of [Grotius' status as] the 'father of international law' must, once and for all, be qualified.").

72. *E.g.,* Thomas Alfred Walker, 1 *A History of the Law of Nations* 278, 282, 286–87 (William S. Hein & Co., photo. reprint 2004) (1899) (describing Grotius's use of "*Jus Gentium Primarium*" as a basis for freedom of commerce and navigation, and Grotius's comparison of *jus gentium* with natural law and civil law).

73. Nussbaum, *supra* note 4, at 109 ("Grotius defines the *jus gentium* as a law *inter civitates* which now definitely means between states."); *accord Brierly's Law of Nations, supra* note 16, at 28 ("[I]n Grotius, [*jus gentium*] has come to be a branch of *public* law, governing the relations between one people and another.").

74. *E.g.,* Nussbaum, *supra* note 4, at 113 ("*On the Law of War and Peace* . . . initiated the doctrine of modern international law [which] was bound to be secular and indiscriminate.").

75. *E.g., Brierly's Law of Nations, supra* note 16, at 32 ("At the heart of his system lay the attempt to distinguish between lawful and unlawful war, *bellum justum* and *bellum injustum* . . . just as national order would be precarious if the laws within the state did not distinguish between the lawful and the unlawful use of force.").

76. *E.g.,* Grewe, *supra* note 65, at 218 (One of Grotius's aims "was to demonstrate and prove that even in war there existed a legal order, the principal task of which was to limit, moderate and humanize the ways and means of conducting wars . . . ."); *see also* Nussbaum,

work has been praised for exhibiting tolerance[77] and for his focus on peace and justice.[78]

Grotius's view was of a unified whole, a legal system rather than a series of pin-prick subjects addressed according to the interests and enthusiasms of the writer.[79] He set forth a general theory of treaties, distinguishing them from mere contracts to be treated as if they were entered into by private parties.[80] He also maintained that ethics should generally triumph over self-interest.[81]

Grotius was also clear on his motivation for using the work of previous commentators. He maintained that he did not cite historical authorities because they were themselves conclusively correct. Rather, he cited them when they were in agreement with each other, because their agreement either meant that they had cumulatively deduced a principle of reason, or that they had discovered a matter on which all states agreed, and hence a rule of the law of nations.[82]

---

supra note 4, at 110–11 ("Grotius . . . urged moderation for reasons of humanity, religion, and farsighted policy.").

77. Nussbaum, *supra* note 4, at 110 ("[T]olerance is the outstanding feature of Grotius' work.").

78. von Redlich, *supra* note 4, at xi ("The keynote of Grotius' *De Jure Belli ac Pacis* was justice. He condemned selfish and aggressive wars. Grotius believed that peace and justice mutually rely upon each other . . . ."); *see also* Grewe, *supra* note 65, at 218 ("[I]n his [*De jure bellli ac pacis*] he gave expression to the deep shock which he suffered in realizing the catastrophic savagery of the wars of religion and the decline of law and morals which followed them . . . .").

79. Nussbaum, *supra* note 4, at 109 ("Grotius' international law . . . was in substance a unified whole, fundamentally different from the conceptions of the scholastics."); *see also* Walker, *supra* note 72, at 334 (comparing Grotius's work to the accomplishment of the biblical Ezekiel, in creating bodies of living flesh out of the valley of bones).

80. Nussbaum, *supra* note 4, at 111–12 ("Surpassing Gentili, Grotius set forth a general theory of treaties, giving a much fuller account. For the first time treaties were distinguished from contracts . . . .").

81. *E.g.,* Walker, *supra* note 72, at 330 (quoting Grotius's ethical exhortation for rulers to obey the law of nations for much the same self-abnegating reasons that a virtuous citizen decides to obey domestic law); *see also* von Redlich, *supra* note 4, at 2 ("[I]t was he who proclaimed that the ethics of right should take precedence over the 'contemporary canons of self-interest.' ").

82. *Brierly's Law of Nations, supra* note 16, at 28–29:

> He [Grotius] used, he tells us, the testimony of philosophers, historians, poets, and orators, not because they were themselves conclusive witnesses, but because when they were found to be in agreement, their agreement could only be explained in one of two ways: either what they said must be a correct deduction from the principles of reason, and so a rule of the law of nature; or else it must be a matter on which common consent existed, and so a rule of the law of nations.

This distinction may be reflected in the modern treatment of *opinio juris*, an aspect of customary international law discussed in chapter 8 of this book.

VII. The Peace of Westphalia and the Period Following

The treaties signed for the Peace of Westphalia in 1648 were signal developments in Western political history, and in the history of international law. Most specifically, the 1648 agreements ended the Thirty Years' War, one of the bloodiest religious wars in European history.[83] For our purposes, the agreements were also important because they embodied a new political framework in Europe.[84] For some time, the conventional view has been that the Peace of Westphalia ushered in the current era of international society composed of modern autonomous nation-states.[85]

With the 1648 Peace, more than 300 member polities of the Holy Roman Empire now had the official right to enter into treaties and conduct their own foreign relations.[86] Beforehand, a principality might be one thing, a dukedom

---

83. Butler & Maccoby, *supra* note 61, at 98 (branding the Thirty Years' War as "the most terrible, devastating and widespread struggle in which the modern nation states of Europe had been yet engaged," and noting the War's primary hostilities as having been between the "Catholic" and the "Protestant" sides); Nussbaum, *supra* note 4, at 115 (referring to the Thirty Years' War as "probably the most devastating European conflict after the barbarian invasion" and as "the climax of, and practically the last of, the religious wars;" also noting that "[t]he war was ended by the Peace of Westphalia").

84. *E.g.,* Stephan Verosta, *History of the Law of Nations 1648 to 1815, in* 2 *Encyclopedia of Public International Law* 749, 749 § A (Rudolf Bernhardt ed., 1995) ("After the Thirty Years War, the 1648 Peace of Westphalia created a new political order in Europe . . . ."); *see also Brierly's Law of Nations, supra* note 16, at 5 ("The Peace of Westphalia, which brought to an end in 1648 the great Thirty Years War of religion, marked the acceptance of the new political order in Europe.").

85. *E.g.,* Leo Gross, *The Peace of Westphalia, 1648–1948*, 42 Am. J. Int'l L. 20, 28–29 (1948):

> In the political field [the Peace of Westphalia] marked man's abandonment of the idea of a hierarchical structure of society and his option for a new system characterized by the coexistence of a multiplicity of states, each sovereign within its territory, equal to one another, and free from any external earthly authority.

86. Verosta, *supra* note 84, at 750 § B.1 ("Through the Peace of Westphalia the members of the Holy Roman Empire—numbering around 300—achieved a status approaching sovereignty; they were granted the right to enter into alliances with foreign powers . . . ."); Nussbaum, *supra* note 4, at 115 ("The members of the Holy Roman Empire, more than

another, an earldom another, and so on. Different kinds of polities might be viewed as having different capacities in their external dealings, and also might have varying degrees of independence from the Roman Church. But the 1648 arrangement provided international recognition for Protestantism,[87] and allowed each of the signatory polities (both Catholic and Protestant) to begin developing toward what we now think of as a nation-state.

This was important because a "law of nations" cannot develop until, first of all, entities properly called "nations" are existing. Secondly, a genuine "law of nations" cannot be effective unless there is a broadly-based system operating among those nations. Before 1648, different polities had different characteristics, capacities and identities, as noted above. There was no awareness of all (or at least most) polities in Europe (much less the world) having the same type of status as a nation-state. Also, there was not a universally-accepted notion of a system of rights and responsibilities among them over a broad variety of subject areas. With the Peace at Westphalia, both these concepts (the nation-state and systematic relations between them) became prominent in political and legal terms.

Accordingly, in the years following the Peace of Westphalia, the need for states to maintain permanent embassies became apparent,[88] states began to maintain consuls in other states,[89] treaties among states began to be considered binding on their own terms, without religious oaths being added to bind their signatories,[90] and there were substantial improvements in international trade and the treaties helping to advance it.[91]

---

three hundred, now officially had the right to enter into alliances with foreign powers—and consequently to wage wars . . . .").

87. Nussbaum, *supra* note 4, at 116 ("[T]he Peace brought forth the first international recognition of Protestantism—or, more precisely, of Lutheranism and Calvinism."); *see also* Verosta, *supra* note 84, at 750 § B.1 (noting that the Peace accorded recognition to the Calvinists and bestowed upon princes the power "to decide on the confession of their subjects").

88. von Redlich, *supra* note 4, at 263 (attributing significance to the Peace of Westphalia for "the establishment of the modern permanent diplomatic missions"); Nussbaum, *supra* note 4 at 125 ("The necessity for permanent embassies . . . was no longer a matter of controversy.").

89. Nussbaum, *supra* note 4, at 125 ("[O]ne hears again during this period about consuls.").

90. *Id.* at 126.

91. *E.g.,* Gross, *supra* note 85, at 25–26 (noting provisions of the Peace treaties restoring freedom of commerce); Nussbaum, *supra* note 4, at 126–28 (tracing the development of certain commercial treaties during the period following the Peace of Westphalia).

VIII. Philosophers of the European Enlightenment

There is no complete consensus on the beginning and ending dates for the European Enlightenment. But for our purposes we can use the time span from about 1650 to the end of the Napoleonic Wars, culminating in the Congress of Vienna in 1815. Not all the Enlightenment philosophers contributed to the development of international law, but many did. We will review the work only of some of those whose contributions were most significant.

A. Thomas Hobbes (1588–1679)

Thomas Hobbes was an English philosopher who published his major works in the mid-seventeenth century. Among these were *Elementa philosophica* (1642) and *Leviathan* (1651).[92] Accordingly, on our time span, he could be viewed as either a precursor to the European Enlightenment or one of its very earliest contributors.

Hobbes posited a hypothetical original condition for humanity called the "state of nature."[93] In this state of nature, humans were motivated only by selfish concerns for power.[94] Hobbes viewed this state of nature as an inherently violent, unstable and undesirable condition. He considered that it comes to an end to the extent humans agree to band together through the social contract to form a state in which all are obligated to obey a sovereign.[95]

---

92. Nussbaum, *supra* note 4, at 144.

93. *See, e.g.,* Thomas Hobbes, *Leviathan* 64–65 (J.M. Dent & Sons 1914) (1651) ("Hereby it is manifest, that during the time men live without a common Power to keep them all in awe, they are in that condition . . . where every man is enemy to every man. . . . In such condition, there is . . . continual fear, and danger of violent death; and the life of man, solitary, poor, nasty, brutish and short."), *referenced in* Nussbaum, *supra* note 4, at 144 (referring generally to Hobbes' concept thus described as the "state of nature").

94. *See, e.g., Leviathan, supra* note 93, at 64 ("And from this diffidence [in the sense of 'mutual distrust'] of one another, there is no way for any man to secure himself, so reasonably, as [by] anticipation; that is, by force, or will, to master the persons of all men he can, so long, till he see no other power great enough to endanger him . . . ."), *referenced in* Nussbaum, *supra* note 4, at 144 (discussing the strife for power as characteristic of the state of nature).

95. *See, e.g., Leviathan, supra* note 93, at 90 ("[T]he essence of commonwealth . . . is one person, of whose acts a great multitude, by mutual covenants one with another, have made themselves every one the author, to the end he may use the strength and means of them all, as he shall think expedient, for their peace and common defense."), *referenced in* Nuss-

Note that Hobbes' "state of nature" is a very different concept from classical or medieval "natural law" theory. Under Hobbes' view, a naturally pristine state is a dangerous, frightening and volatile situation. Classical and medieval natural law theory had a more optimistic view of human character, asserting that naturally within human consciousness (ultimately through divine assistance), a set of rules could be determined for the right governance of society. While Hobbes believed in a version of "natural law" theory,[96] his description of what has become known as the "state of nature" is very different from the established concept of natural law, even as reflected in his own work.[97]

Hobbes was mostly concerned with political philosophy operating within a national society.[98] But he also addressed relations between nations. He felt that the state of nature was suppressed only to the extent an organized community was in place. Where there is no organized community, the state of nature prevails.[99] Thus the relations between the sovereigns of his day exhibited the state of nature, to the extent the sovereigns did not live in an organized community.

He allowed that sometimes even among sovereigns an enlightened concern for self-preservation and self-defense could result in mutual conciliations, and that then a "law of nature" could take hold. This law of nature he called *jus gentium*, using the Roman phrase.[100] It was very different from natural law, since it dealt with practical reconciliation among initially hostile forces, rather

---

baum, *supra* note 4, at 145 (describing a "social contract" as arising when persons in society unite to form a state and obligate themselves to obey a sovereign).

96. *See, e.g., Leviathan, supra* note 93, at 66 ("A law of nature is a precept, or general rule, found out by reason, by which a man is forbidden to do, that, which is destructive of his life, or takes away the means of preserving the same . . . .").

97. *Compare* the quotation from *Leviathan* in note 93 *with* that in note 96, *supra*.

98. *E.g.,* Robinson A. Grover, *Hobbes and the Concept of International Law, in Hobbes on Law* 559, 559 (Claire Finkelstein ed., 2005) (Hobbes' "complete neglect of the topic of international law makes it appear that he considers international law either uninteresting or useless or impossible."); Nussbaum, *supra* note 4, at 146 ("Hobbes's remarks touching on international relations are only incidental to his philosophy of state, and rather perfunctory.")

99. *E.g.,* Grover, *supra* note 98, at 559 ("Hobbes argues for the similarity of the state of nature between individuals and between nations . . . ."); Nussbaum, *supra* note 4, at 145 ("Outside the organized community, however, the state of nature, or war of all against all, persists. This is especially true of relations among sovereigns because they do not live in such a community.").

100. Nussbaum, *supra* note 4, at 145 ("Still, the so-called law of nature—the enlightened desire for self-preservation and defense—operates also among sovereigns (states); in this particular application, Hobbes calls it *jus gentium* . . . .").

than a predetermined benevolent system of rules. It was closer to the meaning of *jus gentium*, referencing a system of law among states, and was a precursor to our current international law. Indeed, he referenced his conception of *jus gentium* as being, in English, the "law of nations."[101]

B. Naturalism and Positivism

As the Enlightenment got into full swing, for many theorists addressing relations between states, natural law took on a much more modern cast. Natural law was becoming a primarily secular concept embodying Enlightenment values.[102] On the one hand, it was possible to view this more secular form of natural law as fundamental to the developing law of nations.[103] On the other hand, a new perspective began to emerge that contrasted with natural law. Under this view, there were primarily two bases for the law of nations. The first was treaties among states, and the second consisted of customary practices followed by states out of a conviction that the law of nations had developed in such a way that it required observance of those customs.[104] The first of these perspectives has often been called "naturalism," while the second has been called "positivism."[105] Sometimes discussions pit writers in the "naturalist" school

---

101. *Id.* at 146 ("Hobbes was the first to reserve the term 'law of nations' (*jus gentium*) for application to international relations.").

102. *See, e.g.,* Verosta, *supra* note 84, at 762 § F (referencing "[t]his secularized theory of natural law"); Nussbaum, *supra* note 4, at 135 ("In the eighteenth century [natural law] became associated with the great movement of the Enlightenment. . . . Thus, the law of nature became more and more imbued with revolutionary tendencies.").

103. *E.g.,* Verosta, *supra* note 84, at 762 § F (emphasizing, in part, the effect on "[i]nternational Law doctrine" of the "the special significance . . . accorded to natural law in the political and legal philosophy in Europe").

104. Grewe is among those referring to this perspective as favoring "positive law," and quotes an earlier authority to illustrate the difference. Grewe, *supra* note 65, at 510 (" 'The most useful and practical part of the Law of Nations is, no doubt, instituted or positive law, founded on usage, consent and agreement.' " (quoting Henry Sumner Maine, *International Law* 32 (1888)); *see also* Nussbaum, *supra* note 4, at 135 (During this period, "one can draw a line between 'naturalists,' who still emphasized [natural law], and 'positivists,' who emphasized treaties and custom, pushing the law of nature into a subordinate position . . . .").

105. *See* Grewe, supra note 65, at 352 (denoting the distinction between the "natural law" school and the "positivist" school); *see also* Nussbaum, *supra* note 4, at 135 ("The reasoning of the positivists was more juridical and more related to concrete situations, whereas that of the naturalists was more philosophical and abstract."). Although the term "positivism" can take on different nuances in different contexts, we can note Grewe's observation that "it is Hobbes who should be regarded as the true father of modern legal positivism." Grewe, *supra* note 65, at 349.

starkly against other writers said to be in the "positivist" school, but many writers of the day saw value in both approaches.[106]

We will see in chapter 4 that both perspectives can be detected in the modern list of sources of international law. The positivist view is reflected in the inclusion of treaties and customary law in that list, while the naturalist view can be seen in the inclusion in that list of general principles of law.

C. Samuel Pufendorf (1632–1694)

A German academician who also briefly served as the Swedish ambassador to Denmark,[107] Samuel Pufendorf has been called the "founder of the so-called 'naturalist' school of writers."[108] As a professor at the University of Lund in Sweden, he published *On the Law of Nature and of Nations* in 1672. The title reconfirms the ascendance of the phrase, "law of nations," to describe the legal relations among states. Pufendorf emphasized the role of a highly moralistic form of natural law.[109] His moral basis for natural law was nevertheless highly secular,[110] which distinguished him from earlier natural-law theorists who deployed Christian morality to support their views.

For Pufendorf, treaties were merely contracts among states, and had no more to do with defining the law of nations than specific private contracts define the rules governing general private relations within a state.[111] Similarly, he held that

---

106. *See* Grewe, *supra* note 65, at 355 ("[T]he name 'positivist' is not particularly descriptive, because they [the early positivists] remained attached to the basic natural law concept of their time . . . ."). Grewe also discerns a third school of the day, a "synthetic" school that completely adopted neither naturalism nor positivism. *Id.* at 352 & 357.

107. Nussbaum, *supra* note 4, at 147. Grewe also casts Pufendorf as a leading naturalist writer, stating that according to Pufendorf, "there was no voluntary or positive law of nations which had the binding force of law in its pure sense . . . ." Grewe, *supra* note 65, at 352.

108. *Brierly's Law of Nations, supra* note 16, at 34.

109. Nussbaum, *supra* note 4, at 148.

110. *See* Walter Simons, *Introduction, in* Samuel Pufendorf, 2 *De jure naturae et gentium libri octo* 11a, 19a (C.H. Oldfather & W.A. Oldfather trans., Clarendon Press 1934) (1688) (declaring that Pufendorf is "explicit in his statement" rejecting Catholic perspectives, and that Pufendorf's "severe criticism of . . . juristic clericalism impresses us as the first bar of the tune which dominated the century of Enlightenment"); *see also* Nussbaum, *supra* note 4, at 148 ("Pufendorf gives the law of nature a new secular twist . . . . [H]e came to be considered as the true founder of a secular law of nature.").

111. Nussbaum, *supra* note 4, at 149; Grewe, supra note 65, at 354 (describing Pufendorf's view that "[t]reaties and custom could not establish legal rules because they were not the expression of a will which was superimposed on the subjects of the law of nations").

the state practice was without importance in determining the law of nations.[112] In considering his dismissal of both treaties and customary practice, it is easy to see why he was considered a consummate "naturalist," rather than a "positivist."

D. Richard Zouche (1590–1660)

One of the prominent positivists of this period was Richard Zouche, an English professor of law at Oxford during the mid-seventeenth century.[113] A contemporary of Thomas Hobbes, he is known for having emphasized the law of peace over the law of war, by discussing the first before discussing the second in his major treatise.[114] This was contrary to the custom at the time.

According to Zouche, the law of nations was based on the customary behavior of states and on treaties.[115] He held that custom, in order to be considered part of the law of nations, needed to conform to reason,[116] but he generally de-emphasized natural law.[117]

E. Emmerich de Vattel (1714–1767)

A Swiss diplomat who also published several works on political philosophy, in international matters he is most known for a treatise titled *Le droit des gens* in 1758.[118] (The title could be translated for our purposes, either strictly as "*The Law of Peoples*," or more loosely (the more common approach), as "*The Law of Nations*.") Vattel appreciated the importance of both the naturalist and positivist perspective.[119] Characteristically of the Enlightenment, his view of nat-

---

112. *Brierly's Law of Nations, supra* note 16, at 34 ("He denied any binding force to the practice of nations and based his system wholly on natural law . . . .").

113. Nussbaum, *supra* note 4, at 165.

114. Grewe, *supra* note 65, at 355; Nussbaum, *supra* note 4, at 166. The treatise is still known by its lengthy Latin name, *Juris et judicii fecialis sive juris inter gentes et quaestionum de eodem explicatio* (1650).

115. Grewe, *supra* note 65, at 355–56; Nussbaum, *supra* note 4, at 167.

116. Grewe, *supra* note 65, at 355–56; Nussbaum, *supra* note 4, at 167.

117. Nussbaum, *supra* note 4, at 167 ("Of the traditional natural-law doctrine his book shows practically no mark.").

118. *Id.* at 156.

119. Emmerich de Vattel, 3 *The Law of Nations* 9 (William S. Hein & Co., photo. reprint 1995) (Charles G. Fenwick trans., Carnegie Institution 1916) (1758) (contrasting "the positive law of nations" with the "natural or necessary law of nations," and noting the importance of features of both). Grewe places Vattel neither with the naturalists nor with the positivists, but rather with his third category, the "synthetic" perspective. Grewe, *supra* note 65, at 357–58.

ural law allowed for broad freedom of states in external affairs, and emphasized the independence of every state.[120]

Having been a diplomat for most of his professional life, his work was known for being notably practical, and perhaps more based in real-world observations than other theorists.[121]

Probably most significantly, Vattel is known for having introduced the doctrine of the sovereign equality of states.[122] The notion that each state in the world is entitled to the same degree of formal respect is fundamental to today's international system, and can be seen to spring readily from Vattel's ideas regarding the external freedom and independence of states.

IX. From the Congress of Vienna to World War I

Napoleon's defeat was memorialized at the Congress of Vienna, the terms of which were solidified in a comprehensive set of treaties in 1815.[123] The Congress signaled the beginning of a period in which trade and communications necessitated greater international communication.[124]

A. The Concert of Great Powers and the Crimean War

Upon the conclusion of the Congress, a "European Concert" of "Great Powers" emerged (also called the "Concert of Europe"), which tried to decide the political destiny of Europe for a good while thereafter.[125]

---

120. *Brierly's Law of Nations*, *supra* note 16, at 36 (For Vattel "natural law itself establishes the freedom and independence of every state, and therefore each is the sole judge of its own actions and accountable for its observance of natural law only to its own conscience.").

121. Nussbaum, *supra* note 4, at 157 ("It is the work of a modern-minded diplomat who . . . systematically sets forth his own opinions on the most diverse topics of international and constitutional law [and] viewed with the eyes of a practitioner of statecraft."); *see also* Grewe, *supra* note 65, at 334 (noting that "Vattel was in closer contact with the realities of political life" than the others).

122. *Brierly's Law of Nations*, *supra* note 16, at 36 (holding Vattel responsible for introducing "the doctrine of the equality of states" into the theory of international law).

123. Butler & Maccoby, *supra* note 61, at 351–52 (discussing the various treaties of 1815 concluded during, and in the months following, the Congress of Vienna); *see also* Nussbaum, *supra* note 4, at 186 (emphasizing the Final Act of the Congress of Vienna).

124. Malcolm N. Shaw, *International Law* 28 (6th ed. 2008).

125. Regarding the Concert of Europe, *see generally* Satow's *Diplomatic Practice* ¶¶ 1.12–1.15, at 11–14 (Ivor Roberts ed., 6th ed. 2009); *id.* ¶ 1.12, at 12 (the "Great Power system of consensus"

Initially this group consisted of Austria, England, Prussia, and Russia. As soon as a traditionalist French state could be established free of Napoleonic influences, France was also included.[126] For a time, the concerted action of the Great Powers provided something of a precursor for the League of Nations arrangement. As will be seen in chapter 3, the Covenant of the League crowned four states as "Principal Allied and Associated Powers," in a configuration that could be seen to echo the nineteenth-century Concert.

The loose affiliation of the European Concert was short-lived. In the mid-nineteenth century, the Crimean War broke out between Russia on the one hand and an alliance of France, England, and Austria on the other.

The 1856 Treaty of Paris ended the Crimean War, and its terms advanced the development of international law in several respects. For example, the Paris Treaty created a Commission of the Danube, a possible a forerunner for modern international conferences and organizations.[127] In its treatment of the Black Sea territories of Walachia and Moldavia (now generally parts of Romania), the Paris Treaty began to suggest modern notions of self-determination.[128]

B. Toward the Development of Modern Treaties and Conventions

During the decades following the Congress of Vienna, key aspects of the modern practice of international conventions began to develop. States began entering into multilateral conventions laying down general rules for the conduct of states.[129] It became more and more accepted for conventions to be

---

which "was to prove a form of proto-European government for the period up to the Crimean War" became known as "the Concert of Europe"); *see also* Nussbaum, *supra* note 4, at 187.

126. Butler & Maccoby, *supra* note 61, at 360 (noting that "the principal result" of an 1818 conference at Aix-la-Chapelle "may be found in the admission of France into the gathering of the great Powers," and quoting a protocol that followed the conference emphasizing that France was then "associated with the other Powers by the restoration of the legitimate and constitutional monarchic authority"); *see also* Nussbaum, *supra* note 4, at 187 (referring to the effect of the addition of France being an expansion of the Great Powers from a "'tetrarchy'" to a "'pentarchy'").

127. Hans-Ulrich Scupin, *History of the Law of Nations 1815 to World War I, in* 2 *Encyclopedia of Public International Law* 767, 779–80 § E (Rudolf Bernhardt ed., 1995) ("In the case of river navigation, the establishment of an international organization for the Danube goes back to the Treaty of Paris of 1856. . . . The idea of the Danube Commission as a separate entity only took shape gradually, however . . . ."); *see also* Nussbaum, *supra* note 4, at 191 (characterizing the creation by the Treaty of Paris of the International Commission of the Danube as "fortunate").

128. Nussbaum, *supra* note 4, at 191–92.

129. Grewe, *supra* note 65, at 512 ("The States which participated in the Congress of

"open" for certain periods of time, allowing later accession by states not originally parties to the negotiation of the conventions.[130]

These features contrasted with earlier practices. First, before this period, multilateral treaties usually served as final resolutions of conflicts, rather than as statements of general legal rules to be followed in the future. And the feature of open accession was also an innovation, since open accession would not have served a direct purpose for treaties that were simply addressing past conflicts between specific parties. The current state of development of legal procedures for negotiating and finalizing treaties and conventions is discussed in chapter 5 of this book.

C. Particular Features of Developing Conventions

A noteworthy feature of many of the new conventions of this era was a focus on humanitarian issues.[131] Largely due to the work of the Swiss activist, Jean Henri Dunant, the International Red Cross movement began in Geneva in 1863.[132] The next year, the Convention for the Amelioration of the Condition of the Wounded in Armies in the Field[133] adopted the symbol of the Red Cross[134] and proclaimed

---

Vienna were, already, not prepared to restrict themselves to concluding treaties concerning specific legal transactions. Instead, they used law-making treaties to regulate fundamental aspects ... of international life . . . ."); Scupin, *supra* note 127, at 783–84 § G (detailing the multilateral law-making conventions of the period); *see also* Nussbaum, *supra* note 4, at 197 (emphasizing the importance of "the spread of multilateral conventions in the state practice of the period," as opposed to "[e]arlier periods," which had witnessed only "a few compacts among more than two parties").

130. Nussbaum, *supra* note 4, at 198. Specific examples of these kinds of conventions during this period were the Universal Telegraphic Union of 1865, the International Convention on Railway Freight Traffic of 1890, and the Convention on the International Circulation of Motor Vehicles of 1909. *Id. See also* Grewe, supra note 65, at 487 (noting the development of "[t]he legal modalities of treaty-making, in particular the function of ratification in the treaty law of the nineteenth century").

131. Scupin, *supra* note 127, at 784 § G ("International law in this period was shaped . . . by the idealism of the century, the legacy of humanism and the Enlightenment, and the fruits of a reawakening Christian sense of responsibility with regard to the suffering in this world."); Nussbaum, *supra* note 4, at 198–99 (noting that a "conspicuous type" of the conventions of the period "was humanitarian in character," citing examples in the fields of public health and the suppression of slavery).

132. *Founding and Early Years of the ICRC (1863–1914)*, International Committee of the Red Cross, http://www.icrc.org/eng/who-we-are/history/founding/overview-section-founding .htm (last updated Sept. 29, 2010); Nussbaum, *supra* note 4, at 225.

133. Aug. 22, 1864, 22 Stat. 940, 129 Consol. T.S. 361, 1 Bevans 7 (entered into force June 22, 1865).

134. *Id.* art. 7.

protections for the wounded, ambulances and military hospitals, among other measures.[135] The current prominence of the International Committee of the Red Cross (the "ICRC"), and its influence over international humanitarian law, is discussed in chapter 10 of this book.

Also during this period, the movement toward the establishment of international organizations became more pronounced.[136] In addition to the ICRC, the Universal Postal Union[137] and the Permanent Court of Arbitration[138] are examples of the international organizations originating from this era. The movement toward the establishment of international organizations has of course grown even more in recent times. We will discuss many international organizations, and research on international law regarding them, in chapter 9 of this book.

Treaties regarding commerce also grew substantially in the decades that followed the Napoleonic period.[139] These included treaties of friendship, commerce and navigation,[140] treaties containing most-favored-nation clauses,[141] and treaties advancing the often-notorious "open door" policy to facilitate the exploitation of resources in developing countries by the interests of more developed countries.[142]

The greater incidence of treaties involving international commerce did not mean that there were no disputes during this period. One feature of the time was the threat or use of force by one state to collect the unpaid debts owed to its nationals by another state. An example was an ill-fated attempt by France

---

135. *Id.* arts. 1–6; Nussbaum, *supra* note 4, at 225. *See generally* Scupin, *supra* note 127, at 780–81 § E (discussing the 1864 convention, Dunant's role in initiating it, and the subsequent development of the Red Cross and Red Crescent).

136. *See generally* Scupin, *supra* note 127, at 779–81 § E (discussing the development of international organizations during this period at length); Nussbaum, *supra* note 4, at 202.

137. Treaty Concerning the Formation of a General Postal Union, Oct. 9, 1874, 19 Stat. 577, 147 Consol. T.S. 136, 1 Bevans 29 (entered into force July 1, 1875). This original treaty has been superseded, and a 1964 convention established the current arrangements for a "Universal Postal Union." Constitution of the Universal Postal Union, July 10, 1964, 16 U.S.T. 1291, 611 U.N.T.S. 7 (entered into force Jan. 1, 1966).

138. *See* text and note at notes 146–47, *infra.*

139. Nussbaum, *supra* note 4, at 203. *See also* Scupin, *supra* note 127, at 782 § F (noting the ascendency of economic interests during the period, which could be "real, but less obvious" than political interests).

140. Nussbaum, *supra* note 4, at 204–05 (emphasizing the role of the Franco-English Treaty of Commerce of 1860).

141. Scupin, *supra* note 127, at 782 § F (tracing the development of most-favored-nation clauses); Nussbaum, *supra* note 4, at 205 (same).

142. Grewe, *supra* note 65, at 477–82; Scupin, *supra* note 127, at 782 § F.

under Napoleon III to use force against the Mexican government to obtain payment of obligations owed to French nationals.[143]

In part as a result of such episodes, the use of arbitration among states also became more common during this period. One of the most famous international arbitrations of the day was the *Alabama* Arbitration, between the United States and England, decided in 1872. The underlying claims arose when England allowed the American Confederacy to build a ship, the *Alabama*, in England, which the Union government in the United States believed to be contrary to England's obligations as a neutral. The arbitral tribunal found in favor of the United States.[144]

Arbitration remains a significant component of conflict resolution among sovereigns today, as detailed in chapter 6 of this book.

D. The Hague Peace Conferences

The first Hague Peace Conference was held in 1899, in large part at the instigation of Russia to try to limit armaments.[145] It is especially well-known for the creation of the Convention for the Pacific Settlement of International Disputes, which established the Permanent Court of Arbitration, or "PCA."[146] The PCA still operates today in the Netherlands, and is also discussed in chapter 6 of this book.

A second Hague Peace Conference was held in 1907, which resulted in the finalization of a large number of treaties, all designed in one way or another to bring more humane conduct into the practice and circumstances of war.[147] The two Hague Peace Conferences help to form the celebrated tradition of the "Law of the Hague" under international humanitarian law.[148]

Still, all of these advancements were not able to counteract the combination of economic adventurism, nationalistic interests, and imperialistic ambitions that, together with a network of sovereign alliances, helped to bring about World War I.[149] In chapter 3, we will continue tracing the development of international law after the end of World War I, and the beginning of the League of Nations.

---

143. Nussbaum, *supra* note 4, at 216. This kind of activity was among the subjects at the Second Hague Peace Conference in 1907, which included a Convention Respecting the Limitation of the Employment of Force for the Recovery of Contract Debts. *Id.* at 217.

144. *Id.* at 218.

145. *Id.* at 227.

146. *Id.* at 221.

147. *Id.* at 229.

148. Frits Kalshoven & Liesbeth Zegveld, Int'l Comm. of the Red Cross, *Constraints on the Waging of War* 21–23 (2001).

149. C. Howard-Ellis, *The Origin, Structure & Working of the League of Nations* 28–33 (1928).

X. Chapter Summary

In this chapter, we review the historical roots of public international law. Knowledge of this historical development of international law can guide practitioners to use its modern forms most effectively.

During the classical period in Greece, the different city-states would sometimes enter into alliances, truces, and other arrangements with one another. Most of the formal agreements during this period were entered into only among the Greek city-states themselves. On the whole the Greeks considered non-Greeks to be barbarians, so that these chiefly Greek-to-Greek agreements would not be considered international in a modern sense. The city-states sometimes also engaged in arbitration. But these were tools of political maneuvering rather than genuine attempts to resolve differences.

In classical Rome, the *jus gentium* was developed to deal with disputes arising between a Roman and an alien, or between aliens. It was supposed to represent all the best common features of any legal system. Gradually the *jus gentium* became more desirable than the domestic Roman legal rules, and ultimately it became the primarily applicable Roman law. But with that development, the phrase, "*jus gentium*," acquired ambiguity. On the one hand, it could refer to the actual rules that were used to resolve conflicts in Rome once it had eclipsed the pre-existing domestic Roman law. On the other hand it could refer to the philosophical precepts underlying the best common features of any legal system.

At the same time, the Roman framework also involved natural law, or *jus naturae*, which concerned itself with how the world worked as a matter of natural physical reality. Sometimes *jus gentium*, in the philosophical sense, was viewed as synonymous with this natural law. It was this philosophical interpretation of *jus gentium*, sometimes conflated with natural law, that began to be a basis for a "law of nations."

During the Middle Ages, two major influences tended to foreclose the development of international law. First, the Roman Catholic Church developed canon law, which was above nations or polities. Its over-arching influence would have eclipsed the development of international law, even if states (in the modern sense) had existed at the time. Second, the feudal system was based on loyalties to particular persons, such as emperors or kings. The system so concentrated on personal hierarchies that it was inconsistent with the modern idea of a state.

Philosophers during the Middle Ages did develop some notions we might now associate with international law, such as the "just war" doctrine. These were viewed as aspects of moral theology, rather than specifically legal concepts. Natural law, continuing from the Roman period, was also seen as an element of moral theology and superior over law itself. Parallels may be observed between these theological concepts and customary international law, general principles of law, and *jus cogens*.

During the early Renaissance, two Spanish clerics introduced theological concepts important for the development of international law: Francisco Vitoria and Francisco Suárez. Vitoria applied the just war doctrine to conflicts between the Spaniards and Indians in the Americas. In so doing, he demonstrated that the just war doctrine could protect non-Christian peoples. Suárez emphasized the distinction between the secular character of the state and the religious character of the Church. His work hinted at the interdependence of states.

Secular scholars also had an influence during the Renaissance. The French legal theorist, Jean Bodin, developed the idea of sovereignty as a means of advancing unified state power, in order to reduce the destructive impact of feudal and religious conflicts. Alberico Gentili, an Italian scholar working in England, published his famous *Law of War*, which was notable for its breadth on the subject of warfare and its related aspects. He declared that a war could be just on both sides, and incorporated a purely secular approach to the ideas that would become part of international law.

Hugo Grotius published the celebrated *On the Law of War and Peace*, and is considered by some (although not all) to be the founder of modern international law. He dealt with *jus gentium* as the law between states, rather than a universal natural law. He further developed ideas regarding just and unjust wars, particularly involving the treatment of prisoners and subject populations. His view was of a unified whole, and set forth a general theory of treaties. He insisted that historical authorities were most significant when their common agreement reflected a common agreement of states. His approach may be reflected in the modern idea of *opinio juris* as an element of customary international law.

The Peace of Westphalia in 1648 was important because it helped establish the modern idea of the nation-state. With the appearance of the nation-state, a "law of nations" could start to develop. Each international polity began to have a similar status as a nation-state, and a system of rights and responsibilities among all of them began to emerge.

Some of the philosophers of the European Enlightenment contributed to the development of international law. Thomas Hobbes allowed that among sovereigns an enlightened concern for self-preservation could result in the predominance of what he called "*jus gentium.*" He was referring to the practical reconciliation among initially hostile forces, rather than a predetermined benevolent system of rules. He referenced his idea of *jus gentium*, as being, in English, the "law of nations."

As the Enlightenment got into full swing, some philosophers determined that natural law was a secular concept, embodying Enlightenment values, that was fundamental to the law of nations. Others insisted that the law of nations was based solely on treaties among states and customary practices followed by states out of a conviction that the practices were required by the law of nations. These two groups have been called "naturalists" and "positivists." The views of the naturalists are reflected in the inclusion of "general principles of law" within modern international law, while the views of the positivists are reflected in the inclusion of treaties and conventions, and of as customary international law.

A leading exponent of the naturalists was Samuel Pufendorf, a German academic who served as the Swedish ambassador to Denmark. He emphasized a highly moralistic, yet secular, view of international law. He minimized the significance of treaties and state practice in determining the law of nations. By contrast, Richard Zouche (a law professor at Oxford) emphasized treaties and the customary behavior of states. He is viewed as an early positivist. Emerich de Vattel was a Swiss diplomat who had a very practical approach to the law of nations. While still believing in natural law, he also focused on the real-world observations, and introduced the doctrine of the sovereign equality of states.

After the Napoleonic wars, the Congress of Vienna in 1815 signaled the beginning of a new period in the history of international law. Briefly the "Concert of the Great Powers" tried to decide the political destiny of Europe. This loose affiliation of states may have been a precursor to the arrangement in the League of Nations, which accorded preeminence to four states as "Principal Allied and Associated Powers."

During the decades following the Congress of Vienna, states began entering into multilateral conventions laying down general rules for the conduct of states. It also became more accepted for conventions to be "open" for certain periods of time, to allow for later accessions. These features contrasted with earlier practices, in which multilateral treaties usually served as final resolutions of conflicts, rather than as statements of general legal rules.

Several particular features of some of the conventions of this period can be noted. Many of the new conventions focused on humanitarian issues. For example, in 1863 the International Red Cross movement began, and the next year its first convention proclaimed protections for the wounded, ambulances, and military hospitals. Also during this period, the movement toward the establishment of international organizations became more pronounced. Finally, many treaties of the era involved international commerce, including those with most-favored-nation and open-door provisions. Arbitration was also on the rise during this period, notably the *Alabama* Arbitration between the United States and England in 1872.

The first Hague Peace Conference in 1899 was called by Russia to try to limit armaments. It is especially well-known for the establishment of the Permanent Court of Arbitration, which still operates today. A second Hague Peace Conference in 1907 resulted in treaties designed to bring more humane conduct into the practice and circumstances of war. Still, all of these advancements were inadequate to forestall the onset of World War I.

XI. Chapter Review Questions

1. What is our purpose in reviewing the historical roots of public international law?

2. Why would agreements among the classical Greek city-states not be considered international in the modern sense?

3. What are the two possible meanings of *jus gentium*, as it developed under Roman law?

4. With what did the Roman idea of natural law concern itself?

5. During the Middle Ages, which two major influences tended to foreclose the development of international law, and why?

6. Who were the two Spanish clerics of the early Renaissance who introduced theological concepts important for the development of international law?

7. Jean Bodin developed the idea of sovereignty as a means to advancing a particular aim. What was that aim?

8. What was the famous publication by Alberico Gentili, and for what was it notable?

9. Who is sometimes (if not always) viewed as the founder of modern international law? What was his celebrated publication, and how did he deal with the concept of *jus gentium*?

10. Why is the 1648 Peace of Westphalia important?

11. When Thomas Hobbes referenced his idea of *jus gentium*, to what did he believe he was referring?

12. Among the Enlightenment philosophers addressing the law of nations, what was the difference between "naturalists" and "positivists"?

13. How could Samuel Pufendorf, Richard Zouche and Emerich de Vattel be contrasted?

14. After the 1815 Congress of Vienna, what loose affiliation of states tried to decide the political destiny of Europe?

15. During the decades following the Congress of Vienna, states began entering into multilateral treaties laying down certain kinds of rules. What would be a general description of these kinds of rules? Also, what did it mean that many of these conventions were "open" conventions?

16. What are some of the particular features of the conventions of the period after the Congress of Vienna?

17. When were the two major Hague Peace Conferences, and what did each accomplish?

XII. Additional Resources and General Bibliographic References

Kinji Akashi, *Cornelius van Bynkershoek: His Role in the History of International Law* (Kluwer Law International 1998).

David J. Bederman, *International Law in Antiquity* (Cambridge University Press 2001).

Matthew Craven, Malgosia Fitzmaurice, & Maria Vogiatzi, *Time, History and International Law* (Martinus Nijhoff Publishers 2007).

Wilhelm Georg Grewe, *The Epochs of International Law* (Michael Byers trans., Walter de Gruyter 2000).

Peter Haggenmacher, Michael Stollies, & Rüdiger Wolfrum, *Journal of the History of International Law* (Kluwer Law International)(periodically published since 1999), *available at* http://www.brill.com/journal-history -international-law-revue-dhistoire-du-droit-international. This source is also commonly referenced by its French title: *Revue d'histoire du droit interntional.*

Ingo J. Hueck, *The Discipline of the History of International Law: New Trends and Methods on the History of International Law*, 3 J. Hist. Int'l L. 194 (2001).

Mark W. Janis, *America and the Law of Nations, 1776–1939* (Oxford University Press 2010).

Mark W. Janis, *The American Tradition of International Law: Great Expectations, 1789–1914* (Clarendon Press 2004).

Douglas M. Johnston, *The Historical Foundations of World Order: The Tower and the Arena* (Martinus Nijhoff Publishers 2008).

Emmanuelle Jouannet, *The Liberal-Welfarist Law of Nations: History of International Law* (Christopher Sutcliffe trans., Cambridge University Press 2012).

Benedict Kingsbury & Benjamin Straumann, *The Roman Foundations of the Law of Nations: Alberico Gentili and the Justice of Empire* (Oxford University Press 2010).

Andree Kirchner, "Law of the Sea, History of," in *Max Planck Encyclopedia of Public International Law* (Rüdiger Wolfrum ed., Oxford University Press 2012), *available at* http://www.mpepil.com/home.

Robert Kolb, "International Organizations or Institutions, History of," in *Max Planck Encyclopedia of Public International Law* (Rüdiger Wolfrum ed., Oxford University Press 2012), *available at* http://www.mpepil.com/home.

Martti Koskenniemi, *The Gentle Civilizer of Nations: The Rise and Fall of International Law, 1870–1960* (Cambridge University Press 2002).

Martti Koskenniemi, "History of International Law Since World War II" in *Max Planck Encyclopedia of Public International Law* (Rüdiger Wolfrum ed., Oxford University Press 2012), *available at* http://www.mpepil.com/home.

Martti Koskenniemi, "History of International Law, World War I to World War II," in *Max Planck Encyclopedia of Public International Law* (Rüdiger Wolfrum ed., Oxford University Press 2012), *available at* http://www.mpepil.com/home.

Randall Lesaffer, *The Grotian Tradition Revisited: Change and Continuity in the History of International Law*, 73 Brit. Y.B. Int'l L. 103 (2002).

Peter Macalister-Smith & Joachim Schwietzke, *Literature and Documentary Sources Relating to the History of Public International Law: An Annotated Bibliography Survey*, 1 J. Hist. Int'l L. 136 (1999).

Stephen C. Neff, "A Short History of International Law," in *International Law* 3 (Malcolm D. Evans ed., Oxford University Press 2010).

Arthur Nussbaum, *A Concise History of the Law of Nations* (rev. ed., Macmillan 1954).

Alexander Orakhelashvili, *Research Handbook on the Theory and History of International Law* (Edward Elgar 2011)(Research Handbooks in International Law Series).

Wolfgang Preiser, "History of International Law, Ancient Times to 1648," in *Max Planck Encyclopedia of Public International Law* (Rüdiger Wolfrum ed., Oxford University Press 2012), *available at* http://www.mpepil.com/home.

Wolfgang Preiser, "History of International Law, Basic Questions and Principles," in *Max Planck Encyclopedia of Public International Law* (Rüdiger Wolfrum ed., Oxford University Press 2012), *available at* http://www.mpepil.com/home.

Christopher R. Rossi, *Broken Chain of Being: James Brown Scott and the Origins of Modern International Law* (Kluwer Law International 1998).

Hans-Ulrich Scupin, "History of International Law, 1851 to World War I," in *Max Planck Encyclopedia of Public International Law* (Rüdiger Wolfrum ed., Oxford University Press 2012), *available at* http://www.mpepil.com/home.

Gerry Simpson, "International Law in Diplomatic History," in *The Cambridge Companion to International Law* 25 (James Crawford & Martti Koskenniemi eds., Cambridge University Press 2012).

Gesina H.J. van der Molen, *Alberico Gentili and the Development of International Law: His Life, Work and Times* (2d ed., A.W. Sijthoff 1968).

J.H.W. Veizjil, *International Law in Historical Perspective* (A.W. Sijthoff 1979)(12 volumes).

Stephan Verosta, "History of International Law, 1648 to 1815," in *Max Planck Encyclopedia of Public International Law* (Rüdiger Wolfrum ed., Oxford University Press 2012), *available at* http://www.mpepil.com/home.

Alan Watson, *International Law in Archaic Rome: War and Religion* (Johns Hopkins University Press 1993).

Chapter 3

The Establishment and Structure of the United Nations

I. Introduction

Modern international law is closely connected with the United Nations (the "UN") and the UN Charter. The Charter determines the legality of many actions that can be taken by states.[1] Some bodies of the UN have the authority to enforce international law.[2] The UN Secretary-General has special responsibilities regarding the administration of many multilateral treaties.[3] In particular, the International Court of Justice, a principal organ of the UN, has substantial judicial responsibilities under international law.[4] There are many other examples of the close relationship between modern international law and the UN.[5]

---

1. The most famous example is Article 2(4) of the Charter, which prohibits "the threat or use of force against the territorial integrity or political independence of any state."

2. One of the most salient examples is the legal ability of the Security Council, under Article 42 of the Charter, to use military force "to maintain or restore international peace and security."

3. Note the discussion of the Secretary-General's role as a "depositary" for many multilateral treaties, provided in chapter 5 of this book.

4. The role and structure of the International Court of Justice (also called the "ICJ" or the "World Court") are discussed later in this chapter 3. Research points regarding its decisions are discussed in chapter 6, and special coverage of Article 38 of its Statute is the subject of chapter 4.

5. For example, Article 102 of the Charter generally requires each UN Member state to register every international agreement it enters into with the Secretary-General. Article 103 of the Charter states that its obligations shall prevail over those of all other international agree-

Therefore, in order to understand how international law works, one needs to understand the UN. Also, many aspects of UN operations relate to the history of the organization. This chapter therefore reviews the basic structure of the UN, with emphasis on the history of its establishment.

This chapter repeatedly makes comparisons between the UN and its predecessor organization, the League of Nations. This is partly because many treaties entered into under the League regime, and many court cases issued under it, are still considered authoritative today. It helps to have some background with the older system when dealing with these treaties and cases. Also, the differences between the League regime and the current UN regime can provide some indication as to why the first was less successful than the second.

II. The League of Nations

Although the League of Nations no longer exists, its creation and operation served as an important precursor for the modern structure of international law. A brief review of its establishment and structure is worthwhile.

World War I ended with the Treaty of Versailles, signed in 1919.[6] The structure and operating methods of the League were set forth in the "Covenant of the League of Nations,"[7] which was a part of the Versailles treaty.[8]

The overriding purpose of the League was to discourage the onset of any further wars that could have the destructive effect of World War I.[9] The major provisions of the Covenant were designed to forestall the possibility of League members going to war.[10] Although the Covenant did not prohibit going to

---

ments (whether entered into in the past or in the future). Article 25 generally requires all UN Member states to "accept and carry out the decisions of the Security Council."

6. Treaty of Peace, June 28, 1919, 225 Consol. T.S. 188 [hereinafter Versailles Treaty].

7. The Covenant of the League of Nations [hereinafter League Covenant] was set forth as "Part I" of the Versailles Treaty.

8. Part I of the Versailles Treaty (setting forth the League Covenant) was the first of 15 "Parts" to the treaty.

9. *See, e.g.,* Alfred Zimmern, *The League of Nations and the Rule of Law 1918–1935* 1 (photo reprint 1998) (1936) (The League of Nations "was devised at the close of the World War in the hope that it would conduce to a better understanding" among states; it was "aimed at providing machinery which would, so far as is humanly possible, prevent the recurrence of such a catastrophe" as World War I.).

10. *See, e.g.,* League Covenant arts. 10 (in which the Members of the League "undertake to respect and preserve as against external aggression the territorial integrity and existing political independence of all Members of the League") & 11 ("Any war or threat of war . . .

war,[11] it imposed requirements on Member states to engage in arbitration and other peaceful means of settling disputes between them.[12]

The Covenant established two main structural components for the League: an Assembly and a Council.[13] The Assembly was composed of representatives from each Member state of the League,[14] while the Council had only eight members; four designated in the Covenant as "Principal Allied and Associated Powers," and four elected for rotating terms.[15] It was envisioned that the Council would have major responsibility for maintaining peace.[16] The League's Assembly was the clear precursor for today's General Assembly in the UN, and the League's Council was similarly a clear precursor for today's UN Security Council. The League officially came into existence on January 10, 1920.[17]

Also envisioned as part of the League framework was a Permanent Court of International Justice, or "PCIJ."[18] This was an early attempt at the creation of

---

is hereby declared a matter of concern to the whole League, and the League shall take any action that may be deemed wise and effectual to safeguard the peace of nations.").

11. *See* Clive Parry, *League of Nations, in* 3 *Encyclopedia of Public International Law* 177, 178 § 2 (Rudolf Bernhardt ed., 1997) ("What was contemporaneously conceived to be the States' absolute right of war was not . . . sought to be excluded altogether . . . ."). Such a prohibition was included in the Kellogg-Briand Pact of 1928. General Treaty for the Renunciation of War, Aug. 27, 1928, 46 Stat. 2343, 94 L.N.T.S. 57.

12. *See, e.g.,* League Covenant arts. 12 (generally requiring League Members to submit "any dispute likely to lead to a rupture" either to "arbitration or to inquiry by the Council," and prohibiting "resort to war until three months after the award by the arbitrators or the report by the Council"); 13 (generally requiring League Members to submit to arbitration "the whole subject-matter" of any "dispute [which] shall arise between them which they recognize to be suitable for submission to arbitration and which cannot be satisfactorily settled by diplomacy") & 15 (generally requiring League Members to submit to the Council "any dispute likely to lead to a rupture, which is not submitted to arbitration in accordance with Article 13").

13. *Id.* art. 2 (providing that the "action of the League . . . shall be effected through the instrumentality of an Assembly and of a Council with a permanent Secretariat").

14. *Id.* art. 3 ("The Assembly shall consist of Representatives of the Members of the League.").

15. *Id.* art. 4. The Preamble to the Versailles Treaty referred to five states as "Principal Allied and Associated Powers" ("the United States of America, the British Empire, France, Italy and Japan"), but since the United States never joined the League, there were in fact only four such powers.

16. *See, e.g., id.* art. 16 ("It shall be the duty of the Council . . . to recommend to the several Governments what effective military, naval or air force the Members of the League shall severally contribute to the armed forces to be used to protect the covenants of the League.").

17. Zimmern, *supra* note 9, at 306.

18. League Covenant art. 14 ("The Council shall formulate and submit to the Members of the League for adoption plans for the establishment of a Permanent Court of International Justice.").

a judicial body to hear disputes between states. It was a precursor to the current International Court of Justice (mentioned earlier in this chapter), established as part of the UN. League negotiators began drafting a "Statute" for the PCIJ almost as soon as the League commenced operations. This Statute was designed as a kind of charter for the PCIJ.[19] The Statute became effective in September 1921, and the PCIJ held its first meeting in January of 1922.

The institutions set up by the Covenant, however, and the procedures it provided for peaceful dispute settlement, were inadequate for the fractious times following World War I.[20] Furthermore, the failure of the United States to ratify the Covenant and become a Member of the League,[21] together with the stresses of the Great Depression,[22] also stood in the way of the League's success. Accordingly, the League fell into disarray and was functionally irrelevant well before the end of World War II.[23]

As noted earlier, awareness of the League's history provides important background for understanding the UN. More importantly from a research perspective, many of the treaties entered into and decisions issued during the period of the League are still in force today. In modern international law research, it is not unusual to encounter treaties and judicial opinions dating from the League's years, and dealing with League institutions.

For example, the International Labor Organization, still very active today, was created as part of the League framework.[24] Important decisions of the PCIJ include the *Chorzów Factory* Case[25] (which addressed state responsibility for wrongful acts) and the *East Greenland* Case[26] (which, among other things, established that oral agreements could be binding among states). PCIJ decisions such as these are still often referred to today.

---

19. C. Howard-Ellis, *The Origin, Structure & Working of the League of Nations* 365 (1928) ("One of the first acts of the Council was . . . at its second session, held in February 1920 . . . to appoint a Committee of Jurists to frame a statute for the proposed Court.").

20. *See id.* at 56 ("[T]he League was crippled at the outset by the exclusion of the ex-enemies and by the fact that the Allies left the chief questions outstanding to inter-Allied bodies" other than the League.).

21. Parry, *supra* note 11, at 183 § 9.

22. *Id.* at 184 § 12.

23. *Id.* ("[T]he last political action of the League was the adoption of the Assembly resolution of December 14, 1939 declaring the Soviet Union to be no longer a member by reason of its refusal to accept mediation of its complaint against Finland.").

24. The ILO was established pursuant to Part XIII of the Versailles Treaty.

25. Factory at Chorzów (Ger. v. Pol.) (Merits), 1928 P.C.I.J. (ser. A) No. 13 (Sept. 13).

26. Legal Status of Eastern Greenland (Den. v. Nor.), 1933 P.C.I.J. (ser. A/B) No. 53 (Apr. 5).

III. Historical Situation at the End of World War II

In 1944, as World War II was drawing to a close, representatives of the United States, the United Kingdom, the Union of Soviet Socialist Republics (the "USSR"), and China met at an estate in Washington, D.C. called Dumbarton Oaks.[27] The League of Nations had actually been a loose association of states, rather than a solid international institution.[28] This was viewed as a shortcoming. Accordingly, the participants at the Dumbarton Oaks Conference proposed a new "General International Organization."[29]

Although this proposal reflected agreement on general principles, some important specific issues (chiefly regarding voting procedures in the Security Council) were resolved in February 1945.[30] This was at the Yalta Conference, held at the Black Sea resort of Yalta, which was then in the USSR and is now part of Ukraine. The leading conferees were Franklin Roosevelt (for the United States), Winston Churchill (for the United Kingdom), and Joseph Stalin (for the USSR).

Finally, in May and June of 1945, nearly 300 delegates from 50 states met in San Francisco and negotiated the final text of the new "Charter of the United Nations."[31] The Charter was signed by representatives from all the states attending in San Francisco on June 26.[32] For the first time, the world had a permanent international organization designed to afford representation to virtually all nations.

IV. United Nations and Its Principal Organs

In current politics, many different people have many different opinions of the UN. Some view it as being very valuable, others view it very negatively, and still others have views somewhere between these extremes. Regardless of the diversity of political views about the UN, its institutions serve a central function in modern international law. Indeed, the UN Charter can be viewed

---

27. *E.g.,* Wilhelm G. Grewe & Daniel-Erasmus Khan, *Drafting History, in* 1 *The Charter of the United Nations: A Commentary* 1, 2 & 8 (Bruno Simma et al. eds., 2d ed. 2002).

28. Parry, *supra* note 11, at 178 § 2 ("In contrast to the [UN] Charter, the Covenant . . . was not so much the constituent instrument of an international organization as a set of undertakings between States.").

29. Grewe & Khan, *supra* note 27, at 8.

30. *Id.* at 9–10.

31. *Id.* at 10.

32. *Id.* The Charter entered into force less than five months later on October 24.

as a "constitution" not only of the UN,[33] but also for much of modern international law.[34] We will see this operating in various contexts throughout this book.

The United Nations is constituted of six principal organs:

(a) General Assembly

(b) Security Council

(c) International Court of Justice

(d) Secretariat

(e) Economic and Social Council

(f) Trusteeship Council

In this chapter 3, we first examine the six principal organs, although we will devote more attention to some than others. We will then look at certain additional UN bodies and the connections that they can have to international law.

A. The General Assembly and the Security Council

Of all the UN principal organs, the General Assembly is the only one that consistently and continually has representatives from all the UN Member states.[35] Each Member state can have as many as five delegates to the General Assembly,[36] and each Member state (regardless of size, population, wealth, or influence) has only one vote.[37] The General Assembly is a deliberative body that operates largely through the passage of resolutions. The UN Charter makes it clear that the General Assembly does not generally have the authority to compel any state to take any particular action. The resolutions it passes do not generally, in and of themselves, have the force or effect of international law.

---

33. *E.g.*, Christopher C. Joyner, *Conclusion: The United Nations as International Law-giver*, in *The United Nations and International Law* 432, 434 (Christopher C. Joyner ed., 1997) ("The Charter, in effect the constitution of the United Nations, embodies the fundamental law of the Organization.").

34. *See, e.g., id.* at 435 ("The Charter of the United Nations is an instrument of international law [that has a] profound influence upon the dynamics of the international process for legal development.").

35. U.N. Charter art. 9(1) ("The General Assembly shall consist of all the Members of the United Nations."). The Charter contains no such language for any of the other UN principal organs.

36. *Id.* art. 9(2).

37. *Id.* art. 18(1).

However, the process of passing these resolutions is important for providing a medium for the exchange of ideas, viewpoints and values among states.

Note the similarity of the General Assembly of the UN to the "Assembly" established by the League of Nations. In both contexts, the body consisted of representatives from all the members of the association or organization. In both contexts, each member state had one vote, although in both contexts there could be a larger number of delegates for each member (three in the League's Assembly, and five in the UN's General Assembly). In both contexts this large body was viewed as being chiefly deliberative, whereas a smaller co-ordinate body was to have more compulsory authority.

For the UN, that body is the Security Council, which consists of representatives from fifteen Member states.[38] Five of these are permanent members of the Security Council, and the other ten are elected by the General Assembly for rotating two-year terms.[39] Half of the non-permanent members of the Security Council are elected each year, on a staggered basis.[40] The Security Council's compulsory authority derives from Article 25 of the UN Charter, which provides that all UN Member states "agree to accept and carry out the decisions of the Security Council." There is no such corresponding provision regarding General Assembly resolutions or decisions.

The UN Charter also provides that the Security Council shall have "primary responsibility for the maintenance of international peace and security."[41] Chapter VII of the UN Charter gives the Security Council the authority, under certain circumstances, to pursue international peace and security through the use of coercive measures. These can include the complete or partial interruption of economic relations,[42] the severance of diplomatic relations,[43] and the use of armed force,[44] all at the direction of the Security Council.

Note that in some of these respects, there are similarities to the "Council" established by the League of Nations. In both contexts, the body is substantially smaller than the body having universal representation (eight members for the League's Council and fifteen members for the UN's Security Council). In both contexts, five of the members of this smaller body would be permanent, with the remainder being elected by the larger body. (Although there were two dif-

---

38. *Id.* art. 23(1).
39. *Id.* art. 23(2).
40. *Id.*
41. *Id.* art. 24(1).
42. *See id.* art. 41.
43. *See id.*
44. *See id.* art. 42.

ferences in this respect: there are ten rotating members for the Security Council,[45] while the League's Council had only four rotating members;[46] and the Charter provides that the rotating members have two-year terms,[47] while the Covenant did not specify the terms of the rotating members.[48])

Another major similarity concerned the missions of the UN's Security Council and the League's Council. As noted earlier, the UN's Security Council has "primary responsibility for the maintenance of international peace and security."[49] It also appears from the League's Covenant that its "Council" was thought of in a similar way. Under the League's Covenant, the League's Council was to provide advice in the event of any aggression against any League Member.[50] Matters that threatened to lead to a "rupture" were to be submitted to an "arbitration or inquiry" arranged with the Council.[51] Any matters not submitted to arbitration or inquiry were to be submitted directly to the Council itself for resolution.[52] Accordingly, the Council also seems to have been charged with some degree of responsibility for encouraging international tranquility.

One difference between the two organs is that the UN Security Council, also as noted earlier, has the power under the Charter to impose economic, diplomatic, and military sanctions on non-complying states.[53] The League's Council had no such express coercive power; it was expected to encourage peace through arbitration and diplomacy.

B. The Secretary-General and the Secretariat

The Secretary-General is the chief administrative officer of the UN.[54] The Secretary-General, or a representative, attends all meetings of the General Assembly, Security Council and ECOSOC (discussed later in this chapter). The Secretary-General also performs such functions as are entrusted to him by these organs.[55] The Secretary-General may bring to the attention of the Security Coun-

---

45. *Id.* art. 23(1).
46. League Covenant, art. 4, para. 1.
47. U.N. Charter art. 23(1).
48. League Covenant art. 4, para. 1.
49. U.N. Charter art. 24(1).
50. League Covenant art. 10.
51. *Id.* art. 12.
52. *Id.* art. 15, para. 1.
53. U.N. Charter arts. 41 & 42.
54. *Id.* art. 97.
55. *Id.* art. 98. (All Secretaries-General have been male so far, although there is no requirement for this.)

cil any matter that he thinks may threaten international peace and security.[56] The Secretariat consists of the Secretary-General and his staff,[57] which the Secretary-General appoints under regulations established by the General Assembly.[58]

The role of the Secretariat is administrative in character, rather than executive. The Secretary-General and the Secretariat are not "executive officers." They do not have independent authority to generally execute any and all rules of any kind. Instead, they operate as facilitators. The Secretariat works behind the scenes to facilitate resolution of controversies and disputes between governments of Member states.[59] And, of course, the Secretariat plans and coordinates more than 5000 meetings and international conferences every year under UN auspices.[60]

The Charter and other UN instruments give the Secretary-General certain duties. For example, the Secretary-General serves as depositary for many multilateral conventions, and the Secretary-General is required to deliver numerous reports to a broad variety of UN organs and bodies.[61] Although significant, these roles are neither directly legislative nor executive. Accordingly, the Secretary-General and the Secretariat have influence over legal rules that arise during UN activities, but the nature of that influence is most often indirect. As we come to work with documents generated by the Secretary-General and the Secretariat, we will need to bear this in mind.

C. The International Court of Justice

Very important among the six UN principal organs is the International Court of Justice, or "ICJ." We saw earlier in this chapter that it is the successor to the PCIJ established under the League of Nations. It is the principal judicial organ of the UN.[62] In that capacity, it regularly hears and resolves disputes between sovereign states through judicial proceedings at its headquarters in The Hague, a city that is the seat of government of the Netherlands. It conducts its operations pursuant to a charter, called "The Statute of the International Court of

---

56. *Id.* art. 99.

57. *Id.* art. 97.

58. *Id.* art. 101(1).

59. Joyner, *supra* note 33, at 447.

60. *Id.*

61. *Id.* at 448. As noted earlier in this chapter, the role of the Secretary-General as depositary for conventions is discussed in chapter 5 of this book. The Secretariat is also generally responsible for administering the internal rules and regulations of the UN as an operating entity. *Id.*

62. U.N. Charter art. 92; ICJ Statute art. 1.

Justice" (or the "ICJ Statute").[63] The ICJ Statute was strongly based on the PCIJ Statute under the League of Nations.

All Members of the UN are automatically states parties to the ICJ Statute by virtue of their UN membership. This does not mean that the ICJ necessarily has jurisdiction over any dispute between any two or more Member states. Jurisdiction of the ICJ over any particular dispute is a complex matter that will be discussed in chapter 6 of this book. However, status as a state party to the ICJ Statute does mean that each UN Member state is obliged to follow any judgment of the ICJ in any case to which it is a party.[64] Upon any failure by any party to comply with an ICJ judgment, the other party may have recourse to the Security Council, which can then decide on measures necessary to effectuate the judgment.[65]

Only states may be parties in cases before the ICJ,[66] although duly authorized UN organs and specialized agencies can request that the ICJ deliver advisory opinions.[67] As a technical matter, ICJ opinions are not supposed to have the effects of *stare decisis*.[68] Nevertheless, the ICJ, and other tribunals dealing with international subjects, frequently cite earlier ICJ decisions as persuasive authority, even if they are not technically binding.[69]

D. ECOSOC and the Trusteeship Council

We will cover these two organs only briefly. At the current time they do not have a central role for purposes of international law. The Economic and Social Council (often called "ECOSOC") consists of representatives from 54 Member states, who are elected for three-year terms.[70] The elections are annual and on a staggered basis, so that a third of the body is subject to election every year.[71]

---

63. Statute of the International Court of Justice, June 26, 1945, 59 Stat. 1055, 3 Bevans 1179 [hereinafter ICJ Statute].

64. U.N. Charter art. 94(1).

65. *Id*. art. 94(2).

66. ICJ Statute art. 34(1).

67. *Id*. arts. 65–68; U.N. Charter art. 96.

68. *Id*. art. 59 ("The decision of the Court has no binding force except between the parties and in respect of that particular case.").

69. *E.g.*, Malcolm N. Shaw, *International Law* 1104 (6th ed. 2008) ("[T]he judgment of the Court . . . is final and without appeal. Although it has no binding force except between the parties . . . , such decisions are often very influential in the evolution of new rules of international law.").

70. U.N. Charter art. 61(1) & (2). ECOSOC originally had 18 Members, but the Charter was amended in 1963 to expand the number to 27, and in 1971 to expand it again to 54.

71. *Id*. art. 61(3).

Under the Charter, many of the responsibilities of ECOSOC are delibera-tive, in much the same way that the General Assembly is primarily delibera-tive. ECOSOC's focus, however, is specifically on "international economic, social, cultural, educational, health and related matters,"[72] rather than the broader range of matters that can be addressed by the General Assembly. ECOSOC is permitted to make studies, reports and recommendations, to pre-pare draft conventions, and call international conferences, regarding its areas of competence.[73] It also has responsibilities regarding the UN specialized agen-cies[74] that will be discussed in part V of this chapter. Furthermore, ECOSOC coordinates links between the UN and non-governmental organizations.[75] Most of these activities are political in character and do not directly involve the mak-ing or enforcement of international law.[76]

Those who worked on the establishment of the UN may have hoped that ECOSOC would achieve a degree of prominence in economic, social, and cul-tural affairs, such as the Security Council has since achieved in international se-curity.[77] Although its coordination with specialized agencies and non-governmental organizations is notable, ECOSOC has generally not achieved the prominence originally contemplated.[78]

The UN's Trusteeship Council generally followed in the steps of the "man-date" system established under the League of Nations.[79] Most of the territories administered by the Trusteeship Council had been mandates under the League[80]

---

72. *Id.* art. 62(1).

73. *Id.* art. 62(1)-(4).

74. *Id.* arts. 63 & 64.

75. *Id.* art. 71.

76. Frederic L. Kirgis, Jr., *United Nations Economic and Social Council, in* 4 *Encyclopedia of International Law* 1089, 1092 § 4 (Rudolf Bernhardt, ed. 2000) (noting that ECOSOC "does not have formal power to make binding decisions, except as to internal matters").

77. *See, e.g.,* Rainer Lagoni & Oliver Landwehr, *The Economic and Social Council, in* 2 *The Charter of the United Nations: A Commentary* 977, 979–80 (Bruno Simma et al. eds., 2d ed. 2002) (describing the concerns of the negotiators at the San Francisco Conference in view of the report of the "Bruce Committee" delivered under the League of Nations framework).

78. Kirgis, *supra* note 76, at 1092 § 4 ("ECOSOC has never satisfied the hopes of those at the San Francisco Conference who saw it as the primary policy-making body for inter-national economic and social cooperation.").

79. Dietrich Rauschning, *United Nations Trusteeship System, in* 4 *Encyclopedia of Inter-national Law* 1193, 1193 § 1 (Rudolf Bernhardt ed., 2000).

80. *Id.* at 1196 § 4(a) (referencing the placement of the League's "B mandates" in Africa under the trusteeship system, as well as the similar placement of the League's "C mandates," island territories in the Pacific Ocean).

and the Trusteeship Council was designed chiefly to assist those territories obtain self-governance or independence.[81] The last remaining UN Trust Territory was Palau, which gained independence on October 1, 1994.[82] The Trusteeship Council suspended its operation effective November 1, 1994, and it no longer meets regularly.[83]

V. Specialized Agencies of the UN

The UN Charter envisions that members of the UN would, by separate multilateral treaties, establish "specialized agencies."[84] Each such specialized agency would have responsibilities defined in the treaty creating it. The Charter provides that such responsibilities would be in "economic, social, cultural, educational, health and related fields."[85] Although each such specialized agency would have its own staff and governing bodies, the UN Charter still provided that the General Assembly would have a degree of approval authority over their financial and budgetary operations.[86]

This system has in fact come into being. Among the most famous of these specialized agencies are UNESCO (the United Nations Educational, Scientific and Cultural Organization), WHO (the World Health Organization), and more recently, the IAEA (the International Atomic Energy Agency). But there are many more.

Many of the specialized agencies have substantial impact throughout the world. However, as with ECOSOC, their influence on the creation of international law is generally indirect. The specialized agencies do not usually have the formal power to legislate binding rules,[87] although there are some exceptions.[88] Nevertheless, many of the specialized agencies can have enormous influence when their work is taken up by other entities, such as the Security Council or indi-

---

81. *See Trusteeship Council*, United Nations, http://www.un.org/en/mainbodies/trusteeship/ (last visited June 8, 2013).

82. *Id.*

83. *Id.*

84. U.N. Charter art. 57(1) & (2).

85. *Id.* art. 57(1).

86. *Id.* art. 17(3).

87. Frederic L. Kirgis, *Specialized Law-Making Processes, in The United Nations and International Law* 65, 76 (Christopher Joyner ed., 1997).

88. For example, the International Civil Aeronautics Organization and the International Maritime Organization each have the authority to directly make rules binding on individual states. Kirgis, *supra* note 87, at 77–79.

vidual Member states.[89] The specialized agencies, and research regarding their activities, are discussed in chapter 9 of this book.

VI. Chapter Summary

After the end of World War I, the Treaty of Versailles established the League of Nations. Although the League was ultimately unsuccessful, it created precursor institutions for the United Nations at the end of World War II.

The UN is constituted of six principal organs: the General Assembly, the Security Council, the Secretariat, the International Court of Justice, ECOSOC, and the Trusteeship Council. Of these, the last two generally have a less central role in the creation of international law than the others. The General Assembly is the only organ that always has representatives from all the UN Member states. Its resolutions generally do not, in and of themselves, state rules of international law, but they can be very important in the development of international law.

The Security Council consists of representatives from fifteen Member states, five of which are permanent members. The Security Council has compulsory authority under the UN Charter, so its decisions have the force and effect of international law. The Security Council has primary responsibility for the maintenance of international peace and security. The UN Charter allows it to order the interruption of economic relations and the use of armed force to help maintain international peace and security.

The Secretary-General is the chief administrative officer of the UN. The Secretary-General performs a facilitating role for the other organs of the UN, rather than a role that is formally executive. The Secretary-General, together with his staff, comprises the Secretariat of the UN.

The International Court of Justice (or the "ICJ") is the principal judicial organ of the UN. It sits in The Hague, the seat of government of the Netherlands. It regularly hears and resolves disputes between sovereign states through its judicial proceedings. The ICJ also gives advisory opinions, which may be requested by duly authorized UN organs and specialized agencies. It operates pursuant to a charter, called the "Statute of the International Court of Justice." Only states may be parties in cases before the ICJ. The ICJ and its Statute were modeled upon coun-

---

89. In recent years, for example, the Security Council has issued resolutions imposing legal consequences, when those resolutions have resulted from reports of the IAEA. *E.g.,* S.C. Res. 1441, U.N. Doc. S/RES/1441 (Nov. 8, 2002) (requiring Iraq to comply with certain informational and other requests posed by the IAEA).

terparts under the League of Nations; the Permanent Court of International Justice (the "PCIJ"), and its Statute.

The Economic and Social Council (or "ECOSOC") is a deliberative body addressing international economic, social, cultural, educational, health, and related matters. It has special responsibilities for coordinating the work of the UN specialized agencies and dealing with non-governmental organizations represented at the UN. However, ECOSOC is generally not directly involved in the making or enforcement of international law rules. The operations of the Trusteeship Council were suspended in 1994 and it no longer holds regular meetings.

Under the UN Charter, there are many specialized agencies, each established by a separate multilateral treaty, and each with responsibilities defined in its treaty. Examples are UNESCO, the WHO and the IAEA. The specialized agencies have substantial impact, but most do not have the authority to legislate binding rules. Other entities, however, such as the Security Council, can take up the work of the specialized agencies in ways that give their work mandatory effect.

VII. Chapter Review Questions

1. What were some of the differences between the League of Nations and the UN?

2. What are some of the differences between the UN General Assembly and the UN Security Council?

3. Is the Secretary-General the chief executive officer of the UN? Why or why not?

4. What is the chief judicial organ of the UN? Where does it sit?

5. What are some examples of UN specialized agencies?

6. Under what circumstances can the work of UN specialized agencies become binding under international law?

VIII. Additional Resources and General Bibliographic References

Franz Cede & Lily Sucharipa-Behrmann, *The United Nations: Law and Practice* (Martinus Nijhoff Publishers 2001).

Simon Chesterman, Thomas M. Franck, & David M. Malone, *Law and Practice of the United Nations: Documents and Commentary* (New York: Oxford University Press 2008).

Benedetto Conforti & Carlo Focarelli, *The Law and Practice of the United Nations* (4th rev. ed., Boston: Martinus Nijhoff Publishers 2010)(vol. 53 of Legal Aspects of International Organization Series).

Robert Kolb, *An Introduction to the Law of the United Nations* (Katherine Del Mar trans., Portland, Or.: Hart 2010).

Oscar Schachter & Christopher C. Joyner, *United Nations Legal Order* (Cambridge: Grotius Publications, Cambridge University Press, 1995)(2 volumes).

United Nations Department of Public Information, *United Nations Today* (New York: United Nations 2008), *available at* http://unic.un.org/aroundworld /unics/common/documents/publications/untoday/UN_TODAY_BOOK _eng.pdf.

Thomas G. Weiss & Sam Daws, *The Oxford Handbook on the United Nations* (New York: Oxford University Press 2009 prtg. & 2007).

Andreas Zimmermann, Christian Tomuschat, Karin Oellers-Frahm & Christian J. Tams, *The Statute of the International Court of Justice: A Commentary* (2d ed., New York: Oxford University Press 2012).

Chapter 4

The Modern Sources of International Law

I. Introduction

This chapter introduces the idea of "sources of international law." Broadly speaking, there are five kinds of sources for international law. This chapter describes what they are and where they come from. To do this, we must first take a closer look at the International Court of Justice (the "ICJ"), and its Statute, both introduced in the preceding chapter 3.

II. ICJ Statute; Comparison with PCIJ Statute

As noted in chapter 3, the modern ICJ was preceded by the former Permanent Court of International Justice (the "PCIJ"), established under the League of Nations. The ICJ Statute is based on the earlier Statute for the PCIJ.[1]

The ICJ Statute specifies that the ICJ consists of fifteen judges, who are elected for renewable nine-year terms.[2] The judges of the ICJ, who are sometimes referred to as "members of the Court," must be very highly qualified. They must "possess the qualifications required in their respective countries for appointment

---

1. U.N. Charter art. 92 (declaring that the ICJ Statute "is based upon the Statute of the Permanent Court of International Justice").

2. Statute of the International Court of Justice, June 26, 1945, 59 Stat. 1055, 3 Bevans 1179 [hereinafter ICJ Statute], arts. 3 & 13; Statute of the Permanent Court of International Justice, Dec. 16, 1920, 6 L.N.T.S. 379 [hereinafter PCIJ Statute], arts. 3 & 13.

to the highest judicial offices" or be "jurisconsults of recognized competence in international law."[3] No member of the Court may exercise any political or administrative function, and no member of the Court may act as counsel or advocate in any case.[4]

Also as noted in chapter 3, the PCIJ fell into disuse during World War II. With the establishment of the United Nations (the "UN") in 1945, the PCIJ was treated as having expired, and the ICJ took its place.[5] The ICJ Statute provides that when earlier treaties give jurisdiction over related disputes to the PCIJ, it is now the ICJ that shall have jurisdiction over such disputes.[6]

While the Statutes for the two successive courts are nearly identical, there are some subtle differences. As noted earlier, the ICJ is clearly the "primary judicial organ of the United Nations," and there are functional links between the ICJ and certain UN bodies, particularly the Security Council with respect to potentially enforcing judgments. By contrast, the link between the PCIJ and the League of Nations was never so tightly drawn.[7] Also, the earlier court's statute provided no means for its own amendment, thus potentially requiring unanimous agreement for any changes. However, the ICJ Statute provides for the terms of its amendment, and they do not require unanimity.[8]

III. Sources of International Law

The sources of international law are listed in Article 38(1) of the ICJ Statute. The list contains four clauses. However, since the fourth clause describes two different kinds of sources, Article 38(1) really lists five types of sources. Article 38(1) reads as follows:

"The Court, whose function is to decide in accordance with international law such disputes as are submitted to it, shall apply:

---

3. ICJ Statute art. 2; PCIJ Statute art. 2.

4. ICJ Statute arts. 16 & 17; PCIJ Statute arts. 16 & 17.

5. *Brownlie's Principles of Public International Law* 721–22 (James Crawford ed., 8th ed. 2012)[hereinafter Brownlie].

6. ICJ Statute art. 37.

7. *See* Brownlie, *supra* note 5, at 722.

8. Article 69 of the ICJ Statute provides that amendments "shall be effected by the same procedure as is provided by the Charter of the United Nations for amendments to the Charter." Under Article 108 of the UN Charter, amendments to the Charter "shall come into force . . . when they have been adopted by a vote of two thirds of the members of the General Assembly and ratified . . . by two thirds of the Members of the UN, including all the permanent members of the Security Council."

(a) international conventions, whether general or particular, establishing rules expressly recognized by the contesting states;

(b) international custom, as evidence of a general practice accepted as law;

(c) the general principles of law recognized by civilized nations;

(d) . . . judicial decisions and the teachings of the most highly qualified publicists of the various nations, as subsidiary means for the determination of rules of law."

Technically speaking, Article 38(1) does not refer to these listed authorities as "sources." However, the lead-in clause directs the ICJ "to apply" these authorities in deciding cases in accordance with international law. Accordingly, most courts and writers refer to the authorities listed in Article 38(1) of the ICJ Statute as "sources of international law."[9]

A. International Conventions

Although the language of Clause (1)(a) does not contain the word "treaties," the broadest meaning of the clause is that it indeed does encompass all treaties. There is a very subtle distinction in meaning between the words "treaty" and "convention," which is discussed in chapter 5 of this book. We will see there that not all treaties are technically "conventions." However, the drafters of the PCIJ and ICJ Statutes intended their use of the word "conventions" to include all international treaties. This item in the Article 38(1) list is best thought of as being composed of "treaties and conventions."

As suggested above, we will be dealing with treaties and conventions in much greater detail in chapter 5.

B. International Custom

We got a glimpse of the development of customary international law during our historical review in chapter 2 of this book. Customary rules develop over periods of time (usually quite lengthy) when the behavior of states be-

---

9. For example, J.G. Starke, Malcolm Shaw and Ian Brownlie all discuss the elements of Article 38(1) under chapter headings referencing the "sources" of international law. *Starke's International Law* (I.A. Shearer ed., 11th ed. 1994) (title and contents of chapter 2); Malcolm N. Shaw, *International Law* (6th ed. 2008) (title and contents of chapter 3); Brownlie, *supra* note 5 (title and contents of chapter 2).

comes consistent in particular ways. Once it becomes clear that the pattern of state practice exists, if it also becomes clear that states engage in the practice out of a sense of mutual legal obligation, then we say that the practice has become a rule of customary international law.

For example, over many centuries it became clear that states would provide diplomatic immunity to foreign ambassadors. Until 1964, however, there was no universal treaty providing for diplomatic immunity.[10] So, for many centuries, the general rule of diplomatic immunity covering ambassadors while on foreign assignment was simply a matter of customary international law.

There are no books that comprehensively list all the rules of customary international law. The existence of such rules is determined through detailed research into state practices, and also detailed research into indications that states may view their behavior as arising from a sense of mutual legal obligation. Although this process can be arduous, courts do enforce rules of customary international law, and many commentators, judges, and diplomats can take them quite seriously.

Of course, the identification of any rule of customary international law, if it is not already well established in court cases and the works of prominent commentators, can be very subjective. There can be disagreement between different authorities as to whether rules of customary international law exist in particular subject-matter areas and, if so, what their precise content might be. This is one thing that makes researching international law especially interesting.

We have much more to say about customary international law, and ways of researching it, in chapter 8 of this book.

C. General Principles of Law

There are various ways to view this category. The most common way is to say that "general principles of law" are basic underpinning legal ideas that are so general (and perhaps so self-evident) that they transcend all national borders and all differences between legal systems. That is to say, they are elemental characteristics of law as law, rather than as the law of any particular legal system.[11]

Thought of in this way, one such "general principle of law" might be the principle of proportionality—that the punishment or other corrective action taken by the law must be proportionate to whatever initial action or event en-

---

10. The 1964 treaty providing for diplomatic immunity was the Vienna Convention on Diplomatic Relations, Apr. 18, 1961, 23 U.S.T. 3227, 500 U.N.T.S. 95 (entered into force Apr. 24, 1964).

11. *See generally* Oscar Schachter, *International Law in Theory and Practice* 50–55 (1991).

gendered the law's application.[12] Another such principle might be the idea that any legal wrong must occasion a legal means of redressing that wrong, or that the law must afford a meaningful opportunity to redress legal wrongs.[13] Decisions of the PCIJ and ICJ have established that these kinds of considerations can constitute general principles of law.[14]

These general principles, as the name implies, might usually be considered to be more general than rules of customary international law. Also, the means of determining their existence would be different from that required for customary international law. To determine the existence of a rule of customary international law, one would need to examine state practice to see if it was general and consistent, and one would need to determine if states engaged in the relevant practices out of a sense of mutual legal obligation.

However, it is not necessary to make such determinations to establish a general principle of law. Such principles could often be established simply by pointing to the works of prominent commentators and judicial decisions that might indicate the presence of such a rule. The direct examination of state practice would not normally be necessary.[15]

D. Judicial Decisions

When Article 38(1)(d) refers to "judicial decisions," the first things most readers may think of would be decisions of the ICJ and the PCIJ. And indeed, decisions of these two courts (the first being the successor to the second) are viewed as persuasive indicators of international law and are often cited in ICJ decisions. They are addressed in detail in chapter 6 of this book.

However, many international organizations maintain judicial bodies that issue decisions that would be included within this category. Examples would be the European Court of Human Rights, which operates as part of the Coun-

---

12. *E.g.*, Shaw, *supra* note 9, at 1140 ("The concepts of necessity and proportionality are at the heart of self-defense in international law.").

13. *Id.* at 801 (confirming the significance of the "basic principle with regard to reparation, or the remedying of a breach of an international obligation for which the state concerned is responsible").

14. *E.g.*, Factory at Chorzów (Ger. v. Pol.)(Merits), 1928 P.C.I.J. (ser. A) No. 13, at 47–48 (Sept. 13) (redress of legal wrongs); Gabčíkokvo-Nagymaros Project (Hung./Slovk.), 1997 I.C.J. 7, 56–57 & 80 (Sept. 25) (respectively, proportionality and redress of legal wrongs).

15. *See* Brownlie, *supra* note 5, at 37 ("these principles . . . are primarily abstractions and have been accepted for so long and so generally as to be no longer *directly* connected with state practice") (emphasis in original).

cil of Europe.[16] Still another would be the Dispute Settlement Body that operates under the auspices of the World Trade Organization.[17]

Furthermore, it is not unusual for states to agree to arbitration, or other dispute resolution methods, on an *ad hoc* basis. That is, states agree to seek resolution of their disputes pursuant to a judicial mechanism that they establish on a purpose-specific basis for the particular dispute. The "judicial decisions" referenced in Article 38(1) would include awards and other decisions issued through arbitration, often generally called "arbitral awards."

Finally, the reference to "judicial decisions" in Article 38(1) also covers domestic tribunals in the different states when they address issues of international law. Of course, various tribunals might decide various issues in various ways, and different decisions on particular matters might not always be consistent. But this is not terribly different from situations that can develop in common-law countries when different courts decide particular matters in different ways. Usually, courts, commentators, and states are able to live with these ambiguities for the purposes of the day-to-day existence and regular activities of states. Possible occasional inconsistencies are relatively insignificant in view of the advantages provided by the ability to resolve disputes judicially.

Decisions by judicial bodies of international organizations, arbitral awards, and decisions by domestic tribunals are all addressed in chapter 6 of this book.

E. Published Works of Prominent Commentators

Article 38(1)(d) refers to "the teachings of the most highly qualified publicists." This is slightly archaic language from the early twentieth century that today means "published works of prominent commentators" in the various subject areas of international law.

This category is usually thought of as referencing the most influential treatise writers in the various geographic areas of the world. Academic authors who publish especially renowned scholarly articles in academic journals or

---

16. *See* Protocol No. 11 to the Convention for the Protection of Human Rights and Fundamental Freedoms, May 11, 1994, 2061 U.N.T.S. 7 (entered into force Nov. 1, 1998) (establishing the European Court of Human Rights).

17. *See* Marrakesh Agreement establishing the World Trade Organization, art. III(2), Apr. 15, 1994, 1867 U.N.T.S. 154, (entered into force Jan. 1, 1995) (directing the WTO to administer the "Dispute Settlement Understanding" included with the WTO Agreement); *id.* art. IV(3) (referring to the discharge of the responsibilities of the "Dispute Settlement Body" provided for in the Dispute Settlement Understanding).

textbooks might also be included, depending on the circumstances. Sometimes the collective work of academic or professional organizations can also be considered to fall within this category. We will discuss these types of authorities, and research regarding them, in chapter 10 of this book.

IV. Perspectives on Sources

It is clear from the text of Article 38(1)(d) that the two sources it names (judicial decisions and commentators' works) have less dignitary weight than the first three types of sources. This is because the language of this provision states that these two sources are included as "subsidiary means" for determining rules of international law.[18]

Some commentators also suggest that there is a general pattern of declining dignitary weight throughout all the items in the Article 38(1) list. That is, these commentators suggest that treaties and conventions are weightier than customary international law, that customary international law is weightier than general principles, and so on.[19] It is clear that this is not universally accepted, however.[20]

V. Chapter Summary

The ICJ has its own Statute of operation, based on the Statute for the PCIJ. One of the most important provisions of the ICJ Statute lists the five sources of modern international law. This is Article 38(1) of the ICJ Statute, and the sources are:

A. Treaties and Conventions
B. Customary International Law

---

18. Shaw, *supra* note 9, at 123 ("Judicial decisions and writings clearly have a subordinate function within the hierarchy in view of their description as subsidiary means of law determination in article 38(1) . . . .").

19. *E.g.,* Brownlie, *supra* note 5, at 22 ("The first question which arises is whether paragraph 1 creates a hierarchy of sources. There is no express hierarchy, but the draftsmen stipulated an order . . . . In practice sub-paragraphs (a) and (b) are the most important [but] it is unwise to think in terms of hierarchy as dictated by the order of (a) to (d) in all cases.").

20. *E.g.,* Shaw, *supra* note 9, at 123–24 ("The question of priority as between custom and treaty law is more complex. As a general rule, that which is later in time will have priority. . . . However, where the same rule appears in both a treaty and a custom, there is no presumption that the latter is subsumed by the former.").

C. General Principles of Law

D. Judicial Decisions

E. Published Works of Prominent Commentators

The language in Article 38(1) stating the first of these categories actually only refers to "conventions." But this term in this context is usually understood to cover virtually all international treaties, whether or not they technically qualify as conventions.

A rule of customary international law arises when a general and consistent pattern of state practice develops that is followed out of a sense of legal obligation. There is no single book or resource that lists all the rules of customary international law. Their existence is usually determined through detailed research and investigation.

There are various ways to interpret the phrase, "general principles of law." One way of viewing these principles is as basic underpinning legal ideas that are so general (and perhaps so self-evident) that they transcend all national borders and all differences between legal systems. Two examples might be the principle of proportionality and the idea that any legal wrong must occasion a legal means of redressing that wrong.

The reference in Article 38(1) to judicial decisions means that decisions of the ICJ and PCIJ can be persuasive indicators of international law. The ICJ often cites earlier ICJ decisions and PCIJ decisions in its opinions. However, the Article 38(1) reference also includes arbitral awards and the rulings of domestic tribunals that pertain to issues of international law.

The last source referenced in the Article 38(1) list is described archaically in the list as "teachings of the most highly qualified publicists." However, in more modern terms, it can be viewed as the published works of prominent academic and professional commentators.

Given the text of Article 38(1), it is clear that the last two of these sources are meant to have a lesser dignitary weight than the first three. Some commentators say that all the items on the list in Article 38(1) should be viewed in descending order of dignitary weight, but this is not a universal view.

VI. Chapter Review Questions

1. What are the names of the two documents that serve (or served) as charters for the ICJ and the PCIJ?

2. What are the five categories of sources for modern public international law listed by the Statute of the ICJ? In which provision of the Statute are they found?

3. In this list of sources, does the use of the word "conventions" include all international treaties?

4. Are there any books that comprehensively list all the rules of customary international law?

5. What are two examples of the "general principles of law" referred to in this list?

6. Can the reference to "judicial decisions" in this list also include arbitral awards and the judicial decisions of domestic courts?

7. The last source in this list is "the teachings of the most highly qualified publicists." How would you describe this in your own words?

8. Do all the sources in this list have the same dignitary weight?

VII. Additional Resources and General Bibliographic References

Samantha Besson & John Tasioulas, *The Philosophy of International Law* (Oxford: Oxford University Press 2010).

Michael Byers, *Custom, Power and the Power of Rules: International Relations and Customary International Law* (Cambridge: Cambridge University Press 1999).

Bin Chen, *General Principles of Law, As Applied by International Courts and Tribunals* (photo. reprint, Cambridge University Press 2006)(1953).

Vladimir Đuro Degan, *Sources of International Law* (Boston: Martinus Nijhoff Publishers 1997)(vol. 27 of the Developments in International Law Series).

L. Goldsmith & Eric A. Posner, *The Limits of International Law* 23 (New York: Oxford University Press 2005).

Brian D. Lepard, *Customary International Law: A New Theory with Practical Applications* (New York: Cambridge University Press 2010)(ASIL Studies in International Legal Theory Series).

Maurice H. Mendelson, *The Formation of Customary International Law*, 272 *Recueil des cours* 159 (1998).

Thomas Skouteris, "The Force of a Doctrine: Art. 38 of the PCIJ Statute and the Sources of International Law," in *Events: The Force of International Law* 69 (Fleur Johns, Richard Joyce, & Sundhya Pahuia eds., New York: Routledge 2011).

H.W.A. Thirlway, "The Sources of International Law," in *International Law* 95 (Malcolm D. Evans ed., Oxford: Oxford University Press 2010).

Tullio Treves, "Customary International Law," in *Max Planck Encyclopedia of Public International Law Online* (Rüdiger Wolfrum ed., Oxford University Press 2008), http://www.mpepil.com/home.

Mark E. Villiger, *Customary International Law and Treaties: A Manual on the Theory and Practice of the Interrelation of Sources* (2d ed., Boston: Kluwer Law International 1997)(vol. 28 of the Developments in International Law Series).

Andreas Zimmermann, Christian Tomuschat, Karin Oellers-Frahm & Christian J. Tams, *The Statute of the International Court of Justice: A Commentary* (2d ed., New York: Oxford University Press 2012).

Chapter 5

Treaties and Conventions

I. The Nature of Treaties

Many of us are already familiar with the idea of treaties and conventions. It is not unusual for news stories, movies, and literary works to refer to treaties and conventions. Most of us have a general idea of what they probably are. (As we will see later, all conventions are treaties, but not all treaties are conventions.) In this chapter, we begin with a few general points to explain in more detail what treaties are and how they operate. Then we provide an overview of how to find them and work with them.

A. Like Statutes or Like Contracts?

A treaty is a certain kind of agreement among states. When a treaty becomes effective, it generally binds the parties to it permanently. These factors can make treaties sometimes look like statutes, and sometimes look like contracts. Most statutes, like most treaties, bind large numbers of persons and are in force for a relatively long period of time. Statutes, like treaties, are generally negotiated by people who have governmental authority. For these kinds of reasons, practitioners of public international law sometimes refer to treaties as "international legislation."

On the other hand, sometimes treaties can seem more like contracts. The terms of contracts, like the terms of treaties, are negotiated by the parties who expect to be bound by them. Most significantly, contracts and treaties only bind those who have agreed to become parties to them. Statutes, on the other hand, generally bind all persons within a domestic society, even those who disagree with and object to them.

Treaties can also look like both statutes and contracts at the same time. For example, statutes, contracts, and treaties can all be (and frequently are) amended. Also, legal capacity can be an issue in treaty practice; only those persons duly authorized by their governments can bind the states they represent to a treaty. Furthermore, some treaties allow only certain types of states to become parties, and not others. These concerns for capacity in treaty practice are similar to capacity rules that operate both for contracts and statutes.

Although these ideas may seem theoretical, it is worthwhile keeping these kinds of things in mind while researching public international law. For example, it will often be important to know if a treaty has been amended, and to what effect. Also, a potential failure of consent or capacity can be material when making arguments about the effectiveness of treaties.

B. The Vienna Convention on the Law of Treaties (the "VCLT"), and Its Definition of a "Treaty"

When working with treaties, it is useful to be familiar with the Vienna Convention on the Law of Treaties.[1] Sometimes called the "treaty on treaties," and often abbreviated as the "VCLT," it was opened for signature in 1969 and became effective in 1980.[2] It is a significant guideline for working with and interpreting treaties.[3] The VCLT prescribes accepted procedures for such matters as conclusion procedures for treaties,[4] the observance, application and interpretation of treaties,[5] and the amendment and modification of treaties.[6] It functions as a guide to the operation of treaties.

---

1. Vienna Convention on the Law of Treaties, May 23, 1969, 1155 U.N.T.S. 331, 8 I.L.M. 679 (1969) [hereinafter VCLT] (entered into force Jan. 27, 1980).

2. Although the VCLT entered into force in 1980, the United States is not a party. Nonetheless, the U.S. State Department has effectively taken the position that portions of the VCLT codify rules of customary international law relating to the operation and interpretation of treaties. Letter from Secretary of State William P. Rogers to President Richard Nixon, *in* S. Exec. Doc. L, 92-1 (1971), *reprinted in* 11 I.L.M. 234 (1972) ("Although not yet in force, the Convention is already generally recognized as the authoritative guide to current treaty law and practice.").

3. *See, e.g.,* Malcolm N. Shaw, *International Law* 903 (6th ed. 2008) ("The 1969 Vienna Convention on the Law of Treaties . . . constitutes the basic framework for any discussion of the nature and characteristics of treaties.").

4. VCLT, *supra* note 1, part II.

5. *Id.* part III.

6. *Id.* part IV.

The VCLT contains a useful definition of the word "treaty." According to the VCLT, a "treaty" is an "international agreement concluded between States in written form and governed by international law."[7] Note that this requires that an agreement be in writing if it is to be a "treaty" covered by the VCLT. Note also that under this definition, only states can be parties to "treaties."[8]

Most importantly, the VCLT's definition also requires that a treaty be "governed by international law." This is significant because of the kinds of agreements it excludes. First, it excludes day-to-day contracts that may exist between states that are intended to be governed by the domestic law of one state or the other. (An example here might be an agreement between two states for the rental of a government-owned apartment building in one state to house citizens of the other. Such a contract would normally be governed by the real-property law of the state in which the building is located, rather than public international law.) Second, this phrase excludes agreements between states that are of a purely political character, which are not intended to be legally binding. (More will be said on this point later in this chapter.)

As significant as the VCLT's definition is, it does not set the outer limits of what type of agreement is enforceable at international law. Other types of agreements, such as oral agreements or agreements that involve parties other than states, can still be enforceable at international law.[9] The VCLT's definition simply delineates which kinds of agreements will be subject to its provisions on conclusion procedures, observance, application, and so on.[10] Nevertheless, it bears emphasizing that the VCLT's definition of a "treaty" is important to our understanding of what a treaty generally is.

---

7. *Id.* art. 2(1)(a).

8. Discussions later in this segment and this chapter emphasize that even agreements that are not "treaties" under the VCLT can often still be enforceable under international law. Accordingly, an agreement between a state and an international organization (such as the World Trade Organization) can be enforceable, even though not a "treaty" under the VCLT. Note also that the UN has promulgated a convention that would largely replicate the provisions of the VCLT for agreements between states and international organizations, but that this convention is not yet in force. Vienna Convention on the Law of Treaties between States and International Organizations or between International Organizations, Mar. 21, 1986, U.N. Doc. A/CONF.129.15 (Mar. 20, 1986) (not yet in force), *reprinted in* 25 I.L.M. 543 (1986) [hereinafter VCIO].

9. *E.g.,* VCLT art. 3(a) ("The fact that the present Convention does not apply to international agreements concluded between States and other subjects of international law or between such other subjects of international law, or to international agreements not in written form, shall not affect . . . the legal force of such agreements.").

10. *See, e.g.,* VCIO, *supra* note 8 (and accompanying discussion in note 8).

C. *Pacta Sunt Servanda*

A general principle that has developed over the centuries is the rule of "*pacta sunt servanda*."[11] This Latin phrase simply means that, when a state becomes a party to a treaty, it is bound by the terms of that treaty for as long as the treaty is in force. That is, when a state becomes a party to a treaty, it is a violation of international law for the state to violate the terms of the treaty during the period the treaty is in force. This may seem self-evident at first, but *pacta sunt servanda* actually serves as an important fundamental limitation on state action, whenever a state becomes a party to a treaty that is in force or later enters into force.

Article 26 of the VCLT also explicitly states the principle of *pacta sunt servanda*.[12] This provision of the VCLT further emphasizes the point that a state that becomes a party to a treaty in force is bound by its terms.

II. Kinds of Treaties and Other Agreements

International treaties can be viewed from various perspectives. They can be subdivided in several ways, and also distinguished from other types of international agreements. It will be crucial to keep these subdivisions and distinctions in mind as you research treaties.

A. Bilateral and Multilateral Treaties

The distinction between bilateral and multilateral treaties is elementary, but also important. Simply stated, a "bilateral" treaty is a treaty between two states, while a "multilateral" treaty is a treaty among three or more states.

One is continually called upon to keep this distinction in mind when researching and working with treaties. Whether a treaty is bilateral or multilateral can affect where and how one searches for it, how it is to be amended, and who is responsible for administering compliance with it, among other things.

---

11. *See, e.g.,* James R. Fox, *Dictionary of International and Comparative Law* 247 (Oceana, 3d ed. 2003)(defining "*pacta sunt servanda*" in part as "one of the oldest principles of international law[,] stating that treaties properly concluded are to be observed").

12. The title of Article 26 is simply: "*Pacta sunt servanda,*" and the Article reads in its entirety: "Every treaty in force is binding upon the parties to it and must be performed by them in good faith." Vienna Convention, *supra* note 1, art. 26; VCIO, *supra* note 8, art. 26 (same).

B. Conventions as Distinct from Treaties

Some treaties are called "conventions." When a treaty is called a convention, this usually means that it sets forth rules of international law applicable in a broad variety of circumstances within its subject matter.[13] Other kinds of treaties often merely set forth more narrowly defined rights between their specific parties, or resolve particular disputes between specific parties.[14] Conventions are also usually multilateral and decided upon through the deliberations of a diplomatic conference.[15] A treaty that is not called a convention is more likely to have been signed and agreed upon through more private or ad hoc methods, without the convening of a widely attended diplomatic conference.[16]

In terms of ultimate legal effectiveness, there is virtually no distinction between an agreement called a "treaty" and an agreement called a "convention." The principle of *pacta sunt servanda* applies to both in the same way. Assuming compliance with the definitional requirements of the VCLT, the VCLT applies to both without distinction.

The status of a treaty as a convention usually *does* affect the way in which it enters into force, and this is discussed later in this chapter. To reiterate, however, once each type of agreement enters into force, there is no distinction in legal effectiveness as between the two types. For this reason, in this book and in others, the terms "agreements," "treaties," and "conventions" can sometimes be used interchangeably.

---

13. *Satow's Diplomatic Practice* 544 (Ivor Roberts ed., 6th ed. 2009).

14. Sometimes these more specific types of treaties are referred to as "treaty-contracts," emphasizing the especially contractual nature of these kinds of treaties. *See, e.g., Starke's International Law* 39–41 (I.A. Shearer, ed., 11th ed. 1994).

15. *But see Satow's Diplomatic Practice, supra* note 13, at 545 ("The designation ['convention'] is also used for a wide range of bilateral treaties, in the fields, for example, of extradition, double taxation, and judicial cooperation.").

16. There are exceptions to this general observation, and some agreements are called "treaties" that press the distinction between treaties and conventions to its limits. *E.g.,* The Treaty on European Union, Feb. 7, 1992, 1992 O.J. (C 191) 1 (the original version of the treaty, introduced as part of the so-called "Maastricht" agreement of the same date, that (among other things) put in motion the adoption of the euro currency for participating members of the European Union). *See, e.g.,* Ralph H. Folsom, *Principles of European Union Law* 20–21 (2d ed. 2009).

C. Treaties as Distinct from Political Agreements

We noted above that treaties and conventions covered by the VCLT are subject to the rule of *pacta sunt servanda*, and are thus legally binding on the states parties to them. We also saw that some agreements not covered by the VCLT (perhaps because they are oral or include parties other than states) may also be legally binding on the parties.

However, some international agreements are not meant to be legally binding. Such agreements generally have only political significance. For example, if one country's national leader (usually a president or prime minister) takes a trip to another country to visit that country's national leader, they may want to sign a document at the end of the visitor's stay to memorialize and solemnize the visit. This document may be in the form of an agreement between the two countries, but may not be meant to impose legal obligations on either. Such an agreement will speak in only vague and general terms, and not include terms of legal obligation or mechanisms for enforcement. It has a purely ceremonial or official function, not a legal function.

Another type of non-binding agreement may be more substantive. Sometimes in newly developing areas of the law, large numbers of states can reach agreement on general principles or aspirations if they are not going to be required to legally comply with them. It can be easier for states to agree that certain behavior patterns are desirable than to promise to follow such behavior patterns. These aspirational agreements are sometimes called "soft law" agreements.[17]

In researching, it is important to know when an agreement is merely political, or is in the nature of a "soft law" agreement. To begin with, of course, since such agreements are not legally binding, they are not "governed by international law" under the VCLT and thus not treaties under the VCLT. This then has consequences for finding them. They are usually not indexed with official treaty sources, and also usually not contained in most official treaty text collections. They must be located through other means, such as privately-compiled treaty sources.

Whether an agreement is binding or not generally depends on the intent of the parties. Sometimes the intent will be expressly stated in the agreement. More often, a political or non-binding intent can be discerned from the type of language in the agreement. The more general and vague the language is, and the less it uses expressions of obligation such as "shall," "must," "will," and "undertakes to," the more likely it is to be political or non-binding. This is not

---

17. Soft law is discussed in greater detail in segment IV.E.2 of chapter 8 of this book.

an exhaustive list of indicators of intent, but is meant as a general description of some of the most elementary indicators.

D. Article II Treaties as Distinct from Executive Agreements (in the United States)

While we are discussing different types of treaties and agreements, it is also necessary to briefly consider an important distinction in U.S. treaty practice. This is the distinction between an "Article II treaty" and an "executive agreement." This distinction is most significant from the standpoint of the U.S. Constitution.

Under Article II, Section 2 of the U.S. Constitution, all treaties must be signed by the president and confirmed by a two-thirds vote of the Senate. Treaties made in this way are often called "Article II treaties." However, over the many political generations ensuing since the establishment of the U.S. Constitution, an alternative means of approving international agreements has developed. This is through the mechanism of an "executive agreement."

An executive agreement is an agreement negotiated and signed exclusively by the president, without the two-thirds vote of the Senate required by Article II, Section 2.[18] Instead, executive agreements are authorized by one of two ways. First, the president may be authorized by a simple federal statute to enter into the agreement. (Such a federal statute will have been passed by a simple majority of both houses of Congress and signed by the president.) These kinds of executive agreements are called "congressional executive agreements," because they have been approved by both houses of Congress.[19] The authorizing federal statute is sometimes passed before, and sometimes passed after, the president signs the agreement.[20]

Second, other executive agreements are negotiated and signed by the president without any specific authorization from Congress. These are called "presidential executive agreements," or "sole executive agreements," because

---

18. *See, e.g.,* Louis Henkin, *Foreign Affairs and the US Constitution* 215 (2d ed. 1996) (Henkin notes, as a means of introducing the concept of "Executive Agreements," that: "Presidents have made some 1600 treaties with the consent of the Senate; they have made many thousands of other international agreements without seeking Senate consent.").

19. *Id.* (introducing the concept of "Congressional-Executive Agreements" by noting that they are "[a]greements made by joint authority of the President and Congress").

20. *Id.* at 215–16 (noting that "Congressional-Executive agreements" can "come about in two ways," and specifying that one way is involved when "Congress has authorized the President to negotiate and conclude international agreements on particular subjects," and that the other way is involved when "Congress has approved Presidential agreements already made").

they are entered into only on the authority of the president, without involvement from either the Senate or the House of Representatives.[21] The subject-
matter scope for these kinds of executive agreements is narrow, however.[22] They
are most likely to be constitutionally permissible when the subject matter of the
executive agreement is within the range of authority that the U.S. Constitution has granted to the president alone.[23]

In addition to having constitutional significance, the distinction between
Article II treaties and executive agreements has had some relevance in the way
U.S. authorities have indexed and compiled treaties. These will be discussed later
in this chapter.

E. Names for Treaties

Treaties are given many kinds of names. We have already discussed the circumstances under which some treaties are called "conventions." However, there
is an array of other names that are sometimes used to describe treaties; these
include "protocols," "concordats," "accords," or even "communiqués."

There can sometimes be subtle distinctions among these labels. For example, the word "protocol" is sometimes (although not always) used to describe
a short later agreement ancillary to an earlier longer agreement, which parties
to the earlier agreement are free to agree to or not, as they prefer.[24]

---

21. *Id.* at 219 (Henkin introduces the concept of "Sole Executive Agreements" by noting that: "Without the consent of the Senate (or authorization or approval by both houses
of Congress), Presidents from Washington to Clinton have made many thousands of agreements [regarding] U.S. foreign relations.").

22. *See id.* at 224 ("The reaches of the President's power to make executive agreements
remain highly uncertain as a matter of constitutional law. . . . But constitutional tradition
as well as other political forces are powerful deterrents.").

23. *See id.* ("If an agreement is within the President's power, there seem to be no formal
requirements as to how it shall be made."). *See also* Youngstown Sheet & Tube Co. v. Sawyer,
343 U.S. 579, 637 (1952) (Jackson, J., concurring) ("When the President acts in absence of
either a congressional grant or denial of authority, he can only rely upon his own independent powers, but there is a zone of twilight in which he and Congress may have concurrent
authority, or in which its distribution is uncertain. . . . When the President takes measures
incompatible with the expressed or implied will of Congress, his power is at its lowest ebb,
for then he can rely only upon his own constitutional powers minus any constitutional powers of Congress over the matter.").

24. *See* Fox, *supra* note 11, at 267 (Fox notes the following as part of the primary definition for "protocol": "A protocol may be an independent agreement, or it may be supplemental to a convention drawn up by the same negotiators explaining or interpreting the provisions
of the convention."). In some cases, a state may become a party to a protocol without having
been a party to the original treaty. For example the United States is a party to the two 2000 pro-

However, in all these cases, whether a treaty is called a "treaty," or a "protocol," or any other name, the same rules would apply to it. For example, it would be subject to *pacta sunt servanda*, and (if the criteria for its definition of a "treaty" were met) to the VCLT. Indeed, for nearly all legal purposes, no important difference hinges on the different types of names that treaties can have.

F. Exchange of Notes or Correspondence

There is a special format that is specifically characteristic of some bilateral treaties. Treaties between two states are occasionally concluded, not by means of a single written agreement simultaneously signed by both parties, but rather by an exchange of diplomatic notes or other correspondence between them. This can be a more informal means of establishing agreement between the two parties, and is specifically recognized by the VCLT.[25] Each item of correspondence must generally be carefully reviewed to determine the areas of agreement between the two parties.

III. Ratification and Its Analogs

In this part III we will introduce the significance of "ratification," which is a key concept for many conventions and sometimes other treaties as well. Since ratification and analogous procedures are most closely associated with conventions, for brevity the following discussion only uses the term, "conventions." However, we should remember that sometimes treaties other than conventions will also require ratification or analogous procedures.

We should also be aware of another linguistic point. The word "ratification" is sometimes used in a domestic sense within the United States. It sometimes is used to refer to the requirement in Article II of the U.S. Constitution that a

---

tocols to the Convention on the Rights of the Child, even though it is not a party to the Convention itself. Convention on the Rights of the Child, Nov. 20, 1989, 1577 U.N.T.S. 3, 28 I.L.M. 1448 (entered into force Sept. 2, 1980); Optional Protocol to the Convention on the Rights of the Child on the Involvement of Children in Armed Conflict, May 25, 2000, 2173 U.N.T.S. 222, 39 I.L.M. 1285 (entered into force Feb. 12, 2002); Optional Protocol to the Convention on the Rights of the Child on the Sale of Children, Child Prostitution and Child Pornography, May 25, 2000, 2171 U.N.T.S. 227, 39 I.L.M. 1285 (entered into force Jan. 18, 2002).

25. Article 2(1)(a) of the VCLT specifies that a treaty can be viewed as being in written form, "whether embodied in a single instrument or in two or more related instruments and whatever its particular designation."

two-thirds majority of the Senate vote to give its consent to any treaty signed by the president. We saw in segment II.D of this chapter that any treaty so confirmed by the Senate is often referenced as an "Article II treaty."

When the Senate so confirms an Article II treaty, people in the United States sometimes say that the Senate has "ratified" the treaty. This, however, is an inexact usage, and should be avoided by careful practitioners and researchers. It is better to say that the Senate has "approved of," or "given its consent to," the treaty. In public international law, "ratification" is best reserved for describing a particular process through which states express their consent to be bound by a convention.

A. Signature and Expression of Consent to Be Bound; Ratification

For most conventions, a state's agreement to the convention normally occurs in two steps—signature and expression of consent to be bound. The signature of the text of a convention generally testifies that the signed convention is the genuine and authentic document agreed to by the negotiating parties.[26] That, however, does not mean that the convention thereby becomes binding on any of the signatories.[27] For that, states must express their consent to be bound.

In public international law, there are several methods for a state to express its consent to be bound by a convention. The most common of these methods is ratification. If a state has signed a convention, and it decides at or after the time of signature that it wishes to be bound by the convention, it may "ratify" the convention. It would do so by submitting, usually at some time after signature, a signed "instrument of ratification."[28] Such an instrument may or may not indicate that the state's legislature has approved of the convention, depending on the constitutional framework of the ratifying state. But it always indicates that the ratifying state consents to be bound by the convention.

---

26. *E.g.*, *Brownlie's Principles of Public International Law* 372 (James Crawford ed., 8th ed. 2012) [hereinafter Brownlie] ("Signature has, as one of its functions, authentication . . . .").

27. The mere signature of a multilateral treaty by a state would result in the expression of its consent to be bound by the treaty only in a limited set of circumstances. These are noted in Article 12 of the Vienna Convention: such an effect would ensue where the treaty provides for that effect, where it is established by agreement among the negotiating states that mere signature should have that effect, or where such an intention in favor of such an effect appears from the full powers of the representatives or was expressed during negotiations.

28. *See* VCLT, *supra* note 1, art. 16(a) ("Unless the treaty otherwise provides, instruments of ratification . . . establish the consent of a State to be bound by a treaty upon . . . their exchange between the contracting States . . . .").

B. Other Kinds of Consent to Be Bound

A state that did not sign a convention when it was originally open for signature may at some later point decide that it wants to be bound by the convention. In that event, it will "accede" to the convention. That state will submit an instrument of accession, which will express its consent to be bound to the same extent that an instrument of ratification would have. If the convention is in force at the time of accession (see below), it will generally be binding on that state from the date of accession.[29]

In some circumstances, conventions allow states to express consent to be bound through methods called "acceptance" or "approval." Under the domestic law of some states, consent to be bound to a convention in some circumstances can be obtained through means other than legislative assent. For example, some states may be allowed to express their consent to be bound to some conventions upon executive action alone.[30] The term "acceptance" allows flexibility for the use of this method,[31] and the term "approval" allows for similar flexibility.[32]

While states may use these other methods in the international arena to express their consent to be bound, the actions involved would still be considered to have the same legal effect.[33] In these other situations, instruments would generally be delivered by states, but would attest to "acceptance" or "approval," say, rather than to "ratification" or "accession."

C. Effectiveness or Entry into Force

Even if a state ratifies or accedes to a convention, that does not guarantee that the convention will in all cases become legally binding on that state. Generally, conventions cannot become binding until they have become effective, or "entered into force."[34]

Modern conventions usually specify the conditions required for their effectiveness or entry into force. These conditions are often stated in an article or segment near the end of the convention. They usually provide that effectiveness,

---

29. Sometimes other terms are used to describe a state's expression of consent to be bound in these circumstances. *E.g.,* Brownlie, *supra* note 26, at 373.

30. *Satow's Diplomatic Practice, supra* note 13, at 589.

31. Yuen-Li Liang, *Notes on Legal Questions Concerning the United Nations,* 44 Am. J. Int'l L. 333, 343 (1950).

32. *Satow's Diplomatic Practice, supra* note 13, at 589.

33. For example, the VCLT prescribes that "ratification," "acceptance," "approval," and "accession" all have broadly equivalent effect. VCLT, *supra* note 1, art. 2(1)(b).

34. Shaw, *supra* note 3, at 925–26.

or entry into force, will occur after the expiration of a specified waiting period after a prescribed number of states have ratified the convention.[35]

For example, the VCLT provides that it "enter[s] into force on the thirtieth
day following the date of deposit of the thirty-fifth instrument of ratification or
accession."[36] (The VCLT became effective on January 27, 1980. This was thirty days
after Togo, the thirty-fifth state to ratify or accede to it, acceded to it on December 28, 1979.) As another example, the UN Convention against Corruption
provided that it would enter into force on the "ninetieth day after the date of deposit of the thirtieth instrument of ratification, acceptance, approval or accession."[37]

There is no general rule for the content of these requirements. The requirements vary greatly from one convention to the next. They are generally
an element of negotiation among the parties, as would be any element of the
treaty on which the parties need to agree. Sometimes these effectiveness requirements are not demanding, because the parties wish the treaty to come
into effect quickly. For other treaties, the requirements can be more onerous.

For example, each of the four 1949 Geneva Conventions on the Law of War
provides that it "shall come into force six months after not less than two instruments of ratification have been deposited."[38] This minimal requirement indicated
a desire on the part of the negotiating parties that the conventions enter into
force as soon as possible. On the other hand, for example, the UN Convention
on the Law of the Sea provided that it would enter into force fully one year after
the sixtieth ratification or accession.[39] The Convention also prescribed categories
of states that would be eligible to become parties.[40]

An additional terminology point is worth noting. The VCLT defines a "contracting State" as a state that has consented to be bound by a treaty.[41] Such

---

35. *Id.* at 925.

36. VCLT, *supra* note 1, art. 84(1).

37. United Nations Convention against Corruption art. 68, Oct. 31, 2003, 2349 U.N.T.S. 41.

38. Geneva Convention (No. I) for the Amelioration of the Condition of the Wounded and Sick in Armed Forces in the Field art. 58, Aug. 12, 1949, 75 U.N.T.S. 31; Geneva Convention (No. II) for the Amelioration of the Condition of Wounded, Sick and Shipwrecked Members of Armed Forces at Sea art. 57, Aug. 12, 1949, 75 U.N.T.S. 85; Geneva Convention (No. III) Relative to the Treatment of Prisoners of War art. 138, Aug. 12, 1949, 75 U.N.T.S. 135; Geneva Convention (No. IV) Relative to the Protection of Civilian Persons in Time of War art. 153, Aug. 12, 1949, 75 U.N.T.S. 287 (all entered into force Oct. 21, 1950).

39. United Nations Convention on the Law of the Sea art. 308(1), Dec. 10, 1982, 1833 U.N.T.S. 3 (entered into force Nov. 16, 1994). The United States is not yet a party to this convention.

40. *Id.* art. 305.

41. VCLT, *supra* note 1, art. 2(1)(f).

states are often referred to as "states parties" or (particularly where membership in an organization is involved) "member states."[42] The VCLT distinguishes such states from "negotiating states," which are merely those states that participated in drafting and adopting the treaty's text.[43] All of these terms can be distinguished from a "signatory state" or simply a "signatory," which is a state that signs a treaty, without (yet) having assented to be bound.[44]

D. Differing Dates for Signature and Effectiveness

Note that two different dates will be most relevant for the legal status of conventions: the dates they are signed and the dates they become effective. Many newcomers to researching treaties do not appreciate the significance of the two dates. Again, the date of signature is simply the date on which the representatives who agreed to the terms of the convention signed the convention, indicating that it indeed expressed the terms that they thought the convention should express. The date of effectiveness, on the other hand, is the date it entered into binding force for those states that had by that time become parties to the convention.

In researching conventions, it is important to keep these two dates distinct. For example, if one is using a signature date to locate a treaty, one must make sure one is working with the signature date rather than the effective date. In addition, when citing a treaty, it is important to indicate the correct dates as required by good citation form, and not to get the two dates confused.

E. Variations on Expression of Consent to Be Bound; Some Bilateral and Multilateral Treaties

The discussion above has focused on the expression of consent to be bound as an aspect of conventions. As noted earlier, sometimes other types of treaties also require a separate procedure, such as ratification or accession, for states to express consent to be bound. On the other hand, sometimes treaties (especially

---

42. *E.g.,* International Covenant on Civil and Political Rights, Dec. 19, 1966, 999 U.N.T.S. 171, 6 I.L.M. 368 (entered into force Mar. 23, 1976) (regularly referring to "States Parties"); Constitution of the United Nations Educational, Scientific and Cultural Organization, Nov. 16, 1945, 4 U.N.T.S. 276 (entered into force Nov. 4, 1946) (regularly referring to "Member States").

43. VCLT, *supra* note 1, art. 2(1)(e).

44. *E.g., Starke's International Law* 411 (I.A. Shearer ed., 11th ed. 1994) (noting that "new signatories [to a convention] can only be allowed with the consent of the original signatories").

bilateral treaties and multilateral treaties with small numbers of parties) provide that they are effective and in force merely from the date of signature.[45]

In another variation, bilateral treaties sometimes prescribe a waiting period between the signature date and the effectiveness date. In such cases, there will again be a difference between the date of signature and the date of effectiveness. (Keep this in mind when searching for the treaty and when citing it.) However, in these cases effectiveness occurs simply through the passage of a specified time, rather than through the accumulation of a specified number of ratifications or accessions followed by the passage of a specified time, as would be the case for most conventions.

F. U.S. Ratifications Internationally

As noted above, the U.S. Constitution requires that Article II treaties be approved by a two-thirds vote of the Senate. We saw that the constitutional doctrine of the United States also requires that executive agreements either be implemented by congressional statutory authorization or qualify as presidential executive agreements. We have also seen that public international law normally requires the delivery of an instrument of ratification or accession in order for a state to express its consent to be bound. The U.S. State Department does not deliver an instrument of ratification or accession unless constitutional requirements have been satisfied.[46]

Note that the two spheres of operation are separate. An approval by the Senate does not automatically result in "ratification" in the international sense. For that, the State Department delivers an instrument of ratification, most probably referencing the action of the Senate.[47] The same is true for accessions.

IV. Special Characteristics for Conventions

Modern conventions can involve certain textual or operational aspects that are not usually involved with bilateral treaties. We address two of them here, which can be important in treaty research.

---

45. *See* United Nations Conference on Trade and Development, Geneva, Switz., 2006, *The Entry into Force of Bilateral Investment Treaties (BITs)*, U.N. Doc. UNCTAD/WEB/ITE/IIA/2006/9, § I (2006), *available at* http://unctad.org/en/Docs/webiteiia20069_en.pdf ("Some BITs . . . provide that the agreement already enters into force upon signature.").

46. 11 *Foreign Affairs Manual of the U.S.* § 735.1 (2006) ("Exchange of Ratifications; Time and Place of Exchange").

47. *Id.* § 748.2 ("Deposit of Ratification").

A. Depositaries

The task of keeping track of signatures, ratifications, accessions, and other procedural matters regarding many conventions is considerable. It is for this reason that most modern conventions provide for a "depositary" to assume the management of such matters. Since 1945, many conventions have appointed the UN Secretary-General to serve as depositary.[48] However, it is also not unusual for multilateral treaties to appoint sovereign states or international organizations as depositaries.[49]

The identity of the depositary (sometimes spelled "depository," with no difference in meaning) is generally a matter of negotiation among the parties. Usually the appointment of the depositary is provided for in a textual provision near the end of the convention.[50] Sometimes the convention names the entity specifically as a "depositary" or "depository," and in other cases the convention simply states that it will be "deposited with" the entity, thereby setting up the depositary relationship.

As indicated above, depositaries generally manage, keep track of, and notify negotiating parties of, signatures, ratifications, accessions, and effectiveness. They also usually manage, keep track of, and issue notifications regarding, amendments and reservations of various kinds (which will be discussed in part V of this chapter).[51]

B. Final Acts

Sometimes a conference of a large number of states will produce, not the text of one convention or treaty, but the text of many interrelated conventions

---

48. A frequently consulted reference is unnecessarily restrictive in offering a defined term only for a "depository state," defined as "a government entrusted to keep and register the original text of the treaty and to prepare certified copies." Fox, *supra* note 11, at 84. In current practice, depositaries are not necessarily governments, and their roles can extend also to amendments, reservations and additional matters. Fox does add that "the depository . . . is now often the United Nations." *Id.*

49. *See* VCLT, *supra* note 1, art. 76(1) ("The depositary may be one or more States, an international organization or the chief administrative officer of the organization.").

50. *See id.* ("The designation of the depositary of a treaty may be made by the negotiating States, either in the treaty itself or in some other manner.").

51. Article 77 of the VCLT lists various "Functions of Depositaries," including keeping custody of the treaty text, receiving signatures and instruments relating to the treaty, providing notice as to the numbers of signatures, ratifications, etc., received, and related matters.

or treaties. When that happens, the conference will often adopt a sort of covering agreement, or "final act," that references all (or nearly all) of the conventions or treaties negotiated by the conference. This can enable the signatories to simply sign the final act, rather than signing originals of all the various conventions or treaties agreed to.[52] On occasion, final acts are also produced in the context of a single treaty that has many parties or for other reasons seems to warrant the additional proclamation effect afforded by a final act.

The final act will generally not include a large number of additional legal obligations not already stated in the constituent conventions or treaties, but it may contain some. Citation to a final act is not the same thing as a citation to one of the constituent conventions or treaties, and the distinction should be kept in mind while working with complex treaty arrangements.

V. Reservations

A state may desire to sign or become a party to a treaty, but at the same time disagree with one or more terms of the treaty. In the context of a bilateral treaty, this disagreement will probably lead to a re-negotiation until both parties agree on all terms.[53] In the context of a multilateral convention with many parties, however, renegotiation with all signatories or parties would often be impractical. Instead, the state with the disagreement might decide to sign or become a party to the convention, but issue a reservation addressing the issue on which it disagrees.

As a general result of the reservation, the provisions of the treaty that the reservation addresses are modified, to the extent of the reservation, in the relations between the reserving state and other parties to the treaty.[54] But all treaty

---

52. Fox defines "final act" as a "document that sums up the work of an international meeting, often including a treaty or other agreement or principles that the meeting has drafted." Fox, *supra* note 11, at 117.

53. Shaw, *supra* note 3, at 915 ("This problem [involving one state's disagreement with terms of a treaty] does not arise in the case of bilateral treaties, since a reservation by one party to a proposed term of the agreement would necessitate a renegotiation."). *See also* Rebecca M.M. Wallace & Olga Martin-Ortega, *International Law* 270 (6th ed. 2009) ("Reservations only apply in respect of multipartite treaties. They cannot apply with regard to bipartite treaties, as the rejection of a proposed provision constitutes the refusal of an offer made and therefore demands a renegotiation of the proposed term.").

54. *Starke's International Law*, *supra* note 44, at 422 ("The effect of a reservation is to modify the provisions of the treaty to which the reservation relates, to the extent of that reservation, in the reserving state's relations with other parties . . . ."). This is only the general result, because different consequences can ensue if one or more states object to the reser-

provisions remain intact regarding the relations of non-reserving states as among each other.[55] The VCLT largely accommodates the issuance of reservations by states, although within certain limits.

A. Variations on Reservations; Different Kinds of Reservations

States engage in a rich diversity of practices regarding the issuance of written instruments when signing or becoming parties to treaties.[56] Different instruments issued by states can have different effects, and states can give several different names and titles to the different kinds of instruments.

Sometimes a state will issue a written instrument describing its interpretation of specified terms in a treaty that it may consider ambiguous or vague. Since such a state views itself as interpreting the treaty rather than making an exception to it, the state will often call such an instrument something other than a reservation. Among the names states use for such instruments are "declaration," "interpretation," "understanding," and "observation."

Sometimes a state will feel the need to issue an instrument, not objecting to particular terms of a treaty, but rather excluding the application of all or part of the treaty to a particular geographical sub-unit of the state. In that situation, the state might call its written instrument an "exclusion," or an "exception," rather than a reservation.

Furthermore, some reservations do not explicitly exclude the operation of treaty terms, but rather warn that all or part of the treaty is "subject to," "notwithstanding," or "not to derogate from," named provisions of the reserving state's constitution or laws. Here again the instrument issued by the reserving state might be called a "declaration" or an "observation," for example, rather than a reservation, since there is no express statement that any treaty provision is definitely inapplicable.

Some authorities make a distinction between "particular reservations" and "general reservations."[57] There is probably room for some variation in interpre-

---

vation, but this will be discussed in segment D of this part V, below. *See also* VCLT, *supra* note 1, art. 21(1)(a).

55. *Starke's International Law, supra* note 44, at 422 (confirming that a reservation "leav[es] intact the treaty relations of non-reserving states inter se"). *See also* VCLT, *supra* note 1, art. 21(2).

56. *Starke's International Law, supra* note 44, at 425 (referring to a practice that "has developed in recent years" regarding the issuance by ratifying or acceding states of "special understandings or interpretations" or "declaration[s]" regarding the treaty concerned).

57. The European Convention for Human Rights affords an illustration of one distinc-

tation of these terms. One defensible interpretation would view a "particular reservation" as one that excludes the operation of a narrowly identified treaty term specifically to the extent that it is inconsistent with a named and cited provision of domestic law. A "general reservation" might simply exclude the operation of particular treaty terms totally, without referencing any countervailing domestic rules.[58] On the other hand, the European Court of Human Rights has interpreted the phrase "general reservation" to mean "a reservation couched in terms that are too vague or broad for it to be possible to determine their exact meaning and scope."[59]

Note that there are usually two points in time at which a state has the capacity to issue a reservation to a treaty. Our discussion up to now has reflected this, but the point bears emphasis here. The first is when a state signs the treaty. The second is when a state ratifies, accedes to, or otherwise expresses its consent to be bound by, the treaty.[60] At this second point in time, the state is often said to "become a party" to the treaty. It is probably more common for states to issue reservations at the second stage, but it is also generally possible at the first stage.

B. Permissibility of Reservations

As suggested in the introduction to this part V, the VCLT is fairly permissive regarding reservations, within certain limits. Broadly speaking, the VCLT allows any state when signing or expressing its consent to be bound by any

---

tion between particular and general reservations. In the current version of the Convention, Article 57(1) allows a state to "make a reservation in respect of any particular provision of the Convention to the extent that any law then in force in its territory is not in conformity with the provision." However, in the next sentence of the same sub-paragraph, the Convention declares that: "Reservations of a general character shall not be permitted . . . ." In the originally executed version, the same language appeared as Article 64(1). Convention for the Protection of Human Rights and Fundamental Freedoms art. 64(1), Nov. 4, 1950, 213 U.N.T.S. 221, E.T.S. No. 5 (entered into force Sept. 3, 1953). The articles were renumbered pursuant to Protocol No. 11 to the Convention. Protocol No. 11 to the Convention for the Protection of Human Rights and Fundamental Freedoms of 4 November 1950, Restructuring the Control Machinery Established Thereby art. 2(1), May 11, 1994, 2061 U.N.T.S. 7, E.T.S. No. 155 (entered into force Nov. 1, 1998).

58. This might be a fair construction based on commentary from the former UN Human Rights Committee, which discouraged "general" reservations, in favor of reservations that "refer to a particular provision of the [treaty] and indicate in precise terms its scope in relation thereto." General Comment 24 (52), *infra* note 65, ¶ 19.

59. Belilos v. Switzerland, 10 Eur. Ct. H.R. (ser. A) 466, 485 ¶ 55 (1988).

60. Aust suggests that the UN Secretary-General, when acting as depositary for conventions under which he has been so appointed, will sometimes accept "late" reservations, issued by states parties after expressing consent to be bound. But Aust concedes that this is at variance with the VCLT. Anthony Aust, *Handbook of International Law* 72 (2d ed. 2010).

treaty to make any reservation, except in three circumstances. According to VCLT Article 19, those circumstances are when:

(a) the reservation is prohibited by the treaty;

(b) the treaty provides that only specified reservations, which do not include the reservation in question, may be made; or

(c) in cases not falling under sub-paragraphs (a) or (b), the reservation is incompatible with the object and purpose of the treaty.

This is a permissive regime because the treaty does not need to specifically authorize reservations in order for them to be permissible. Instead, the situation is the reverse: reservations are permissible except to the extent the terms of the treaty prohibit them, unless they are incompatible with the object and purpose of the treaty.[61]

Of course, there are some treaties that do limit reservations, as referenced in sub-paragraphs (a) and (b) of Article 19. We could note two of the more well-known examples. Article 19 of the 1997 Ottawa Land Mines Convention generally prohibits reservations,[62] and is thus an example of sub-paragraph (a). Article 98 of the UN Convention on Contracts for the International Sale of Goods prohibits reservations "except those expressly authorized" in the Convention,[63] and would thus be an agreement of the type envisioned in sub-paragraph (b). Nevertheless, many conventions contain no provisions on reservations, one way or the other, and so subparagraphs (a) and (b) to VCLT Article 19 do not limit reservations regarding them.

The final sub-paragraph of Article 19 does sometimes raise issues. On occasion a state may issue a reservation that is unpopular with other states, international organizations, commentators, or activists. The complaining parties

---

61. Even before the drafting of the VCLT, the ICJ determined that the lack of an authorization for reservations in a treaty's text should not be interpreted as an implicit prohibition of them. Reservations to the Convention on the Prevention and Punishment of the Crime of Genocide, Advisory Opinion, 1951 I.C.J. 15, 22 (May 28) ("[I]t could certainly not be inferred from the absence of an article providing for reservations in a multilateral convention that the contracting States are prohibited from making certain reservations.").

62. Convention on the Prohibition of the Use, Stockpiling, Production and Transfer of Anti-Personnel Mines and on Their Destruction art. 19, Dec. 3, 1997, 2056 U.N.T.S. 211, 36 I.L.M. 1507 (entered into force Mar. 1, 1999) ("The Articles of this Convention shall not be subject to reservations."). The United States is not a party to this Convention.

63. UN Convention on Contracts for the International Sale of Goods art. 98, Apr. 11, 1980, 1489 U.N.T.S. 3, 19 I.L.M. 668 (entered into force Jan. 1, 1988). The CISG Convention expressly authorizes specific "declarations," otherwise in variance to the text of the Convention, in Articles 92 through 96.

then have an incentive to argue that the reservation is "incompatible with the object and purpose" of the treaty, and therefore impermissible. This is a relatively frequent topic of debate.

Commentators commonly complain that various reservations to human rights treaties are incompatible with the treaties' objects and purposes, and occasionally take aggressive stances on the consequences of such determinations.[64] The former UN Human Rights Committee famously, and controversially, made such a determination regarding certain reservations issued by the United States and other states under the International Covenant on Civil and Political Rights.[65] The UN's International Law Commission, among others, later questioned various aspects of the Committee's stance,[66] but the incident is prominent in the recent history of treaty affairs.

C. Significance of the Definition of the Term "Reservation"

Article 2(1)(d) of the VCLT defines a reservation as "a unilateral statement, however phrased or named, made by a State, when signing, ratifying, accept-

---

64. *See* Aust, *supra* note 60, at 70 & n.79 (referencing questions involving reservations for human rights treaties and the "*huge*, and increasing, literature" regarding such questions); Shaw, *supra* note 3, at 922 (also referencing a recent "trend" concerning impermissible reservations with regard to human rights treaties).

65. U.N. Human Rights Committee, General Comment No. 24 (52) on Issues Relating to Reservations Made upon Ratification or Accession to the Covenant or the Optional Protocols Thereto, or in Relation to Declarations under Article 41 of the Covenant, U.N. Doc. No. CCPR/C/21/Rev.1/Add.6 (Nov. 11, 1994). The committee asserted that several kinds of reservations issued in connection with the International Covenant on Civil and Political Rights were incompatible with its object and purpose. In its especially controversial paragraph 18, the committee maintained that it was the committee's own responsibility to determine when a reservation is incompatible with the covenant's object and purpose. In that paragraph it also determined that the committee would consider such an incompatible reservation as severable, so that the reserving state would be bound by the reserved-against treaty provision notwithstanding the attempted reservation.

66. Rep. of the Int'l Law Comm'n, 49th Sess., May 12-July 18, 1997, U.N. Doc. A/52/10; GAOR, 52d Sess., Supp. No. 10 (1997). The ILC asserted that the competence of "monitoring bodies" (such as the former UN Human Rights Committee) did not "exclude or otherwise affect" the role of states in accepting or rejecting reservations under the VCLT. *Id.* ¶ 6. The ILC also noted that "in the event of inadmissibility of a reservation, it is the reserving State that has the responsibility for taking action," *id.* ¶ 10, thus suggesting that it was not the role of the former UN Human Rights Committee to embark upon its severability analysis. The General Comment was also criticized by the governments of the U.K. and the U.S. Shaw, *supra* note 3, at 923.

ing, approving or acceding to a treaty, whereby it purports to exclude or to modify the legal effect of certain provisions of the treaty in their application to that State."

We saw above that states often issue written instruments while signing or becoming parties to treaties that they might call "declarations," "interpretations," "understandings," "observations," "exclusions," "exceptions," or by other names. Article 2(1)(d) means that, as long as the instrument, whatever the issuing state calls it, "purports to exclude or modify the legal effect" of the treaty in its application to the issuing state, the instrument is a "reservation" under the VCLT.[67]

The primary legal consequence here is for permissibility. If for any of the three reasons provided in VCLT Article 19, a reservation is impermissible under a certain treaty, that reservation will be impermissible even if it is called something other than a reservation. If a reviewing court or arbitral tribunal finds that an instrument called a "declaration" or an "understanding," for example, is in fact a reservation, and that such a reservation is impermissible under the treaty involved, the court or tribunal will most likely hold the instrument to be impermissible.[68]

Another type of consequence depends for its effect on the reactions of other states parties to the reserving state's reservation. To discuss this, we need to turn generally to the significance of other states' reactions to reservations.

---

67. *See, e.g.*, Delimitation of the Continental Shelf (U.K./France), First Decision, 54 I.L.R. 6, 49–50 (Spec. Ct. Arb. 1977). In this special arbitration ruling, France had issued a reservation regarding its obligations under the 1958 Convention on the Continental Shelf. The U.K. argued that the reservation was "not a true reservation but an interpretative declaration." *Id.* at 49 ¶ 54. The Court of Arbitration cited the VCLT's definition of a reservation, and emphasized that the character of a statement as a reservation depended on whether it purported to exclude or modify the legal effect of treaty provisions. *Id.* at 50 ¶ 55. The Court of Arbitration thus gave weight to the legal effect of the French instrument, rather than relying on the title of the instrument, to determine that it was in the character of a reservation.

68. *E.g.*, Belilos v. Switzerland, 10 Eur. Ct. H.R. (ser. A) 466. *See supra* note 59 and accompanying text. In this case, Switzerland had issued a "declaration" regarding its obligations under the fair-trial provisions of the European Convention for the Protection of Human Rights and Fundamental Freedoms (the "ECHR"). The European Court of Human Rights noted that "[i]n order to establish the legal character of such a declaration, one must look behind the title given to it and seek to determine the substantive content." *Id.* at 483 ¶ 49. The court, in examining the validity of the declaration, then treated the declaration as though it were a reservation. *Id.* The court concluded that the declaration did not satisfy the requirements for reservations stated in then-Article 64 of the ECHR, and invalidated the declaration. 10 Eur. Ct. H.R. at 487 ¶ 60.

D. Acceptance and Objection by Other States

Technically, under the VCLT a reserving state is not generally a party to a treaty in relation to any other state party to the treaty unless and until the other state accepts the reservation.[69] And the reserving state cannot be a party to the treaty at all until at least one other state party accepts the reservation.[70]

However, these requirements are not as onerous as they might seem. This is because in most cases the VCLT provides that acceptance by other states of a reserving state's reservation is almost automatic. For these purposes, any state is assumed to have accepted a reservation if it has not raised an objection to it before a specific point in time. That point in time is the end of the twelve-month period beginning on the date the non-reserving state is notified of the reservation, or the date on which the non-reserving state expresses its consent to be bound by the treaty, whichever is later.[71]

So, broadly speaking, unless a non-reserving state takes the active step of objecting to a reservation within a year, the reserving state is a party to the treaty vis-à-vis the non-reserving state. The reservation is effective as between the reserving state and the non-reserving state on a reciprocal basis as provided in VCLT Article 21(1)(b).

When a state objects to a reservation, the reservation will not be effective as between it and the reserving state. Beyond that, the objecting state has the choice as to whether it wants the treaty to enter into force between it and the reserving state.[72] If the objecting state expresses its intention for the treaty not to enter into force between it and the reserving state, that intention will govern, and the objecting and reserving states will not be parties in relation to one another under the treaty. (The objecting state will still be a party to the treaty vis-à-vis other state parties, and the reserving state will still be a party vis-à-vis accepting states.)

---

69. VCLT, *supra* note 1, art. 20(4)(a) ("acceptance by another contracting State of a reservation constitutes the reserving State a party to the treaty in relation to that other State if or when the treaty is in force for those States"). On the other hand, no acceptance is required by any state party when the treaty expressly authorizes the reservation. *Id.* art. 20(1).

70. *Id.* art. 20(4)(c) ("an act expressing a State's consent to be bound by the treaty and containing a reservation is effective as soon as at least one other contracting State has accepted the reservation").

71. *Id.* art. 20(5) ("a reservation is considered to have been accepted by a State if it shall have raised no objection to the reservation by the end of a period of twelve months after it was notified of the reservation or by the date on which it expressed its consent to be bound by the treaty, whichever is later").

72. *Id.* art. 20(4)(b) ("an objection by another contracting State to a reservation does not preclude the entry into force of the treaty as between the objecting and reserving States unless a contrary intention is definitely expressed by the objecting State").

If the objecting state does not oppose the entry into force of the treaty as between itself and the reserving state, then the two states remain parties to the treaty vis-à-vis one another, but the treaty provision(s) to which the reservation relates do not apply as between the two states, to the extent of the reservation.[73]

E. An Example Illustrating Acceptance and Objection by Other States

The reservation articles of the VCLT can sometimes be complex, and there can be room for interpretation as to their applicability, depending on specific facts. However, the following is probably a defensible example illustrating how the discussion in the preceding segment V.D could play itself out.

Posit a multilateral convention under which each state party guarantees to the citizens of the other states parties access to its own national parks free of all charges and fees. Suppose that the United States, Singapore, South Africa, and Switzerland are all signatories, that they all ratified the convention on the same day, that they are the only parties to the convention, and that the convention is now in effect. Next suppose that the United States, in ratifying the convention, had issued a reservation stating that citizens of the other states parties must pay one half the published entry fees for those U.S. national parks established within the last five years. Finally, suppose that all four states were notified of this reservation on their common date of ratification, that the reservation is permissible under VCLT Article 19, and that no other reservations have been issued under the convention.

Now, suppose that Singapore, from the common date of the ratification, neither says nor does anything about the U.S. reservation for a year. Singapore will thus have accepted the reservation. This means that Singapore will be a party to the convention in relation to the United States, and vice versa, and that the reservation will be in reciprocal effect as between them. Accordingly, both Singapore and the United States need guarantee to citizens of the other free access only to those national parks that are more than five years old, and can charge to citizens of the other one half the published entry fees for access to newer parks.

Suppose that South Africa objects to the U.S. reservation, but does not express an intention, one way or the other, as to whether it wants the convention to enter into force as between it and the United States. In that event, South

---

73. *Id.* art. 21(3) ("When a State objecting to a reservation has not opposed the entry into force of the treaty between itself and the reserving state, the provisions to which the reservation relates do not apply as between the two States to the extent of the reservation.").

Africa will be an objecting state, but the convention will still be generally in force between the United States and South Africa, with the exception of the provision to which the reservation relates, to the extent of the reservation.

This means that there will be no U.S. obligation of any kind regarding access by South African citizens to U.S. national parks that are five years old or less, and there will be no South African obligation of any kind regarding access by U.S. citizens to South African national parks that are five years old or less. (For example, each state could completely bar citizens of the other from its newer parks.) However, the free-access provision will still apply as between the two states for those national parks that are older than five years, and are thus not subject to the reservation.

Finally, suppose that Switzerland objects to the U.S. reservation, and expresses the intention for the convention not to enter into force as between it and the United States. Switzerland will also be an objecting state, but in this case, neither state will have any obligation regarding access of the other's citizens to any of its national parks.

And in all three cases above, each of the non-reserving states will still have the full free-access obligation vis-à-vis each of the other non-reserving states.

F. Additional Points About Objections

In segment V.C above, we noted that the major significance of a determination that an instrument was a reservation concerned the possibility that, as a reservation, the instrument could be determined to be impermissible. At the end of that segment, we noted that another major consequence could arise from a determination that an instrument is a reservation. Now we can briefly address this additional situation. Recall that a state that objects to a reservation can decide that the treaty will not enter into force between it and the reserving state.[74] This is an option that the objecting state clearly has if the instrument is a reservation. However, if the instrument is not determined to be a reservation, the objecting state would generally not have as strong a legal basis for such a decision.[75]

Note also that in earlier decades, objections to reservations by non-reserving states parties were much more significant than under the current VCLT

---

74. *See supra* notes 72–73 and accompanying text.

75. *See* Antonio Cassese, *International Law* 174 (2d ed. 2005) ("[T]he objection may have a considerable legal effect if the objecting State so wishes: this State may oppose the entry into force of the treaty between itself and the reserving State.").

regime. Many authorities traditionally held that reservations needed to be accepted by all states parties if the reserving state were to be a party to the treaty.[76] However, in its 1951 *Reservations to the Genocide Convention* advisory opinion,[77] the ICJ rejected the traditional approach. Instead, it essentially decided that, even if one or more states object to a reservation, the reserving state should still generally be viewed as a party to a convention, as long as the reservation is compatible with the object and purpose of the convention.[78] When the VCLT became effective in 1980, its provisions authoritatively reversed the traditional approach, largely adopting the ICJ perspective,[79] and providing the current more lenient arrangement.

VI. A General Note on Researching Treaties: Indexes as Distinct from Collections; General Electronic Searching

Parts I through V of this chapter have reviewed certain basic features of treaties and conventions. Before moving on to specific guidance on methods of treaty research, some general notes are in order.

First, researchers should be aware that there are generally two types of research tools in dealing with treaties. These are index tools and treaty textual collections. Index tools are simply resources that provide information as to where a particular treaty can be found. One generally starts a search for a treaty by looking up aspects of the treaty (such as its title, general subject matter, or

---

76. *See, e.g., id.* at 173 ("Traditionally, . . . reservations . . . had to be accepted by *all* other contracting parties for the reserving State to become bound by the treaty."); Shaw, *supra* note 3, at 918 ("The general rule that became established [traditionally] was that reservations could only be made with the consent of all the other states involved in the process.").

77. 1951 I.C.J. 15 (May 28).

78. *Id.* at 29 ("a State which has made and maintained a reservation which has been objected to by one or more of the parties to the Convention but not by others, can be regarded as being a party to the Convention if the reservation is compatible with the object and purpose of the Convention").

79. *See supra* note 69 and accompanying text. That discussion in text describes the approach under VCLT Article 20(4)(a), providing that "acceptance by another contracting State of a reservation constitutes the reserving State a party to the treaty in relation to that other State if or when the treaty is in force for those States." Note that under this VCLT arrangement, as long as there is at least one accepting state, the treaty has entered into force as between the reserving state and that accepting state, no matter how many other states parties object. *See also* VCLT, *supra* note 1, art. 20(4)(c).

party names) in an index tool. The index tool then informs the researcher of where the complete text of the treaty can be found. This is usually in a textual collection. The researcher then goes to that textual collection to retrieve the actual treaty text. This is true no less online than it is with print sources.

Second, in the modern information age, there can be a tendency to locate treaty documents through electronic generalized search methods, using search engines like Google or Google Scholar. We discussed the disadvantages of electronic generalized search methods in the preface to this book. We recommend that any reader who is encouraged to use them in researching treaties review the preface thoroughly. All the cautionary notes in the preface regarding accuracy, currency, and authenticity apply especially to work with treaties.

The results of treaty searches found through electronic generalized search methods may or may not be accurate. It is quite possible that generalized search methods will retrieve a treaty other than the one intended that is nevertheless similar to the intended treaty in name, date, subject matter, and parties. (Multiple treaties with confusingly similar names, dates, and parties are in fact quite common.)

Additionally, the subject matter of some treaties may not be fairly reflected in their names, or even some of their key provisions. Relying solely on word searches (as generalized search methods usually do) can result in unsatisfactory outcomes when these kinds of treaties are involved.

Currency is also an issue because a treaty text electronically received from generalized search methods may have been amended since the retrieved site was last updated. The use of a more deliberate and analytical approach, using official indexing tools and treaty textual collections, helps minimize these kinds of difficulties.

Finally, authenticity is important because treaties and other related material retrieved through unofficial websites can be erroneous. Errors can arise either through negligence of the unofficial website or through malevolence of one kind or another. Again, use of determinate analytical searching minimizes these kinds of dangers.

VII. Treaties to Which the United States Is a Party

We consider first those treaties to which the United States is a party because there is a broad variety of sources regarding these treaties that are readily available to researchers in the United States. Historically, the U.S. Department of

State was rather proficient in publishing treaty-related materials, although funding and practical limitations have reduced this proficiency now. There are other privately-produced resources that also make U.S. treaties especially accessible for U.S. researchers.

A. Indexing Tools for U.S. Treaties

1. Treaties in Force

The most prominent indexing tool for U.S. treaties is *Treaties in Force* (or "TIF"), which is published by the U.S. State Department. Originally, it was published in print format annually, but now it is also presented on the Treaty Affairs page of the State Department website. (See below for general information on the State Department website.) This electronic version is updated frequently, although information regarding particular treaties may be incomplete.

TIF has two main sections: one each for bilateral treaties and multilateral treaties. The bilateral treaty section is composed, of course, only of those bilateral treaties to which the United States is a party. The bilateral section can be searched for the name of the other state party, and then within each state's entries, treaties are listed by subject matter in reverse chronological order. For multilateral treaties, one searches the multilateral section of TIF by subject matter. (Recall that TIF includes only those multilateral treaties to which the United States is a party.) Subject matter headings are listed in the table of contents at the beginning of TIF. The electronic version of TIF is in pdf format, permitting full-text searching.

Once you have found the entry in TIF for a particular treaty, the TIF entry provides you with the names of the parties, the signature date of the treaty, the date on which it entered into force (effective date), if different, and (often) a variety of citations to treaty textual collections in which the referenced treaty can be found. These citations are important, of course, because TIF is merely an indexing tool, and does not contain the text of any treaty itself. Entries in TIF may include a treaty's TIAS number, a UST citation or a citation to a historical collection such as Bevans. Each of these citations is discussed in more detail below.

2. Kavass Indexing System

In certain cases, especially with more recent treaties, the citation information in TIF can be incomplete. (Indeed, TIF may not supply any citations for some of the most recent treaties it lists.) In these circumstances, reference can be made to private indexing tools, the most prominent of which is the Kavass indexing system. This system was originally designed by Igor I. Kavass and Adolf Sprudzs, and is now published by William S. Hein & Co., Inc. The Kavass system often supplies separate "KAV" numbers for treaties, which can be used as locator numbers when a TIF entry does not contain citations. The KAV numbers can then be used to find the treaty texts in the Kavass treaty collection, which is available through HeinOnline. These KAV numbers are also useful for finding treaties that are too recent to have even been entered into TIF.

The Hein company also produces an annual set of volumes called *Kavass's Guide to the United States Treaties in Force*. These volumes contain, each year, over a dozen separate indexes of the U.S. treaties in force that year. These indexes include, in addition to indexes of the most recent treaties as referenced above, indexes of non-binding international agreements.

B. Text Collections for U.S. Treaties

Index tools such as TIF and the Kavass indexing system do not contain the actual texts of treaties. Instead, the indexing tools provide (or should provide) citations or locator numbers. The researcher can then go to treaty textual collections, and with the citations or locator numbers provided in the indexing tools, find the actual treaty text in one of the available collections.

1. Statutes at Large

From 1778 to 1949, the official source of collected U.S. treaties was *Statutes at Large*, the session law volumes for U.S. federal statutes. (Session law volumes of statutes are volumes that contain all statutes passed by the legislature chronologically by year, rather than codifying the statutory sections by subject matter, as is done by statutory codes.) Treaties from 1778 to 1945 were also published in a special-purpose collection of treaties called the *Treaty Series*, and they are usually assigned a "TS" locator number corresponding to their position in the *Treaty Series*. The *Treaty Series* is no longer published, however, having been replaced by the TIAS system in 1945, and starting in 1950 by UST (see below), but it is available through HeinOnline.

If an entry for a treaty in TIF has a citation to *Statutes at Large* (signified by the abbreviation "Stat."), or to a TS locator number, then the citation or locator number can be used to find the treaty in *Statutes at Large* or the *Treaty Series*, respectively.

2. United States Treaties and Other International Acts *Series & TIAS Numbers*

Since 1945, the U.S. State Department has assigned a locator number to each treaty to which the United States has become a party. This is the treaty's "TIAS" number, which stands for *"Treaties and Other International Acts."* Historically, all treaties in the TIAS series were published initially as slip pamphlets, although these pamphlets may ultimately be discontinued.

These pamphlets collectively constituted the initial text collection for the TIAS series. The Treaty Affairs page of the State Department website now provides a text collection for recently signed treaties. This feature is useful for finding recent treaties that have not appeared in pamphlet form. These treaties are listed, and linked, there in numerical order under their TIAS numbers. However, there can be a substantial gap between the most recent treaties actually entered into by the United States and those appearing at the Treaty Affairs web page.

The title for the TIAS series references *"Other International Acts"* because it includes executive agreements, as well as Article II treaties. Before institution of the TIAS system, executive agreements were included in a separate textual collection called the *Executive Agreement Series*, which was published between 1922 and 1945. Agreements in this series were assigned "EAS" locator numbers, which can still be used by some indexing tools, and can still be used to locate agreements in the electronic version of the EAS on HeinOnline.

3. United States Treaties and other International Agreements *("UST")*

Beginning in 1950, the U.S. State Department compiled, at more or less regular intervals, all the treaties initially published in the TIAS pamphlet series into print volumes. These volumes were called the *United States Treaties and Other International Agreements* series. A large proportion of the treaties listed in TIF provide a "UST" citation as a source.

The State Department has not published any print UST volumes dated later than 1984. Production of print UST volumes may progress in the future, but the timing involved is uncertain. In the interim, to find the text of a treaty not appearing in UST or a TIAS pamphlet, recourse must be had to the TIAS links at the Treaty Affairs web page, if a treaty is available there, or to a private text collection, such as the Kavass treaty collection.

4. Kavass Treaty Collection

We noted above that the Hein company publishes an indexing tool called *Kavass's Guide to the United States Treaties in Force*. However, Hein also publishes several other works within the Kavass treaty framework. The Kavass project has also accumulated a Kavass treaty textual collection, which is available on HeinOnline. Titled there as the *"KAV Agreements"* collection, it consists of agreements that have been given KAV locator numbers. They are linked in numerical order.

5. Other Historical Collections

At various points in the diplomatic history of the United States, various private persons (before Igor Kavass) have for particular periods indexed and collected U.S. treaties. These treaty textual collections are often termed "unofficial" sources, since they are not compiled or maintained by an agency of the U.S. government, such as the State Department.

None of these other indexes or collections is complete, but they can be useful references for the periods they cover. Probably the most common is a 13-volume collection prepared by Charles I. Bevans, covering the years 1776 through 1949. Many of the treaty entries included in TIF provide citations to the Bevans treaty textual collection. His materials make complete use of the TIAS numbering system, to the extent chronologically applicable.

Bevans is available in print form, but is also available electronically through HeinOnline. Also available through HeinOnline are other private unofficial treaty textual collections pertaining to earlier time periods. These include those compiled by William M. Malloy (1776–1937; four volumes) and Hunter Miller (1776–1863; eight volumes).

It is also possible to try locating a treaty in *International Legal Materials* ("ILM"), described in more detail in part VIII of this chapter, below.

C. State Department Website

Reference has been made above to the Treaty Affairs page of the State Department website, http://www.state.gov/s/l/treaty. At that page, there are links to many important treaty materials. The site contains links to the current electronic version of TIF, and links to more recent treaties that have been assigned TIAS numbers but which might not yet appear in other treaty textual collections.

The Treaty Affairs web page also has links to materials regarding treaties awaiting Senate confirmation and to State Department Circular 175, which is a sort of rules and instruction manual for treaty practice within the Department of State.

VIII. General Finding Methods, Regardless of U.S. Party Status

When the United States is not a party to a treaty, researchers in the United States will generally be using different indexing tools and text collections. These will most often included UN electronic materials, the Kavass system, and private sources such as *International Legal Materials*.

A. United Nations Treaty Collection

The United Nations maintains a separate website for the United Nations Treaty Collection. This site is very complete and accessible, and is an immensely helpful source for researching treaties that have been entered into since 1945. The URL is currently http://treaties.un.org.

At the UN Treaty Collection home page, a researcher is asked to make an initial choice between a database called "Status of Treaties" and another database called "United Nations Treaty Series" (or "UNTS"). The Status of Treaties option links to an active list of all "Multilateral Treaties Deposited with the Secretary-General" (or "MTDSC"). As noted above, many conventions appoint the UN Secretary-General as depositary. At this MTDSC database, all the conventions so appointing the Secretary-General are listed, and for each such convention there are many helpful links. These include a bibliographic history of the convention (including dates of signature and effectiveness), a list of current states parties and their dates of ratification, and the text of any reservations. Also, the text of each covered treaty is available through appropriate links. Accordingly, this MTDSC function serves both as an indexing tool and a treaty textual collection.

The second link option at the home page, UNTS, is related to Article 102 of the UN Charter. Article 102 provides that any treaty that has not been registered with the Secretary-General may not be invoked before any organ of the UN. Accordingly, UN members have registered almost every treaty they have entered into since 1945 with the Secretary-General. The collection of all these treaties so registered is called the "United Nations Treaty Series" (or "UNTS"). The print volumes of UNTS are produced (with a substantial time lag) by the publications services of the UN. However, the entire UNTS is also available through this second major link option at the UN Treaty Collection home page.

Accordingly, if a researcher is going to work with a convention for which the Secretary-General is depositary, the MTDSC database at the UN Treaty Collection website is a sort of "one-stop shop." It provides much of the information that most researchers would want to know.

A researcher working with any other treaty, as long as it is after 1945, and as long as it is not too recent to have been catalogued by the Secretary-General, can usually find it in the UNTS database at the UN Treaty Collection. In this database, one will not find information that is as complete as that provided for the MTDSG database. But always basic information as to dates of signature and effectiveness, and the names of the initial parties, as well as the official treaty text(s), will be available. The UNTS collection is also available as part of the *United Nations Law Collection* in HeinOnline.

B. Kavass System

Hein publishes a detailed multi-volume print indexing tool called the "United Nations Cumulative Treaty Index." These volumes offer the researcher indexes according to KAV number, chronological order, party names (for bilateral treaties), and subject matter (for multilateral treaties and conventions). This set is of course solely an indexing tool, relying on KAV numbers to locate the actual treaty texts themselves.

C. Additional Online Sites with Access to Treaties

There are several other websites maintained by various organizations, governmental entities, and academic institutions that link to particular treaties or collections of treaties. These references are often grouped according to subject matter, member state, or some other unifying characteristic. Their scope can be less broad than that of an encyclopedic collection such as the UN Treaty Collection. But they may be useful nonetheless. There are many such sites and this listing is only representative.

1. *United Nations Audiovisual Library for International Law* (AVL) collections. At this site there are collections of treaties or treaty information posted by individual states and international organizations. Some of the collections posted by some of the states are complete, or nearly so, while other state collections pertain only to specific subject areas, such as trade law. The collections posted by the international organizations tend to relate to only the subject matter addressed by the organizations. http://untreaty.un.org/cod/avl/researchlibrary.html#states

2. *World Legal Information Institute* ("World LII") *International Treaties Collection*. This site accumulates links to the treaty collections of various states and international organizations, with an apparent emphasis on states of the British Commonwealth and international

organizations having such states as members. It is maintained by the law faculties at two Australian universities. http://www.worldlii.org /int/special/treaties/

3. American Society of International Law website, "*Electronic Resource Guide*," Treaties File, Segment on Non-U.S. Treaties. (This was authored by Jill McC. Watson, and was last updated on March 23, 2010.) At this segment, there are links to treaty information posted on websites maintained by Belgium, Canada, China, Costa Rica, Portugal, Switzerland, and the United Kingdom. Some of these country sites afford treaty content, while some principally provide ancillary information about treaties involving the posting countries. http://www.asil .org/treaty1.cfm#sect22

4. LLRX website, Article on "*Researching Non-U.S. Treaties and Agreements*," segment on "Researching Non-U.S. Treaties and Agreements." LLRX is a private, independent web journal designed to provide free information to professionals in legal and various other fields. (This article was authored by Stefanie Weigman, and is posted with a publication date of May 14, 2001.) http://www.llrx.com/features/non_ustreaty.htm

5. *Australian Treaty Series*. This is a database maintained by the Australasian Legal Information Institute, affiliated with the World Legal Information Institute referenced above. This is a complete collection of treaties and agreements to which Australia is a party. It is searchable by words and phrases. The database also contains ancillary catalogs, such as lists of treaty actions, although these are listed in purely chronological order. http://www.worldlii.org/au/other/dfat/treaties/

6. *Australian Treaties Library*. This is a companion database to the *Australian Treaty Series*. It has links to the *Australian Treaty Series*, but also to additional information prepared by the Australasian Legal Information Institute, such as primers on various aspects of treaty law and practice. It would be of most use regarding treaties to which Australia is a party. http://www.austlii.edu.au/au/other/dfat/

7. *Canadian Treaty Series*. This is a database maintained by the Commonwealth Legal Information Institute, also affiliated with the Australasian Legal Information Institute. It provides the texts of treaties to which Canada is a party, from 1812 to (at press time) 2010, and is searchable by words and phrases. http://www.commonlii.org/ca/other /treaties/CATSer/

8. *Canada Treaty Information*. This is a database maintained by the Treaty Law Division of the Department of Foreign Affairs and International

Trade of the Canadian government. One needs to find a treaty through a keyword search, subject search or (for bilateral agreements) a country search. One can look for treaties about which one does not know by also choosing one of these search categories. Once a treaty has been located, signature and effectiveness information is presented, as well as a link to the treaty text. (Although the text may not be available for more recent treaties.) http://www.treaty-accord.gc.ca/Index.aspx

9. *UK Treaties Online.* This is a database maintained by the Foreign and Commonwealth Office of the government of the United Kingdom. Treaties can be located through searches by title, signature date, and other features. Some records that are then retrieved will contain links to status information and the treaty text, although some records may not contain one or the other, or either. (The database also has links to Treaty Command Papers and treaty lists.) http://www.fco.gov.uk/en/publications-and-documents/treaties/uk-treaties-online/

10. *Flare Index to Treaties* (FIT). This is a database of source entries maintained by the Institute of Advanced Legal Studies, which is a research institute attached to the University of London. The online database allows for searching by title, date of signature, and place of signature (or by any such criterion). The entries retrieved from a search will generally include links to the sought treaty text on other online databases. Status information may or may not be available at these links. An interesting feature of the index is that, unlike most of the other databases noted in this list, it is not limited to treaties involving a particular state or group of states. It emphasizes multilateral over bilateral treaties. http://ials.sas.ac.uk/library/flag/introtreaties.htm

11. *World Treaty Index* (WTI). This was a leading print index that was extremely comprehensive and considered quite useful before the advent of the electronic age. It has taken some time for it to be modified into usable electronic formats, and the process is apparently still ongoing. The two websites below can be useful at this point. The first provides background, while the second allows for searching title keywords, dates of signing, countries, or topics (using the topic lists provided at the first site). There are two significant limitations: This database (like the original WTI) is only an index to sources, and does not contain links to treaty texts or status information, and it covers only twentieth-century treaties. http://worldtreatyindex.com/history.html http://worldtreatyindex.com/index.html

D. Collections Maintained by International Organizations

Many international organizations maintain detailed and comprehensive websites regarding international treaties in subject-matter areas relevant to their activities. One of the most extensive is the "International Humanitarian Law—Treaties and Documents" database maintained at the website of the International Committee of the Red Cross. This database includes signature, effectiveness, party status, reservation, and other information about a large number of treaties concerning the law of war. The full text of each document is also available. Chief among the documents presented are the four 1949 Geneva Conventions, but many other treaties and conventions are covered as well. The current URL is: http://www.icrc.org.

Another example is the website of UNESCO, the United Nations Educational, Scientific and Cultural Organization. At its website, there is a "Legal Instruments" database that includes signature, effectiveness, party status, reservation, and other information for many conventions regarding cultural heritage, education, and artistic and scientific development. The full texts of all these conventions are also available. The current URL is: http://www.unesco.org.

Sites such as these can serve both as indexing tools and text collections. Many treaties on these sites may also be available through the UN Treaty Collection, UST, the TIAS system, or through other means. However, if one is doing a large amount of research in a specialized subject area, these specialized sites can be useful. There are also many other organizations and private entities that maintain treaty information. When searching for treaties of regional organizations such as the Organization of American States, remember to check the websites of those organizations.

Although they are rich sources of information, these international organization sites are most apt to be "unofficial sources" for citation purposes. (For a discussion of official and unofficial sources, note part XI of this chapter.)

There are also websites that link to treaty databases maintained by international and regional organizations. See, for example, the websites listed in points 1 and 3 of segment VIII.C of this chapter, from the UN Audiovisual Library for International Law, and the American Society of International Law.

E. Other English-Language Collections of Treaties

Potentially significant can be *International Legal Materials* (or "ILM"). This is a bimonthly periodical published by the American Society of International Law (or "ASIL"). It accumulates treaties, arbitral rulings, reports, resolutions, and other documents, judged by the editors to be significant, and issued or released during each successive two-month period. It has been published since 1962, and before that year, similar material was included in the ASIL's editorial journal, the *American Journal of International Law*. In recent years, the ILM has included useful commentary to explain the importance of most of the documents it publishes.

Searching in the ILM can be performed analytically through the annual indexes at the end of each volume, and decennial indexes are also sometimes prepared. The ILM is also available, although sometimes with date limitations, on commercial legal databases such as WestLaw and LexisNexis. The ILM is considered an "unofficial" source for treaties, since it is issued by a private organization. However, especially for researchers in the United States, it is often the most accessible means of retrieving more recent treaties that are not yet included in UNTS, TIF, UST, or other official sources.

IX. Finding Treaties Entered into Before 1945

As helpful as the online UN Treaty Collection is, treaties under the UN began only in 1945. This leaves the question of how best to locate treaties entered into before this date. If the United States is a party, then TIF, UST, the TIAS system, and related sources discussed above, can be helpful. But if the Unitred States is not a party, and particularly if the treaty dates from before the nineteenth century, different approaches must be considered.

A. League of Nations Treaty Series

During its existence, the League of Nations maintained a *League of Nations Treaty Series* (cited as "LNTS") as well. Although initially published in print format, it is now accessible through the UNTS menu at the UN Treaty Collection. Searching is available by key words, dates, and other parameters. There are 205 numbered volumes and several index volumes. While many of the agreements in the LNTS are now only of historical interest, others are still in force and can retain notable significance.

The LNTS is also available electronically through HeinOnline. Statistical and disarmament documents from the LNTS are included in the online database for the library at Northwestern University in Evanston, Illinois. But many of the documents available here are secondary resources, rather than primary resources.

http://digital.library.northwestern.edu/league/

B. Private and Special-Purpose Collections

Perhaps the most prominent print source for historical treaties is the multi-volume *Consolidated Treaty Series*, prepared under the supervision of Clive Parry and published by Oceana Press. Textual and citation references to the series are usually given as either CTS (especially in textual references) or Consol. T.S. (especially in citations). Although there are several index volumes, most of the indexes are organized by date, as are the volumes themselves.

There are many privately maintained online treaty collections, and collections of historical documents including treaties. One of the most useful for researchers of international law is the Avalon Project website maintained by Yale University. This is especially useful for ancient treaties. It is linked at several of the databases referenced in the discussions above, and its URL currently is:

http://avalon.law.yale.edu/

X. Researching Reservations

The optimal method for retrieving reservations often depends on the identity of the depositary of the relevant convention. This makes sense, since it is usually part of a depositary's role under any convention to keep track of the reservations that have been issued under the convention.

Many depositaries use the phrase "treaty action" to describe any action taken by any party to a treaty relative to that treaty's legal effect. For example, a state's accession, acceptance, or approval of a treaty would be a treaty action, as would be its issuance of a reservation or its withdrawal of a reservation. Accordingly, a search for reservations among materials issued by some depositaries is often considered a search for a certain kind of "treaty action."

The online UN Treaty Collection has complete data for treaty actions regarding conventions for which the Secretary-General is depositary. For other conventions, the broader UNTS database provides some search features that can be helpful in researching reservations. After reviewing these resources, we briefly describe retrieval methods for some of the other most active depositaries.

A. UN Secretary-General as Depositary

As noted earlier, the database in the online UN Treaty Collection for those conventions under which the Secretary-General is the depositary is called "Multilateral Treaties Deposited with the Secretary-General," or "MTDSC,"

for short. Links to the MTDSC are easily observable at the UN Treaty Collection website.

To retrieve reservations under any convention for which the Secretary-General is depositary, one first needs to find the status page for that convention in
MTDSC. The status page for any convention appears after choosing the link
for that convention in the subject-matter index of conventions maintained in
MTDSC. At the top of the status page for each convention, there is a bibliographic history for the convention, generally including signature date(s), the
date(s) of entry into force, and citations to the text of the convention in UNTS,
followed by an alphabetical list of parties.

After the alphabetical list of parties, reservations to the convention generally
appear by country, according to the countries' names in alphabetical order. For
some conventions, there are separate lists for reservations, on the one hand, and
other types of instruments (such as declarations, interpretations, and so on) on
the other hand.

As noted in the substantive discussion of reservations in part V of this chapter, however, the legal character of a reservation depends more on its actual effects than on whether or not it is called a reservation. Accordingly, if one is
interested in reservations, all such lists should be investigated, rather than simply relying on lists with the word "reservations" in the title. Indeed, for the remainder of the discussion in this part X, we will use the term "reservation" to apply
to any supplemental instrument issued upon signature, ratification, accession,
acceptance, or approval, regardless of the name of the instrument. (That is, in
discussing reservations in this segment, we are also referencing instruments called
"declarations," "interpretations," "exceptions," and so on.)

B. Other Conventions in UNTS

If a convention does not have the Secretary-General as a depositary, but
is included within the UNTS database, the UN documentation system may
still provide some assistance. Generally, of course, conventions concluded
after 1945 should be included within UNTS, in view of Article 102 of the UN
Charter. (See the discussion in part VIII, segment A, of this chapter, for review of this point.)

The text of each convention in UNTS will often include the text of any reservations issued under that convention up to the date of its entry into force.
Since treaties are generally included in UNTS only once they have entered into
force, it is practical for the UNTS text of the convention to include reservations issued up to that date. Sometimes the reservations are included after the
text of the convention as part of the convention's signature pages, and some-

times they are included in footnotes at the bottom of the initial pages of the convention. They may appear in other locations as well, such as at the end of the convention's text and before the signature pages begin.

However, this still leaves the question of reservations issued by later acceding states after the date of a convention's entry into force. In general, reservations issued under such later accessions would not appear in the UNTS text of the convention. This is because the UNTS text only reflects the status of the convention as of the date of its entry into force, or at least as of the date of publication of the relevant UNTS volume.

Later accessions are published as separate agreements within UNTS, but retrieving them requires more effort than necessary under the MTDSC database. The different search options available for the UNTS database can be helpful. The search option that will often have the most analytical precision for this purpose is the "Actions Search" option (for "treaty actions").

One effective way to use the Actions Search feature is to retrieve the registration number for the relevant convention from its text in UNTS. (The registration number is the number the Secretariat assigns to any treaty upon its registration with the Secretary-General, and it always appears at or near the treaty's title at the beginning of the treaty's text in UNTS.)

A search by registration number in the Actions Search function yields a chart of all treaty actions for the treaty (or treaties) with that treaty number. (There will sometimes be multiple treaties with the same registration number. This can occur when a later amendment is in the form a full-text subsequent treaty, and in a small number of other instances. Care needs to be taken to check the treaty actions for the correct treaty.)

Some actions are listed in these charts as "reservations," "declarations," or the like, and so are easily detectable. But more often reservations are included within instruments of ratification, accession, acceptance, or approval. In those cases, one will generally only know about the reservation by selecting the instrument of ratification, accession, etc. appearing in the chart, and then checking the instrument's text to see whether it includes a reservation. This can be laborious, but should at least yield relatively accurate results.

Depending on the type of information being sought, searches in the other UNTS search functions, such as "Participant Search," "Advanced Search," or even "Full-Text Search," can be useful. But if one has only minimal information about the convention, and one needs a full text for all reservations to it, the procedure outlined above is usually the most direct and economical.

Also available at the UNTS database are recent editions of the UNTS cumulative indexes. (The UN is adding new volumes of the cumulative indexes, in reverse chronological order, as they become available.) Libraries with more comprehensive international collections will have the full print set of UNTS cumulative indexes.

Within each cumulative index, one needs to search for new treaty actions occurring in the years covered by that index. Each cumulative index volume has both an alphabetical and chronological index, but for more recent conventions, the new treaty actions are only included in the chronological index. Searching in the chronological index is by the signature date of the original convention. Of course, if one knows the date of a particular reservation to begin with, this narrows the search considerably. Using the cumulative indexes to find treaty actions is more involved than checking the electronic "Actions Search" function at the UNTS database, and is not practicable electronically for indexes not yet posted online. But in some instances the cumulative indexes could be useful as back-up tools.

C. States as Depositaries

For some significant international conventions, sovereign states serve as depositaries. This is particularly true of states that have been prominent in international affairs during various periods (such as the United States and the United Kingdom). Also, the Kingdom of the Netherlands is the depositary for many important conventions that have been signed in The Hague.

When a state serves as depositary for a significant number of conventions, its foreign ministry usually maintains a website and database (in English) containing information relevant to its depositary duties. These generally include a current status table for each convention, and possibly links to the conventions' texts. They should also include the texts of all treaty actions, including reservations.

Of course, different countries vary widely as to the usefulness of the information they post in this connection. But three of the most complete and most helpful are the websites and databases offered for depositary functions by the three states names above. That is:

1. The Treaty Affairs Section of the U.S. State Department:

    http://www.state.gov/s/l/treaty/depositary/index.htm

2. The Foreign & Commonwealth Office of the United Kingdom:

    http://www.fco.gov.uk/en/publications-and-documents/treaties/depositary

3. The Ministry of Foreign Affairs of the Kingdom of the Netherlands:

    http://www.minbuza.nl/en/key-topics/treaties/depositary-duties-of
    -the-kingdom-of-the-netherlands

While these are only three states, their depositary functions cover a large range of the most major conventions whose depositary data are not available by other means discussed in this part X.

D. International Organizations as Depositaries

Many international organizations, including UN specialized agencies, serve as depositaries. Again, these organizations usually maintain websites and databases in English that provide information reflecting their duties as depositaries. Such information generally includes a status table for each convention under which the relevant institution is depositary, including the texts of reservations. Among the more prominent examples are:

1. The UN Educational, Scientific and Cultural Organization ("UNESCO"):

    http://portal.unesco.org/en/ev.php-URL_ID=12025&URL_DO=DO
    _TOPIC&URL_SECTION=-471.html

2. Food and Agriculture Organization of the UN ("FAO"):

    http://www.fao.org/legal/treaties/treaties-under-article-xiv/en/

3. The International Committee of the Red Cross ("ICRC"):

    http://www.icrc.org/ihl

The Government of Switzerland is actually the depositary for many of the most major conventions covered at the ICRC database. However, the ICRC maintains exceptionally detailed information on these conventions nonetheless. The ICRC information is often considered authoritative. The ICRC is discussed in more detail in chapter 10.

E. Secondary Sources as Indicators

Secondary sources, such as treatises and law-review articles on particular topics, often constitute an additional fallback method for obtaining information on reservations.

XI. Citations for Treaties and Conventions

In the United States "*Bluebook*" citation manual (19th ed.), the general rule for citing public international law sources is rule 21, for "International Materials." Treaties are covered in sub-rule 21.4, for "Treaties and Other International Agreements." A primary example of the citation form for a bilateral treaty appears at the beginning of sub-rule 21.4. More particular information is then provided for guidance in citing the name of the treaty or agreement (sub-rule 21.4.1), the parties to it (sub-rule 21.4.2), subdivisions (sub-rule 21.4.3), date of signing (sub-rule 21.4.4), and sources (sub-rule 21.4.5).

The closing portion of the *Bluebook* consists of various "tables," and several of these are regularly used in citing foreign and international materials.

Most generally, table 10 is devoted to "Geographical Terms." Sub-table 10.3 lists abbreviations for "Foreign countries and regions," and should be used when referring to countries in treaty citations. Table 4 specifically lists "Treaty Sources," and should also be consulted for prescribed abbreviations, as well as guidance as to which sources are appropriate. Table 3, on "Intergovernmental Organizations," will also be of use for some treaty citations. Even months of the year have prescribed abbreviations in table 12!

One variation that we believe is warranted regards the *Bluebook*'s prescriptions for "Treaty Sources," in table 4. The *Bluebook* specifies certain sources in rule 21.4.5, and requires that only those sources be used. These required sources are usually in some sense "official," and the *Bluebook* allows "unofficial" sources to be used in a citation only if a given treaty is not available in an official source.

We think that unofficial sources should also be included when reference to the official source is impractical. This would include those cases in which the official source is in *Statutes at Large*, and the treaty also appears in Bevans or *International Legal Materials*. We think that the Bevans volumes and other private collections are much easier to work with than *Statutes at Large*, and so recommend a parallel cite to one of these sources when a treaty has an official source in *Statutes at Large*.

Another of our recommended variations involves the titles of treaties. Regardless of format specifications in the *Bluebook*, if the title of a bilateral treaty contains the names of both states parties, we do not believe it should be necessary to state the names of the parties twice in the same citation. Accordingly, unless the usefulness of the citation would dictate otherwise, we generally recommend editing the names of the parties out of the name of any bilateral treaty in which they appear, and allowing the party designation in the citation to perform its normal function of identifying the parties.

XII. Chapter Summary

Treaties and conventions share some of the attributes of statutes, and some of the attributes of contracts, in domestic law. The Vienna Convention on the Law of Treaties ("VCLT") is a significant convention in treaty practice. It defines a "treaty" for its purposes as an "international agreement concluded between states in written form governed by international law." Among other values, it incorporates the principle of *pacta sunt servanda*, which requires states that have become parties to treaties in force to abide by their terms.

Bilateral treaties are those between two parties, while multilateral treaties are those among three or more parties. When a treaty operates as a "convention," it is first signed by the parties that negotiated its text, and then all states that wish to become parties express their consent to be bound by its terms.

Some international agreements are not intended to be legally binding, and are meant to have solely political significance; these are not generally considered "treaties," in a legal sense. In the United States, there is a constitutional distinction between "Article II treaties" and "executive agreements," although both are usually "treaties" within the meaning of public international law. Executive agreements are either "congressional executive agreements" or "presidential executive agreements."

Different binding international agreements can go by different names, such as "protocols," "concordats," "accords," and the like. The names they are given do not affect their status either as binding instruments, or (where they meet the convention's criteria) as "treaties" under the VCLT. Some treaties are in the form of exchange of correspondence (usually diplomatic in character) among representatives of the parties.

Most normally, states express their consent to be bound by a convention, after having signed it, through "ratification." This would be in distinction to accession (which would be undertaken by a state that was not an original signatory to the convention) or such actions as "acceptance" or "approval," which might be offered by means other than domestic legislative approval.

For most conventions, two different dates have legal significance: the date the convention is initially signed and the date it becomes effective. (Most conventions specify the conditions for their effectiveness, which usually involve a minimum number of ratifications or accessions and the passage of a prescribed period of time thereafter.) Conventions and multilateral treaties often make use of depositaries as a means of their administration, and sometimes "final acts" are entered into in connection with the signature of conventions and treaties.

A reservation is a unilateral statement made by a state when signing a convention, or when agreeing to be bound by a convention, that purports to modify the legal effect of the convention as applied to that state. There are many different names that might be given to a statement made in these circumstances, such as "declaration," "interpretation," and so on. But any statement made in these circumstances that has this effect is a reservation, regardless of its name.

Reservations to conventions are permissible only in some circumstances, and never when they would be incompatible with the object and purpose of the convention. Other states parties to a convention may accept or object to a reservation by any state party to the convention. When a state party objects to a reservation it has the choice as to whether the remainder of the convention will remain in force as between itself and the reserving state.

Generalized search methods can be used in very informal settings, but for professional research, analytical researching should be employed. Otherwise, errors regarding accuracy, currency, and authenticity are likely to occur.

There are broadly two kinds of tools for treaty research, indexing tools and treaty textual collections. When the United States is a party to a treaty, primary indexing tools are *Treaties in Force*, the Kavass indexing system, and the TIAS locator system. Sources serving as collections of treaties to which the United States is a party include *Statutes at Large*, the TIAS pamphlet series, the UST collection volumes, the Kavass treaty collection, and other historical and electronic sources. Which source is used depends largely on the date of the treaty concerned.

When the United States is not a party to a treaty, the online UN Treaty Collection can be immensely helpful. One of its two major databases provides detailed information regarding those treaties for which the UN Secretary-General serves as depositary. The other major database provides somewhat less detailed information regarding all treaties that have been registered with the Secretary-General pursuant to Article 102 of the UN Charter. Both of these databases can serve both an indexing and textual collection function. The Kavass treaty system, collections maintained by certain international organizations, and the ASIL's *International Legal Materials* can be other valuable treaty textual collections.

Older treaties can be retrieved using the *League of Nations Treaty Series* (which is accessible through the UN Treaty Collection website), or through private and special-purpose collections. A leading private print collection for historical treaties is Parry's *Consolidated Treaty Series*, while the Avalon Project website, maintained by Yale University, is a leading electronic source.

Reservations are best researched through the use of websites or other materials made available by the depositary for the relevant convention. The online UN Treaty Collection is valuable when the Secretary-General is the convention's depositary. When sovereign states or international organizations act as depositaries, they also publish information useful for researching reservations.

XIII. Chapter Review Questions

1. In what ways are treaties like statutes? In what ways are they like contracts?
2. What is the definition of a "treaty" under the Vienna Convention on the Law of Treaties?
3. What is meant by the phrase, "*pacta sunt servanda*"?
4. In general terms, how does a treaty that is called a "convention" usually become effective?
5. What is the difference between a treaty and an international agreement that is political in character?
6. What is the difference between an "Article II treaty" and an "executive agreement"?
7. What are the two kinds of "executive agreements"?
8. What are some other words that are commonly used to describe procedures analogous to the ratification of a convention?
9. What does it mean for a convention to become "effective" or "enter into force"?
10. What is a "depositary" for a convention?
11. What is meant by a "final act" regarding a convention?
12. What legal term would you use to describe a unilateral statement made by a state when signing a convention, or when agreeing to be bound by a convention, that purports to modify the legal effect of the convention as applied to that state?
13. When a state party to a convention objects to a reservation made by another state party, what additional choice does the objecting state have regarding the extent to which the remainder of the convention will remain in force?
14. What are some of the dangers of relying on generalized search meth-

ods for professional research in public international law?'

15. What is the difference between an "indexing tool" and a "treaty textual collection"?

16. How would you describe the publication, *Treaties in Force*?

17. What are some of the treaty textual collections for treaties to which the U.S. is a party?

18. What are the two main databases provided online by the UN Treaty Collection?

19. How would you describe the contents of the database in the UN Treaty Collection titled "*Status of Treaties*"?

20. What is the significance of Article 102 of the UN Charter in connection with treaty research?

21. What are some international organizations that provide treaty textual collections at their websites?

22. How would you describe the reference work, *International Legal Materials*?

23. How would you describe the *League of Nations Treaty Series*, and where would you get access to it online?

24. What would be some prominent treaty textual collections for more historical treaties, say dating from before the nineteenth century?

25. Why is the identity of a convention's depositary important when researching reservations to the convention?

XIV. Additional Resources and General Bibliographic References

Anthony Aust, *Modern Treaty Law and Practice* (2d ed., New York: Cambridge University Press 2007).

Enzo Cannizzaro, *The Law of Treaties Beyond the Vienna Convention* (Oxford: Oxford University Press 2011).

Olivier Corten & Pierre Klein, *The Vienna Convention on the Law of Treaties: A Commentary* (New York: Oxford University Press 2011)(2 volumes).

Samuel B. Crandall, *Treaties, Their Making and Enforcement* (2d ed., Washington, D.C.: J. Byrne & Co. 1916).

Oliver Dörr & Kirsten Schmalenbach, *Vienna Convention on the Law of Treaties:*

A Commentary (Berlin: Springer 2012).

Monroe Leigh & Merritt R. Blakeslee, *National Treaty Law and Practice: France, Germany, India, Switzerland, Thailand, United Kingdom* (Washington, D.C.: American Society of International Law 1995).

Monroe Leigh, Merritt R. Blakeslee, & L. Benjamin Ederington, *National Treaty Law and Practice: Austria, Chile, Colombia, Japan, The Netherlands, United States* (Washington, D.C.: American Society of International Law 1999).

————, *National Treaty Law and Practice: Canada, Egypt, Israel, Mexico, Russia, South Africa* (Washington, D.C.: American Society of International Law 2003).

————, *National Treaty Law and Practice: Dedicated to the Memory of Monroe Leigh* (Leiden: Martinus Nijhoff 2005).

Shabtai Rosenne, *The Law of Treaties: A Guide to the Legislative History of the Vienna Convention* (Dobbs Ferry, N.Y.: Oceana Publications 1970).

Ian Sinclair, *Vienna Convention on the Law of Treaties* (2d ed., Dover, N.H.: Manchester University Press 1984).

United Nations Office of Legal Affairs, Treaty Section, *Treaty Handbook* (United Nations 2006).

United States Congress, Senate Committee on Foreign Relations, *Treaties and Other International Agreements: The Role of the United States Senate: A Study* (Washington, D.C.: Congressional Research Services; U.S. G.P.O. 2001), *available at* http://www.gpo.gov/fdsys/pkg/CPRT-106SPRT66922/pdf/CPRT 106SPRT66922.pdf.

University of Minnesota Law Library, *Frequently-Cited Treaties and Other International Instruments*, http://library.law.umn.edu/researchguides/most-cited.html (last updated March 27, 2013).

Mark E. Villiger, *Commentary on the 1969 Vienna Convention on the Law of Treaties* (Boston: Martinus Nijhoff Publishers 2009).

Ralf Günter Wetzel & Dietrich Rauschning, *The Vienna Convention on the Law of Treaties: Travaux Préparatoires* (Frankfurt am Main: Metzner 1978).

Chapter 6

Judicial and Arbitral Decisions

I. Introduction

The role of judicial decisions in stating international law is a bit self-contradictory. On the one hand, authorities agree that judicial decisions of various kinds can be authoritative evidence of the law.[1] Judicial decisions are usually concrete and tangible, and easily consulted. That is, they do not present the problems of indefiniteness that can be involved when dealing with customary international law, for example. Judicial decisions are readily cited by treatise authors and tribunals.[2]

On the other hand, Article 38(1)(d) of the ICJ Statute refers to judicial decisions as a "subsidiary means" for determining rules of law.[3] This brands judicial decisions as being only supplemental sources of law. As such, they are supposedly less direct indicators of rules than the other categories of sources listed in Article 38(1): treaties and conventions, customary international law,

---

1. *Brownlie's Principles of Public International Law 37* (James Crawford ed., 8th ed. 2012) [hereinafter Brownlie] (Judicial decisions "in many instances ... are regarded as evidence of the law," and an especially coherent set of judicial decisions "will have important consequences in any given case.").

2. *E.g., id.* at 39 ("The literature contains frequent reference to decisions of arbitral tribunals."); *id.* at 40 (A decision of the ICJ or PCIJ, "especially if unanimous or almost unanimous, may play a catalytic role in the development of the law.").

3. The ICJ Statute was introduced and discussed at length in chapter 3 of this book, and Article 38 of the Statute was discussed in detail in chapter 4 of this book. For ease of reference, we provide a citation to the ICJ Statute here as well. Statute of the International Court of Justice, June 26, 1945, 59 Stat. 1055, 3 Bevans 1179 [hereinafter ICJ Statute].

and general principles of law. While we need to keep this supplemental status of judicial decisions in mind, we should still make complete use of judicial decisions whenever they are relevant to an issue being researched. It seems fairly clear that their designation as "subsidiary" in Article 38 does not prevent them from being very useful in many instances.[4]

Broadly, three types of judicial decisions are involved in this chapter: decisions of domestic courts regarding international law, decisions of international courts, and international arbitration awards. All are included under the concept "judicial decisions" as used by the ICJ Statute. The rulings of domestic courts can be useful in establishing elements of customary international law. Or they might directly address issues of international law, providing their perspectives on what the rules are.[5] International courts apply international law more regularly. They include various types of courts, including regional human rights courts, international criminal courts, and other specialized courts and tribunals. International arbitration can also take many forms, and frequently addresses issues of international law.

In this chapter, we first discuss these three types of judicial decisions in more detail, taking them in order. Then we return to each of the types of decisions a second time, specifically addressing research techniques for each of them. Although we discuss all three types of decisions, by far the most emphasis is placed on the primary international court in today's system, the International Court of Justice, or ICJ.

While there are many courts and tribunals that can judge matters of international law, each such court and tribunal operates only within its own field of authority. Domestic courts can generally affect only the persons and objects over which they have jurisdiction. International courts also generally relate only to a particular subject-matter or a particular region, or have restrictions on parties over whom they may exercise jurisdiction. (The ICJ, for example, hears disputes only between states, and between only those states that consent to its jurisdiction.) Arbitration panels address only those matters that are referred to them, and frequently each panel is constituted to deal with only one particular matter before it.

---

4. *See, e.g.,* Brownlie, *supra* note 1, at 37 ("The significance of the word 'subsidiary' here is not to be overstated."). Researchers and advocates should also remember that Article 38(1) of the ICJ Statute applies to the sources of law that the ICJ will consult for its own decisions. That statute will not necessarily limit the sources of international law that may be relevant and cited by other international tribunals or by advocates and academics.

5. *See, e.g., Starke's International Law* 42–43 (I.A. Shearer ed., 11th ed. 1994).

Accordingly, there are gaps in coverage among the various courts and tribunals. Some international disputes that develop are within the purview of one court or tribunal or another, but many are not subject to any judicial means of redress. This is not a desirable situation, and it is one that international law institutions are trying to address.[6] It does make resort to judicial and arbitral decisions less effective than it might otherwise be. But despite this shortcoming, in those situations where such decisions are available, they can be very useful.

We now turn to a general discussion of the three different types of judicial decisions covered in this chapter.

II. Domestic Court Cases Regarding International Law

The domestic courts of most countries have the authority to enforce international law, pursuant to their domestic constitutional systems. While not an every-day occurrence, it does happen that a domestic court of a particular country will apply an international treaty, or some other rule of international law.[7] A domestic court in a particular country may even find that nationals or the national authorities of that country have violated international law, and impose judgment accordingly.[8]

Researching international law decisions in domestic courts is carried out the same way that researching any other types of issues in domestic courts would be carried out. In the United States, for many researchers this means through Westlaw, LexisNexis, and print case reporters. Domestic key-numbering systems and digest headings tend to include internationally-related top-

---

6. This can be viewed as an aspect of the "fragmentation" of international law. *See Fragmentation of International Law*, Rep. of the Study Grp. of the Int'l L. Comm'n, 58th Sess., May 1-June 9, July 11-Aug. 11, 2006, UN Doc. A/CN.4/L.682 (Apr. 13, 2006).

7. To provide a classic example, in 1924 the U.S. Supreme Court invalidated a Seattle city ordinance as violating a treaty between the United States and Japan. Asakura v. City of Seattle, 265 U.S. 332 (1924) (interpreting and enforcing Treaty of Commerce and Navigation, U.S.-Japan, Feb. 21, 1911, 37 Stat. 1504 (proclaimed Apr. 5, 1911)). *See also* Hamdan v. Rumsfeld, 548 U.S. 557, 625-35 (2006) (holding that procedures the U.S. federal government adopted to try the detained petitioner in that case violated the 1949 Geneva Conventions).

8. In the United States, no doubt the most famous example is the U.S. Supreme Court's invalidation, as a violation of customary international law, of the capture of Cuban fishing vessels by U.S.-flag vessels during the Spanish-American War. The Paquete Habana, 175 U.S. 677 (1900).

ics along with domestic topics. And of course electronic word searching of domestic cases can be undertaken as effectively for words involving international law as it is for words involving domestic law.

There are also major print sources that reproduce the most important international law cases decided by domestic courts from various jurisdictions. Three sources frequently consulted are *International Law Reports*, *American International Law Cases*, and *International Legal Materials*. These are discussed in greater detail in part VII of this chapter.

III. International Courts in General

We have briefly noted that there are many types of international courts. In this chapter we focus primarily on the ICJ and its predecessor, the Permanent Court of International Justice, or PCIJ. These two international courts were first introduced in chapters 3 and 4 of this book. However, an overview of some of the other more influential international courts may be useful at this point.

One prominent group is composed of regional international human rights courts. The most influential is probably the European Court of Human Rights, which sits in Strasbourg, France.[9] Also well-known are the Inter-American Court of Human Rights (in San José, Costa Rica)[10] and the African Court on Human and People's Rights (in Arusha, Tanzania).[11]

International criminal courts have also become significant in recent years. The most famous and most prominent of these is the International Criminal Court ("ICC"), located in The Hague. The ICC was established pursuant to an international convention, the Rome Statute for the International Criminal Court.[12]

---

9. The European Court of Human Rights was established through the European Convention on Human Rights, which currently has 47 states parties throughout Europe. Convention for the Protection of Human Rights and Fundamental Freedoms, Nov. 4, 1950, 213 U.N.T.S. 222 (entered into force Sept. 3, 1953) (as amended).

10. The Inter-American Court of Human Rights was established through the American Convention on Human Rights, which currently has over 20 states parties in North, South and Central America and in the Caribbean. American Convention on Human Rights, Nov. 22, 1969, 1144 U.N.T.S. 144 (entered into force July 18, 1978).

11. The African Court on Human and People's Rights was established by a Protocol to the African Charter of Human and People's Rights, which was signed on June 10, 1998 and which entered into force on January 25, 2004. The text, signature and ratification information concerning the Protocol are available at the website of the African Union. *See OAU/AU Treaties, Conventions, Protocols & Charters*, African Union, http://www.au.int/en/treaties (last visited June 10, 2013).

12. July 17, 1998, 2187 U.N.T.S. 3, 37 I.L.M. 999 (entered into force July 1, 2002).

Also influential have been the International Criminal Tribunal for the former Yugoslavia ("ICTY," sitting in The Hague)[13] and the International Criminal Tribunal for Rwanda ("ICTR," sitting in Arusha).[14] There are also several other "hybrid" courts that have been established with the assistance of the Security Council but also involve substantial local elements in their proceedings.

A third grouping of international courts would include specialized courts and tribunals that have been created to resolve disputes in particular regions or particular subject areas. Two examples here would be the Court of Justice of the European Union[15] and the specific arm of the World Trade Organization ("WTO") referred to as its Dispute Settlement Body.[16]

While all these regional human rights courts, criminal courts, and specialized courts and tribunals are significant, for our purposes the most important international court is the ICJ, including its predecessor PCIJ.

IV. The International Court of Justice

We saw in chapter 3 of this book that the ICJ was created as part of the UN framework in 1945.[17] We also saw that the ICJ is the principal judicial organ of the UN.[18] Also as noted in chapter 3, the ICJ sits in The Hague,[19] which is a city in the Netherlands that happens also to be the "seat of government" of the Netherlands.[20] The ICJ is housed in a building called the Peace Palace, which

---

13. The ICTY was established by the UN Security Council. S.C. Res. 808, U.N. Doc. S/RES/808 (Feb. 22, 1993).

14. The ICTR was also established by the UN Security Council. S.C. Res. 955, UN Doc. S/RES/955 (Nov. 8, 1994).

15. The Court of Justice as currently constituted is provided for in the current, "Lisbon" version of the Treaty on European Union. Consolidated Version of the Treaty on European Union art. 19, Mar. 30, 2010, 2010 O.J. (C 83) 13.

16. *See* Marrakesh Agreement establishing the World Trade Organization, Apr. 15, 1994, 1867 U.N.T.S. 154 [hereinafter WTO Agreement] (entered into force Jan. 1, 1995); *id.* arts. III(2) (directing the WTO to administer the "Dispute Settlement Understanding" included with the WTO Agreement) & IV(3) (referring to the discharge of the responsibilities of the "Dispute Settlement Body" provided for in the Dispute Settlement Understanding).

17. Chapter XIV of the UN Charter establishes the ICJ. UN Charter arts. 92–96.

18. *Id.* art. 92.

19. ICJ Statute art. 22.

20. *The Statesman's Yearbook 2012* (Barry Turner ed.), at 908. The Council of State and Parliament of the Netherlands, along with all foreign embassies in the Netherlands, are all located in The Hague. However, under the Constitution of the Netherlands, Amsterdam has the title of "Capital City" of the Netherlands.

was built, following the First Hague Peace Conference in 1899, with funds donated by the U.S. philanthropist Andrew Carnegie.[21]

The ICJ operates not only under the authority of the UN Charter, but also pursuant to the ICJ Statute, referred to earlier in this chapter and introduced in chapters 3 and 4 of this book.[22] All states that are members of the UN are automatically parties to the ICJ Statute.[23] Article 39(1) of the Statute provides that the official languages of the ICJ are French and English.

The ICJ, even though it is the principal judicial body of the UN, is not a "supreme court" with appellate authority over any other international tribunals. Rather, all the regional and criminal courts referenced above stand on their own legal foundations. That is, neither the ICJ, nor any other court or tribunal, is "senior" over any of the regional or other international courts or tribunals described in part III of this chapter. All the international courts are supposed to give significant respect to the rulings of all the others out of general comity.

Several aspects of the ICJ's operations are worth noting while beginning research into its work.

A. Judges and Chambers

There are fifteen judges on the ICJ at any particular time, no two of whom may be nationals of the same state. Each judge serves a term of nine years, and the terms are staggered so that the terms of five judges end every three years. Terms are renewable. The judges are selected by a complicated procedure that ultimately results in obtaining the joint consent of the General Assembly and the Security Council at the UN.[24]

Generally all fifteen judges sit for ICJ proceedings. However, if the parties to a particular dispute desire a smaller number of judges, the ICJ Statute allows the formation of a smaller chamber, with a number of judges approved by the parties.[25]

---

21. Howard N. Meyer, *The World Court in Action* 24, 29–30 (2002).

22. Article 92 of the UN Charter specifies that the ICJ shall function in accordance with the ICJ Statute, which was annexed to the originally signed text of the UN Charter, and states that the ICJ Statute "forms an integral part of the present Charter."

23. UN Charter art. 93(1).

24. *See* ICJ Statute arts. 2–13 (setting forth the number of judges, their terms, their manner of selection and possible reelections upon the expiry of terms).

25. ICJ Statute art. 26(2) & (3). A smaller chamber also exists under Article 29, and additional chambers can be created under Article 26(1), but these are not generally significant for the ICJ's most prominent work.

When a state is a party before the ICJ, and none of the fifteen sitting judges is a national of that state, the state may choose its own judge as an additional judge for that case.[26] You will see these judges described as "ad hoc" judges in opinions issued by the Court.

B. *Stare Decisis* in the ICJ

Article 59 of the ICJ Statute says that a decision of the ICJ "has no binding force except between the parties and in respect of that particular case." This provision is usually taken to mean that the ICJ is not bound to recognize the doctrine of binding precedent, also called *stare decisis*. Nevertheless, the ICJ does carefully keep track of its prior decisions, and will frequently cite prior decisions in its judgments and other rulings. The distinction is simply that, while the Court is not technically bound by its earlier decisions, it does cite them in later rulings and considers them persuasive authority for later results.[27]

C. Two Types of Proceedings

The ICJ Statute provides that the Court will have jurisdiction over two types of proceedings: contentious cases[28] and proceedings for advisory opinions.[29] Contentious cases involve disagreements between states with adverse interests. Most contentious cases are between two states, but the ICJ Statute provides that additional states may request permission to intervene when they feel their interests are affected by cases between other states.[30] Any such intervention is subject to the agreement of the Court.[31]

---

26. *See* ICJ Statute art. 31(2)-(3).

27. *See* Malcolm N. Shaw, *International Law* 110 (6th ed. 2008).

28. Article 36 of the ICJ Statute describes the extent of the Court's jurisdiction regarding contentious cases.

29. Chapter IV of the ICJ Statute sets forth the means of operation for the Court's proceedings for advisory opinions.

30. ICJ Statute art. 62(1) ("Should a state consider that it has an interest of a legal nature which may be affected by the decision in the case, it may submit a request to the Court to be permitted to intervene.").

31. ICJ Statute art. 62(2) ("It shall be for the Court to decide upon this request."). Articles 81 through 86 of the Court's rules also prescribe specific procedures for intervention requests. Rules of Court, 2007 I.C.J. Acts & Docs, 91, 141–47, available at http://www.icj -cij.org/documents/index.php?p1=4&p2=3&p3=0 [hereinafter ICJ Rules of Court].

By contrast, when the Court renders an advisory opinion, there are generally no states before it and there may not even be a live controversy between any states at all. Rather, the Court simply addresses a specific question, or a set of specific questions, posed to it as a general matter. Under the ICJ Statute and the UN Charter, the General Assembly, the Security Council, and other duly authorized UN organs and specialized agencies have the authority to request advisory opinions.[32] As noted in part VIII of this chapter, both advisory opinions and opinions in contentious cases are available at the ICJ website.

D. States as Parties to the ICJ Statute versus States as Subject to ICJ Jurisdiction

We saw above that all states that are members of the UN are automatically parties to the ICJ Statute. However, this does not mean that all UN Member states have consented to all suits against them before the ICJ. Far from it. The ICJ Statute basically provides three ways in which the Court can obtain jurisdiction over a particular dispute. All three ways require the consent of all parties in order for the Court to have jurisdiction.

First, the parties to the dispute can agree on a one-time-only basis that the ICJ will have jurisdiction over one particular dispute. (This is relatively common; the parties will agree to submit their dispute in an agreed-upon statement of the case called a *compromis*.)[33] Second, various treaties and conventions contain clauses requiring parties to the treaty or convention to submit to ICJ jurisdiction regarding disputes arising under the treaty or convention.[34] These two methods would clearly require the consent of both parties to the dispute, either specifically for the dispute itself or in connection with having entered into the relevant treaty or convention.

The third way in which the ICJ can obtain jurisdiction over a dispute is if both states have deposited with the UN Secretary-General special instruments called "declarations of compulsory jurisdiction." These declarations have been

---

32. Article 65 of the ICJ Statute authorizes the ICJ to give advisory opinions "on any legal question" at the request of bodies that are authorized pursuant to the UN Charter to make such requests. Article 96(2) of the UN Charter provides that, in addition to the General Assembly and the Security Council, any other organ of the UN and its specialized agencies "which may at any time be so authorized by the General Assembly," may also request advisory opinions.

33. ICJ Statute art. 36(1) ("The jurisdiction of the Court comprises all cases which the parties refer to it . . . .").

34. *Id.* ("The jurisdiction of the Court comprises . . . all matters specially provided for in the Charter of the United Nations or in treaties and conventions in force.").

controversial over the years,[35] and cases based on them have not been as common recently as cases founded on jurisdiction through one of the other two methods.

E. Several Types of Rulings

The final opinion that the Court issues in the resolution of a contentious case is referred to as the Court's judgment.[36] The judgment normally contains the Court's reasoning and final disposition of all the issues. It generally ends with a mathematical tally of how many judges voted for each aspect of the result in the case and indicating which judges wrote separate opinions. Accordingly, the judgment will often be the most significant document the Court issues in a contentious case.

However, the Court also issues many ancillary rulings regarding most of its contentious cases. Examples would include rulings granting or denying requests for extra time to file pleadings, rulings on requests for permission for other states to intervene, and rulings on requests for provisional measures.[37] All these rulings are published by the Court in its official records, and they all generally appear in connection with each case on the Court's website.[38] Researchers thus need to be alert to which ruling they would like to review. If one is interested only in the Court's ultimate result and rationale, only the judgment will generally be of interest. If one is interested in one or more ancillary matters, then of course the ancillary rulings can be relevant.

Sometimes there is more than one significant judgment in a case. This can occur in a variety of situations. For example, when there is a substantial doubt as to whether the Court has jurisdiction in a particular case, it may issue a separate judgment on "jurisdiction" before going on to the case in chief and ultimately issuing a judgment on the "merits."[39] Or an initial judgment might be issued on

---

35. *See, e.g.,* Military and Paramilitary Activities in and Against Nicaragua (Nicar. v. U.S.), Jurisdiction, 1984 I.C.J. 392 (Nov. 26). In this case, the Court engaged in a lengthy discussion (over 60 numbered paragraphs and over 25 pages) on the effects of several such declarations submitted by Nicaragua and the United States. *Id.* at 397–426, ¶¶ 12–76.

36. ICJ Rules of Court, *supra* note 31, art. 94.

37. *See, e.g.,* ICJ Statute art. 41(1) ("The Court shall have the power to indicate, if it considers that circumstances so require, any provisional measures which ought to be taken to preserve the respective rights of either party.").

38. This can be distinguished from the practice of current federal case reporters in the United States, in which such intermediate procedural orders are generally not published.

39. In one famous case, the Court issued two Judgments on "Jurisdiction and Admissibility" before going on to issue a Judgment on the Merits. Maritime Delimitation and Ter-

the petition of a third state to intervene, or with regard to other preliminary objections of a party.[40] Sometimes there is a separate judgment on the issue of damages or compensation to be paid, as well.[41]

F. Several Types of Opinions

Article 57 of the ICJ Statute provides that judges are entitled to deliver separate opinions for any judgment that is not unanimous. Article 95 of the Court rules further specifies that such separate opinions can, but do not need to, represent dissents from the majority opinion.[42] Article 95 also allows judges to make declarations of concurrence or dissent without stating reasons for their views.[43]

The breakdown of judges' names and votes is usually provided in the closing paragraph of a judgment for the Court. Any short-form declarations usually immediately follow the text of a judgment. Dissenting opinions and separate opinions (the word "concurring" is seldom used), as well as the occasional longer declaration, then follow.

The judges follow similar procedures, and similar conventions are observed, for the issuance of advisory opinions as for judgments in contentious cases.[44]

V. The Permanent Court of International Justice (the "PCIJ")

As noted in chapter 3 of this book, the ICJ Statute is based on the statute of the earlier Permanent Court of International Justice (the "PCIJ"),[45] which was established under the ill-fated League of Nations regime.[46] Although the League of Nations has not existed for many years, the ICJ has taken the place of the PCIJ; and commentators, courts and litigants still cite decisions of the PCIJ as

---

ritorial Questions (Qatar v. Bahr.), Jurisdiction and Admissibility, 1994 I.C.J. 112 (July 1), Jurisdiction and Admissibility, 1995 I.C.J. 6 (Feb. 15), Merits, 2001 I.C.J. 40 (Mar. 16).

40. *E.g.,* Temple of Preah Vihear (Cambodia v. Thai.), Preliminary Objections, 1961 I.C.J. 17 (May 26), Merits, 1962 I.C.J. 6 (June 15).

41. *E.g.,* Corfu Channel (U.K. v. Alb.), Merits, 1949 I.C.J. 4 (Apr. 9), Assessment of Amount of Compensation, 1949 I.C.J. 244 (Dec. 15).

42. ICJ Rules of Court, *supra* note 31, art. 95(1).

43. *Id.* art. 95(2).

44. *Id.* art. 102(2).

45. UN Charter art. 92 (ICJ Statute "based upon the Statute of the Permanent Court of International Justice").

46. *See* chapter 3, *supra,* part II.

authoritative.[47] The published decisions of the PCIJ are available online at the website of the ICJ, along with those of the ICJ, as described in more detail in part IX of this chapter.

VI. International Arbitrations

The definition of "arbitration" for international law is "the settlement of differences between states by judges of their own choice and on the basis of respect for law."[48] The essential features are that arbitration is consensual, and is the result of a specific agreement in the nature of a contract.[49] This usually means that two or more states have agreed to submit a specific dispute to arbitration. Their agreement would generally be in writing, and would specify the precise questions to be resolved, the number of arbitration judges (or "arbitrators") who will be sitting, the manner of selecting them, the language(s) to be used, and other key points.[50]

Arbitrations between states can be distinguished from adjudication between states in the ICJ. The ICJ is a permanently-constituted body established to hear a large variety of cases, and intended to continue operating indefinitely. International arbitrations between states, on the other hand, are established through the contractual-type agreements described above. The number and identity of the arbitrators, the language(s) of the proceedings, and other key procedural features, are decided by the parties, rather than set forth in the ICJ Statute.[51]

There are several reasons why states might choose to arbitrate rather than pursue adjudication before the ICJ. The dispute may involve one or more private or non-state parties, in addition to one or more states. The ICJ Statute precludes any entity other than a state from being a party,[52] but there is no such

---

47. *E.g.*, Shaw, *supra* note 27, at 110.

48. *Id.* at 1048–49 (citing Convention for the Pacific Settlement of International Disputes art. 15, July 29, 1899, 32 Stat. 1779, 1 Bevans 230). Shaw notes that this "became the accepted definition of arbitration in international law." Shaw, *supra* note 27, at 1049.

49. *E.g.*, W. Michael Reisman, *Systems of Control in International Adjudication and Arbitration* 5–6 (1992) ("arbitration is a creature of contract").

50. *E.g.*, Convention for the Pacific Settlement of International Disputes art. 52, Oct. 18, 1907, 1 Bevans 577 (entered into force Jan. 26, 1910).

51. It has been suggested that, since ICJ proceedings are also subject to the consent of the parties, ICJ proceedings are themselves a kind of arbitration. Mauro Rubino-Sammartano, *International Arbitration: Law and Practice* 151 (2d ed. 2001). But the differences noted above are significant for our purposes.

52. ICJ Statute art. 34(1).

restriction for arbitrations. States also sometimes believe that arbitration provides greater speed and flexibility than ICJ proceedings.[53] Arbitration also can
be attractive when some sort of special technical expertise on the part of the
judges is desirable.[54]

There have been well-noted arbitrations between states for some time. The
Alabama Claims arbitration of 1874[55] between Britain and the United States, as
well as the mixed commissions between the same two states that emerged in
1794, are examples.[56]

International arbitration proceedings among sovereign states were especially prominent in the early- to mid-twentieth century. Through the Hague
Conventions for the Pacific Settlement of International Disputes,[57] the Permanent Court of Arbitration (or "PCA") was established. The PCA is still in existence, and is housed in the Peace Palace in The Hague, along with the ICJ.

Many arbitrations of the early twentieth century, and beyond, have been
instituted under the auspices of the PCA. The PCA, despite its name, is not really a court. Rather, it is an institute that maintains lists of prospective arbitrators, and facilitates the arbitration of particular disputes as they arise. It is
"permanent" in the sense that it permanently maintains its lists of arbitrators
and consistently stands ready to facilitate arbitration. But the arbitral panels
that it helps to establish with respect to any particular dispute are ad hoc in the
same manner as other arbitrations.

Another influential entity that facilitates arbitration in an international context is the International Chamber of Commerce (or "ICC"), headquartered in
Paris. It maintains a set of influential arbitration rules, and also fields a notable
roster of arbitrators. Its arbitrations most often involve private parties engaged
in international commercial disputes. Similarly, the International Center for the
Settlement of Investment Disputes (or "ICSID") is well known as an arbitral
facility for disputes involving direct investment by private parties in the terri-

---

53. Shaw, *supra* note 27, at 1055.

54. *Id.*

55. 5 J.B. Moore, *International Arbitrations* 4639 (1898).

56. *See* 3 J.B. Moore, *International Adjudications* (photo. reprint 1996) (modern series
1931) (regarding mixed commission under Article VI of the Jay Treaty of 1794, on the subject of recovery of pre-Revolutionary War debts); 4 J.B. Moore, *International Adjudications*
(photo. reprint 1996) (modern series 1931) (regarding mixed commission under Article
VII of the Jay Treaty of 1794, on the subject of the violation of neutral rights and the failure to perform neutral duties).

57. There were two such conventions bearing this title, which were substantially identical to each other. *See supra* notes 48–50. The circumstances surrounding the adoption of
these two conventions are also discussed in part IX.D of chapter 2 of this book.

tory of foreign states. As with the ICC, ICSID arbitrations generally involve private individuals or companies.

While arbitrations under the auspices of entities such as the PCA, the ICC, and ICSID have been influential, some important arbitration tribunals are established on an entirely ad hoc basis. A prominent example of such ad hoc arbitration is the "Iran-United States Claims Tribunal," headquartered in The Hague, which has jurisdiction to decide certain claims of U.S. nationals against Iran and of Iranian nationals against the United States. The tribunal was established in 1981 as part of the settlement of the crisis that began when a group of Iranian nationals seized control of the U.S. embassy in Tehran in 1979.

In this chapter, we will be concerned only with arbitrations between and among sovereign states.

VII. Domestic Court Materials Addressing International Law

To uncover those cases in which domestic courts have applied or otherwise addressed international law in a particular subject area, it is generally sufficient to use the same searching methods that one would use for a standard domestic-law issue.

For example, in the United States the liability of commercial airlines to injured passengers is substantially covered by one of two international treaties: either the Warsaw Convention of 1929,[58] or the Montreal Convention of 1999.[59] The Warsaw Convention applied until the effectiveness date of the Montreal Convention, which was November 4, 2003. The U.S. Supreme Court had several occasions to address, interpret, and apply the Warsaw Convention.[60] These cases usually involved airline passengers, allegedly injured while on board aircraft, suing airline companies in the United States. (The Supreme Court has not yet issued any opinions applying the Montreal Convention, but the Court will surely do so in the future.)

---

58. Convention for the Unification of Certain Rules Relating to International Transportation by Air, Oct. 12, 1929, 49 Stat. 3000, T.S. No. 876 (1934).

59. Convention for the Unification of Certain Rules for International Carriage by Air, May 28, 1999, S. Treaty Doc. No. 106-45, 2242 U.N.T.S. 309 (entered into force Nov. 4, 2003).

60. *E.g.,* Zicherman v. Korean Air Lines Co., 516 U.S. 217 (1996), Eastern Airlines, Inc. v. Floyd, 499 U.S. 530 (1991); Chan v. Korean Air Lines, Ltd., 490 U.S. 122 (1989); Olympic Airways v. Husain, 540 U.S. 644 (2004).

To find the most recent case in which the U.S. Supreme Court interpreted the Warsaw Convention, a researcher could use standard U.S.-law research tools such as Westlaw, LexisNexis, or print digests to obtain results. Key words and phrases might be "Warsaw Convention," or "airline liability," for example, and results for one or more of these phrases would normally be successful.[61] Analogous techniques could be used when state courts or lower federal courts refer to international law.

Most questions of international law do not find their way into domestic courts, for a variety of reasons. Most treaties and customary rules probably do not afford a basis for private relief. Additionally, most rules of public international law bind states as sovereign entities. Due to sovereign immunity rules and other considerations, most domestic courts would generally not have jurisdiction over foreign sovereigns regarding the types of issues covered in most treaties and customary rules. But when private relief is provided for in the relevant international rules, and jurisdiction exists, domestic courts have their role to play.

As noted earlier in this chapter, there are major print sources that reproduce important international-law cases decided by domestic courts from various jurisdictions. On occasion researchers can find these quite useful. The first is *International Law Reports* (often referred to as the "ILR"), a multi-volume series published on an ongoing basis that is maintained by most comprehensive law libraries in the United States. The ILR began in 1919 as a publication edited at the University of London, when it had the earlier name of *The Annual Digest of International Law*. Its name was changed to its current form with the volumes published in 1950. At the present time, it is published by Cambridge University Press. The ILR is also available as a subscription database via Justis, a commercial electronic legal publisher based in the United Kingdom.

Another prominent work is also a multi-volume, continuously published series, but focuses specifically on U.S. domestic cases involving international law. It is called (appropriately) *American International Law Cases* (or "*American ILC*"). Both of these series have periodic indexes, although mostly they are useful as repositories if one already knows the case exists and one has a citation to it in the series. They are not as suitable for the initial phases of research.

Finally, recent domestic court cases (from various countries) involving international law are often published in *International Legal Materials*, or "ILM." This is a bimonthly publication of the American Society of International Law.

---

61. Of course, the same procedure could be used for the Montreal Convention, if a researcher either knew of a recent case applying it, or wanted to know if there was one.

The ILM was introduced and discussed at length in segment VIII.E of chapter 5 of this book. The advantages and disadvantages of using ILM are addressed there. Also as noted there, ILM is available through Westlaw and LexisNexis.

VIII. Locating and Working with ICJ Materials

Since its inception, the ICJ has published a print reporter series officially including the definitive texts of most of its orders, judgments, and other rulings. The title of the series is *Reports of Judgments, Advisory Opinions and Orders*. Under rule 21.5.1 of the 19th edition of the *Bluebook*, this title is abbreviated in case citations as "I.C.J." In normal discourse, this series is often referenced simply as the "*ICJ Reports*." Reprinted editions of the earliest volumes of the *ICJ Reports* have been made available through the offices of William S. Hein & Co., and many U.S. law libraries have taken advantage of this service.

The concept evidently used in compiling the volumes of these reports is similar to that used in compiling decisions in U.S. reporters, such as *United States Reports* ("U.S.") and the federal and regional reporters. That is, in *ICJ Reports*, the decisions in each case are reported, followed by any concurring or dissenting opinions. Cases are presented in roughly chronological order, and are captioned by party names and dates. The volumes serve solely as reporters and contain little or no additional secondary substantive material. Accordingly, U.S. lawyers, law students, and legal professionals, at least at a basic level, should feel fairly comfortable using the *ICJ Reports*.

However, there are several points of difference between standard U.S. reporters and the *ICJ Reports*. Most noticeably, the *ICJ Reports* are bilingual, generally with the English text of each decision on the left-hand pages and the corresponding French text on the opposite right-hand pages. This, of course, is in keeping with the specification in Article 39 of the ICJ Statute. Although this may take some getting used to, it should not present a problem for most researchers.

Of more significance is the limited indexing available for the print *ICJ Reports*. Unfortunately, there are no digests or head-note numbering systems that might facilitate searching the internal portions of the reported decisions. Therefore, material in the print *ICJ Reports* can only be visually searched or scanned by date, title, or other summary features of each decision.

In addition, the mechanisms for locating opinions even by date and title are limited. The only finding aids included in the print *ICJ Reports* are indexes and tables of contents at the end of each yearly compendium. A further difficulty is that the indexes and tables of contents appear only in this annual format; there is no cumulative indexing or listing of contents.

A. ICJ Website

Fortunately, use of the ICJ website, currently at www.icj-cij.org, alleviates many of these problems. The website contains a "Cases" file, and in this file, there are separate databases for "Contentious Cases" and "Advisory Proceedings." Appropriate links in the "Cases" file make each database available. For both databases, cases or proceedings appear by default in reverse chronological order according to the year in which they were commenced or introduced.

A major improvement resulting from this database is that all ICJ rulings are now searchable for words and phrases, on a document-by-document basis. This is a big improvement over the print reporters. Similarly, when printing a particular bilingual document, the printing function on your computer normally allows you to print either "even" or "odd" pages, and this should usually allow you to print only those pages in English, if you wish.

However, as convenient as the ICJ case databases are, several points are worth noting about their use.

First, as of the date of this printing, searching by word or phrase is still only possible within each document. Accordingly, a single word, phrase, or concept cannot be electronically searched at the website through all the rulings that the ICJ has issued.

Second, note that there are searching links at the top of each page, allowing the reader to list cases according to party names and according to year of culmination, rather than year of commencement (or introduction). Many researchers could find these alternative formats to be useful.

For example, suppose you wanted to find a case brought by Costa Rica against Nicaragua in 2005. The default yearly list, which operates by the year of introduction of the case, lists the following under the contentious cases in 2005: "Dispute regarding Navigational and Related Rights (Costa Rica v. Nicaragua)." The title "Dispute regarding Navigational and Related Rights" is assigned by the ICJ shortly after the case begins. So, even if you didn't know the case title, but you knew the countries involved and the year it commenced, you could find the case quickly.

If, on the other hand, you didn't know the year it commenced, but only knew the year in which the judgment was issued, using the default list would not be as helpful. (The ICJ actually issued the judgment in the case on July 13, 2009.) You could then select the alternative searching link for listing by "date of culmination" rather than "date of introduction." The case would then also be relatively easy to find using the judgment date as a basis for retrieval.

Also, be aware that the same two states may have been involved in different cases at different points in time. For example, Costa Rica also brought an action against Nicaragua in 2010. Using the "See by State Party to a Case" function can help keep these cases distinct, and help assure that you retrieve the correct case materials.

A third point worth noting is that the ICJ tends to publish numerous decisions concerning the same case. In the first place, the ICJ publishes on its website many procedural documents, such as interim orders and applications for extensions of time. Accordingly, each case can involve as many as a dozen or more reported orders, judgments, and other rulings, appearing in various different annual lists. By selecting the link for "Judgments," one can usually go directly to the ruling(s) of the Court having the most final and substantive effect.

However, even this may not be completely specific. As noted above, the ICJ on occasion will publish a separate judgment or order on key procedural matters, such as jurisdiction. Then, a judgment on the "merits" will appear separately, and be so denominated. Also as noted above, on occasion there is a separate judgment regarding the award of damages or other adjectival matters. There are even some cases that the ICJ has dismissed without any judgment of any kind, but which it has retained in its reporting records (and therefore on its website databases).

B. Commercial Electronic Databases

Opinions issued by the ICJ are also available on Westlaw, LexisNexis, and HeinOnline. All the documents are in searchable form. Accordingly, this medium may be useful for researchers with access to one or more of these databases who are also comfortable with their search methodologies.

Although these databases can thus present an attractive means for accessing ICJ decisions, some of the inconveniences described above regarding the hard-copy *ICJ Reports* necessarily carry through to the electronic format. For example, searching on the basis of a mere case name will still yield search results encompassing all decisions issued for that case, including procedural and adjectival decisions. The researcher may still need to determine which of several, perhaps many, decisions of the same name listed in the search results will be most useful. Also, Westlaw and LexisNexis documents in this area are generally not in pdf format.

IX. Locating and Working with PCIJ Materials

Although the PCIJ no longer exists, its judgments and advisory opinions are still frequently cited. Thorough research of international legal questions will often involve recourse to its judgments and opinions. The published judgments, opinions, and other rulings of the PCIJ are available at the ICJ website, in a separate set of files linked under the category, "Permanent Court of International Justice."

The case reports of the PCIJ are provided in three separate files, labeled "Series A, Series B, and Series A/B." Series A contains those judgments, orders, and other materials regarding contentious cases before the PCIJ dated from 1923 through 1930. Series B contains advisory opinions, and other orders and materials regarding advisory opinions, dated from 1922 through 1930. Series A/B contains judgments, orders, advisory opinions, and certain related materials dated from 1931 through 1940.

X. Locating and Working with Arbitration Materials

There is no comprehensive published set of international arbitration awards. However, the UN publishes a very prominent multi-volume series that compiles selected significant arbitral awards. It is called the *Reports of International Arbitral Awards* (or frequently, the "RIAA" for short). Many of the most recent arbitral reports published in the RIAA derive from PCA proceedings, although many others do not. In particular, several volumes of the RIAA contain arbitral awards that were issued prior to the establishment of the UN. The reports are published in either French or English, but unfortunately often not both. There are often headnotes and each volume has an index. There can at times be a considerable delay in publishing the reports.

An invaluable finding aid for some PCA arbitral awards is a one-volume index work, *The Permanent Court of Arbitration: International Arbitration and Dispute Resolution*, edited by P. Hamilton, H.C. Requena, L. van Schletinga and B. Shifman (The Hague: Kluwer Law International, 1999). This volume lists, summarizes, and digests many of the most significant PCA awards and decisions. It also contains references to the RIAA and other sources in which original awards (or reports of them) can be found. It is to be emphasized, however, that this work applies only to arbitral awards and decisions rendered under the PCA framework.

The PCA also maintains a database of "cases" on its website (www.pca-cpa.org). This database is not necessarily complete, and may not contain all materials for each arbitration listed. However, it can be useful to the extent relevant arbitration decisions or awards are included.

International Law Reports, referenced in part VII of this chapter, also contains reports of arbitrations as well as judicial opinions. Especially recent arbitral decisions or awards are often published in *International Legal Materials*, also discussed in part VII.

The volumes of the RIAA are now available electronically through the UN website. The URL for their access point is http://www.un.org/law/riaa. Researchers are cautioned that, although each award and decision is generally searchable, volumes as a whole are not searchable. And the series as a whole is not searchable. Accordingly, investigation will need to proceed volume-by-volume, unless for some reason the volume number is known at the outset. The RIAA is also included with HeinOnline's United Nations Law Collection and its Foreign & International Law Resources Database.

XI. Citations for Judicial and Arbitral Decisions

Citations to opinions and other documents issued by the ICJ and the PCIJ are covered by *Bluebook* rule 21.5.1. According to this rule, abbreviations pursuant to table 10 (Geographical Terms) should be used to name litigating states for the parentheticals in ICJ and PCIJ citations that identify the parties. However, when the name of a state is part of the title of the case, it should not be abbreviated.

The cited titles of cases should not include article adjectives, such as "The." Also, the word "Case" and phrases such as "Case concerning" should not appear as part of the title of the case in the citation. (*Bluebook* rule 21.5.1(a).) Strict adherence to rule 21.5.1 could sometimes require the double-entry of the names of states parties to a case. This could happen if the title of the case contains the names of both parties. In that event, rule 21.5.1 would require that the parties' full names appear in the title, and that their abbreviated names then appear in the identification parenthetical. As a common-sense variation from the *Bluebook*, we think that the identification parenthetical is usually unnecessary in this circumstance.

Note that the pages of the *ICJ Reports*, whether in print or online, frequently have two page numbers. (One number is usually in the outside upper corner, and the other is usually in the outside lower corner, of the page.) The smaller of the two numbers refers to the page of the slip opinion, and the larger number refers to the page in the volume of *ICJ Reports* in which the case appears. The volume page number should be used in a citation identifying the case, although the slip opinion page numbers can be useful when working with cases electronically.

Rule 21.6 of the *Bluebook* directs that citations to arbitral decisions be cited "by analogy" to the rule 21.5, which applies to the ICJ and other permanent established international courts. While for most purposes this is reasonably self-explanatory, note that the *Bluebook* contains a separate table (table 5) listing abbreviations for sources of arbitral decisions.

XII. Chapter Summary

Judicial decisions can be authoritative evidence of international law, and are often cited by treatise authors and tribunals. This is true even though Article 38(1) of the ICJ Statute refers to them as a "subsidiary means" for determining rules of international law. There are three basic types of judicial decisions in researching international law: decisions of domestic courts involving international law, decisions of international courts, and international arbitration awards.

Domestic courts in most countries have authority to enforce international law, subject to their domestic constitutional systems. While not necessarily an everyday occurrence, domestic courts in individual countries will sometimes interpret and enforce rules of international law. Researching international law decisions in domestic courts is carried out the same way that researching any other types of issues in domestic courts would be carried out.

There are many types of international courts, such a regional international human rights courts, international criminal courts, and specialized regional or subject-matter courts. However, at this point we focus primarily on the ICJ and its predecessor, the PCIJ.

The ICJ is the principal judicial organ of the UN, and sits in The Hague, the seat of government of the Netherlands. It operates under the authority of the UN Charter and the ICJ Statute. Generally fifteen judges sit on the ICJ, and each judge has a nine-year term. The ICJ Statute provides that the ICJ is not required to recognize the doctrine of binding precedent, but the ICJ nevertheless cites its earlier decisions in its later rulings and considers them persuasive authority.

The ICJ conducts two types of proceedings: contentious cases and advisory proceedings. Contentious cases generally result in the issuance of a judgment, while advisory proceedings generally result in the issuance of an advisory opinion. On the way to a judgment or advisory opinion, however, the ICJ may issue supplemental orders and rulings of various kinds. And individual ICJ judges often issue separate or dissenting opinions or declarations.

The PCIJ was the chief judicial organ of the League of Nations, and so no longer exists. However, its judgments and opinions are still frequently cited as authoritative.

Many modern arbitrations between states are conducted under the auspices of the Permanent Court of Arbitration (or "PCA"). The PCA is not actually a court, but rather an institute that maintains lists of prospective arbitrators, and facilitates the arbitration of particular disputes as they arise. While many arbitrations conducted under PCA auspices have been influential, other significant international arbitrations are still sometimes conducted on an ad hoc basis.

Judgments, opinions, and other rulings of the ICJ are available in the *ICJ Reports* and online at the ICJ website. They are also available through commercial databases, such as Westlaw, LexisNexis, and HeinOnline. Judgments, opinions, and rulings of the PCIJ are also available at a specially-linked section of the ICJ website.

The print *ICJ Reports* are similar in design and function to case reporters published in the United States and other common-law countries. However, there are certain differences, including their publication in bilingual format and the absence of any digests or head-note system. The ICJ website allows for searching by word and phrase within each document, but single words or phrases cannot be electronically searched through all the ICJ rulings on the website.

Working with the ICJ website also requires users to keep in mind that a judgment for a contentious case is usually rendered in a different year from that in which the case commenced. This will affect which manner of listing of cases a reader selects at the website. Readers also need to remember that the same countries can be parties in different cases. Accordingly, attention often needs to be paid to the case title and subject matter, to make sure one is dealing with the correct case. Finally, ICJ cases often generate many different orders and rulings, and sometimes more than one judgment. Care needs to be taken to make sure one is dealing with the correct document, even within a particular case file.

Electronic databases, such as Westlaw and LexisNexis, can provide a basis for searching by words and phrases more broadly. However, such searches can also retrieve a large array of related (or unrelated) materials that can require sorting before the correct reference is actually obtained.

Many significant arbitration awards are reported in the *Reports of International Arbitral Awards* (or "RIAA"). The RIAA collects both significant modern arbitration awards and prominent awards issued before the establishment of the UN. The RIAA is available on the UN website, but words and phrases can presently be searched in text only for each report, rather than for the whole volume or the whole series. The PCA also maintains a database of cases on its website, but availability there may not be complete.

XIII. Chapter Review Questions

1. Do the domestic courts of individual countries ever have the authority to decide issues of international law?

2. Which court is the primary judicial body of the UN?

3. Are the decisions of arbitral tribunals, in addition to court decisions, considered "judicial decisions" that can be sources of international law?

4. What are the two different types of proceedings conducted by the ICJ?

5. Do decisions of the PCIJ still have any relevance under international law today?

6. Is the Permanent Court of Arbitration an actual court?

7. In what ways is the *ICJ Reports* series different from a domestic case reporter series in a common-law country such as the United States?

8. In addition to the *ICJ Reports*, at what electronic sources (via a website or databases) could you find decisions and orders of the ICJ and PCIJ?

9. How does the organization of cases at the ICJ website present issues that need to be taken into account when searching for judgments or other documents related to ICJ cases?

10. What is a primary source in which one would expect to find reports of arbitral awards issued by arbitral tribunals conducted under the auspices of the PCA?

XIV. Additional Resources and General Bibliographic References

Alexander P. Fachiri, *Permanent Court of International Justice: Its Constitution, Procedure and Work* (2d ed., London: Oxford University Press: H. Milford 1932).

Claire M. Germain, "Germain's International Court of Justice Research Guide," in *Germain's Transnational Law Research* (1997), *available at* http://www.lawschool.cornell.edu/library/whatwedo/researchguides/icj.cfm (last visited June 12, 2013).

Terry D. Gill, *Rosenne's The World Court: What It Is and How It Works* (6th ed., Brill Academic Publishers 2003)(vol. 41 of the Legal Aspects of International Organization Series).

Manley O. Hudson, *Permanent Court of International Justice 1920–1942: A Treatise* (New York: Macmillan 1934).

Ijaz Hussain, *Dissenting and Separate Opinions at the World Court*, 3 *Legal Aspects of International Organization* (Martinus Nijhoff Publishers 1984).

John Bassett Moore, *History and Digest of the International Arbitration to which the United States has been a Party* (Washington D.C.: G.P.O. 1898)(6 volumes), http://archive.org/stream/historyanddiges02moorgoog#page/n4/mode/2up.

Oxford Reports on International Courts of General Jurisdiction (New York: Oxford University Press 2006).

Oxford Reports on International Law in Domestic Courts (New York: Oxford University Press 2006).

Shabtai Rosenne, *Law and Practice of the International Court, 1920–2005* (4th ed., Boston: Martinus Nijhoff Publishers 2006)(4 volumes).

James Brown Scott, *Hague Court Reports* (New York: Oxford University Press, American Branch 1916–1932).

David Sloss, *The Role of Domestic Courts in Treaty Enforcement: A Comparative Study* (New York: Cambridge University Press 2009).

Summaries of Judgments, Advisory Opinions, and Orders of the International Court of Justice, 1948–2007, http://www.un.org/law/ICJsummaries/ (last visited June 12, 2013).

Chapter 7

UN Security Council and General Assembly Resolutions

I. Introduction

Given the significance of the UN in modern international law, familiarity with UN documents is important in international law research. We first devote particular attention to resolutions of the Security Council and the General Assembly, because they can be a source, directly or indirectly, of international legal obligations. In chapter 9, we look at other kinds of UN documents, which can also affect international legal obligations.

UN resolutions are important because they are "formal expressions of the opinion or will of United Nations organs."[1] As discussed more fully below, many resolutions of the Security Council state binding obligations under international law. Resolutions of the General Assembly can be important in developing rules of customary international law. Accordingly, we emphasize working with these resolutions now.

First, we will briefly consider the structure of resolutions issued by these two organs.

---

1. Dag Hammarskjöld Library, *UN Documentation: Overview: Resolutions & Decisions*, United Nations Research Guides & Resources, http:// research.un.org/en/docs (last visited June 12, 2013) [hereinafter UN Resolutions Research Guide].

II. Structure of Resolutions

A. Preamble and Operative Paragraphs

Resolutions of both the Security Council and General Assembly usually consist of two parts. The UN calls these the "preamble" and the "operative part."[2] The preamble consists of a set of introductory paragraphs. These state historical and background material serving as a foundation for the resolution. Each of these introductory paragraphs generally begins with an italicized word or phrase, often ending in the suffix "-*ing*," for example, "*noting*," or "*observing*," or "*deploring*."

After the preamble, the operative part begins, usually without any separate break or heading. This consists of a set of numbered paragraphs, which are the paragraphs of the resolution that are intended to have substantive effect. These numbered paragraphs also usually begin with an italicized word or phrase. But the first word of each of these italicized introductions is more likely to end in the suffix letter "-*s*," as in (for example) "*determines that*," "*concludes that*," or "*endorses*."

Which of these two types of paragraphs is more important can be a thorny consideration. On the one hand, only the operative paragraphs are intended to "move the matter forward," stating new substantive positions or (in the case of binding Security Council resolutions) new legal obligations.

However, the preamble paragraphs can be quite significant. They can include definitions of significant terms. They also often list prior relevant resolutions that can be helpful for research. The main point is for researchers to be aware of the two parts of resolutions and their distinct functions. Either kind of paragraph can be the subject of a cogent citation, depending on the purpose of the citation.

B. Attachment of Annexes

Resolutions of both bodies frequently attach one or more additional documents as annexes. These annexes can be important. General Assembly resolutions may attach declarations, which are usually observations or assertions made by the General Assembly on important issues of international affairs. As noted in part III of this chapter, these can have a role in creating binding international law rules, even if they are usually not binding in themselves.

---

2. *Id.*

Annexes to Security Council resolutions can be quite significant also. When a Security Council resolution is binding, often the most detailed and salient terms of its legal obligations are stated in annexed documents.

In particular, when citing material, one needs to be specific in the citation about whether one is citing the text of the resolution or a document (or documents) annexed to the resolution. We have more to say about the citation of annexes to resolutions in segment V.C of this chapter.

C. Masthead Versions & Official Records

A UN resolution will be adopted by a vote on a particular date, and then issued for broader distribution as an intermediate step before publication in the Official Records. When it is initially issued for distribution, the resolution will appear as a "masthead" document, under an official first-page "masthead" header including the UN logo. It is this masthead version that is the first public pronouncement of the full text of the resolution.

When working with masthead versions, researchers need to be aware that the date of the masthead version is often a later date than the date on which the resolution was voted on and adopted. For General Assembly resolutions, the date of adoption is given at the end of the resolution's text (and before any annexes). For Security Council resolutions, the date of adoption is given after the title of the resolution.

The date on which the organ submits the resolution to the Secretariat for distribution is the "imprint date" of the resolution. It is given on the masthead document in the upper-right hand corner of its first page. Citations to the resolution should generally include the adoption date, rather than the imprint date on the masthead version. One might also include the imprint date, for example, if the purpose of the citation is to attest to the fact of distribution.

In due course, resolutions are then published in the "Official Records" of the organ that has adopted them. When resolutions appear in the Official Records, masthead graphics are eliminated, and resolutions appear only as they were adopted. In this format, generally only the adoption date is given, and there is less opportunity for confusion. For especially recent resolutions, often only the masthead version is available.

The Official Records of each principal body of the UN consist of meeting records, resolutions, reports (both of the principal organ itself and any of its committees or commissions), budget and financial reports, and reprints of other documents. The printed resolutions for each General Assembly session are accumulated together in separately numbered "Supplements," distinct from most other components of the General Assembly Official Records. This becomes significant when we discuss citation form for resolutions later on in this chapter.

D. Sessions for the General Assembly, but Not the Security Council

Since its inception in 1945, the General Assembly has met in a series of annual regular sessions, beginning in September that year.[3] Each session begins on a Tuesday, in the third week of September, counting from the first week of the month that has at least one working day.[4] The session beginning on September 17, 2013 was the 68th session of the General Assembly. The General Assembly meets from the beginning of the session until its agenda items are completed, and sometimes this means working through to the beginning of the next session.[5] The session during which the General Assembly adopts a particular resolution can be important for determining the resolution's UN document symbol and its citation, both of which are discussed below.

Depending on unusual needs, the General Assembly sometimes meets for "special sessions" at various times or, when it considers that a suitable emergency exists, in an "emergency session."[6]

By contrast, however, the Security Council does not view itself as operating in annual sessions. Rather, it views itself as operating continuously from one year to the next. Indeed, the UN Charter requires that the Security Council "shall be so organized as to be able to function continuously."[7] It further specifies that each Security Council member state "shall for this purpose be represented at all times at the seat of the Organization."[8]

---

3. Article 20 of the UN Charter specifies that the General Assembly "shall meet in regular annual sessions, and in such special sessions as occasion may require."

4. *Past Sessions*, General Assembly of the United Nations, http://www.un.org/en/ga/sessions/ (last visited June 12, 2013).

5. *Id.*

6. Article 20 of the UN Charter also specifies that "special sessions shall be convoked by the Secretary-General at the request of the Security Council or of a majority of the Members of the United Nations."

7. UN Charter art. 28(1).

8. *Id.*

III. Legal Status of Resolutions

A. Security Council Resolutions

1. Possibility of Binding Character

As noted earlier, the UN Charter requires all Member states to "accept and carry out the decisions of the Security Council in accordance with the . . . Charter."[9] In view of this language, many Security Council resolutions contain operative paragraphs beginning with the italicized phrase "*decides that.*" This can denote that the terms following are "decisions" of the Security Council that Member states are required to "accept and carry out." An historic example was Security Council resolution 1373, following shortly after the terrorist attacks on September 11, 2011. Paragraph 1 provided that, among other things, the Security Council:

1. *Decides* that all States shall: (a) Prevent and suppress the financing of terrorist acts; [and] (b) Criminalize the willful provision or collection . . . of funds by their nationals or in their territories with the intention that the funds should be used . . . in order to carry out terrorist acts . . . .[10]

The use of the initial phrase, "*Decides that,*" clearly signaled that the obligations to prevent and suppress terrorist financing and to criminalize the provision and collection of terrorist funds were mandatory for all Member states.

Other kinds of operative paragraphs can have legally binding consequences. For example, when the Security Council authorized the creation of a standing UN military force in Afghanistan, the relevant paragraphs of the resolution used the italicized term "*Authorizes*" to signal that the military units thus envisioned would be operating at the behest of the Security Council.[11]

On the other hand, many Security Council resolutions do not have these kinds of binding consequences. The initial phrases in the operative paragraphs of these resolutions may indicate that the Security Council "*Calls on*" a state or entity to behave in a certain way, or "*Expresses*" its determination as to a particular matter, or "*Notes with concern*" another matter. Operative paragraphs

---

9. U.N. Charter art. 25. *See* chapter 3 *supra*, segment IV.A.

10. S.C. Res. 1373, ¶ 1, U.N. Doc. S/RES/1373 (Sept. 28, 2001).

11. S.C. Res. 1386, U.N. Doc. S/RES/1386 (Dec. 20, 2001). For example, operative paragraph 1 stated that the Security Council: "*Authorizes* . . . the establishment . . . of an International Security Assistance Force to assist the Afghan Interim Authority in the maintenance of security . . . ." And operative paragraph 3 stated that the Security Council: "*Authorizes* the Member States participating in the International Security Assistance Force to take all necessary measures to fulfill its mandate."

stated in these terms are meant to be taken seriously, but generally do not carry binding legal obligations. Of course, some resolutions contain operative paragraphs of both kinds; in that event, the paragraphs containing the mandatory language are binding and the others are not.

2. Basis for Binding Character

Careful readers may note that Security Council resolutions do not appear anywhere in the list of sources of international law in Article 38(1) of the ICJ Statute.[12] If Security Council resolutions are not listed in Article 38(1), how can they be sources of binding law?

Different answers are possible for this query, but probably the most accepted is the notion that the mandatory character of binding Security Council resolutions derives from the origin of the Security Council's power in the UN Charter. And the Charter itself is of course a "convention" within the meaning of Article 38(1)(a) of the ICJ Statute. Accordingly, it is suggested with some authority that Security Council resolutions are "secondary treaty (or Charter) law."[13]

3. Limits on Security Council Power; Security Council Legislation

There are limits on the scope of the Security Council's power to issue binding resolutions. The most important of these is a subject-matter limitation. According to the UN Charter, the UN Member states have conferred on the Security Council "primary responsibility for the maintenance of international peace and security."[14] All of its activities should probably be viewed as encompassed by this grant of authority. If a Security Council resolution were not grounded within this scope of authority, it would probably be ultra vires. Any binding Security Council resolution should therefore be meaningfully related to the maintenance of international peace and security.

Furthermore, since the end of the Cold War, the Security Council has been issuing resolutions of a broadly applicable character. One example is another

---

12. *See* chapter 4, *supra*.

13. Stefan Talmon, *The Security Council as World Legislature*, 99 Am. J. Int'l L. 175, 179 (2005). It could also be noted that Security Council resolutions can be binding for the simple reason that the Security Council often has authority to enforce them by armed action under Chapter VII of the UN Charter. An example here would be the Security Council resolution authorizing the forceful expulsion of Saddam Hussein's forces after they invaded Kuwait in 1990. S.C. Res. 678, U.N. Doc. S/RES/678 (Nov. 29, 1990). The issue discussed above relates more to the reconciling of the binding character of the Security Council resolutions with the exclusive list of sources set forth in Article 38(1) of the ICJ Statute.

14. U.N. Charter art. 24(1).

provision of Security Council Resolution 1373. The operative part of the resolution also included the directive that the Security Council:

1. *Decides* that all States shall: . . . (c) Freeze without delay funds and other financial assets or economic resources of persons who commit, or attempt to commit, terrorist acts or participate in or facilitate the commission of terrorist acts . . . .[15]

Note that compliance with this resolution requires UN Member states to take certain actions with respect to the property of individual persons within their jurisdiction. At the same time that the resolution effectively imposes legal impediments on individuals, it is also directed broadly to all UN Member states. That is, its obligations have effects on individual persons, while at the same time being general in character and abstract in their language. In these respects the resolution appears to be legislative in character. Indeed, some commentators have referred to such resolutions as "Security Council legislation."[16]

The legal consequences of the Security Council issuing legislative resolutions are still being explored. Of course, all Security Council resolutions (as noted above) must be within its scope of authority under the Charter if they are to escape being ultra vires. However, there may well be other limits on Security Council legislation. For example, the "general principles of law" referenced in Article 38(1)(c) of the ICJ Statute may impose limits in the legislative context. Among these might be a principle of proportionality.[17] And basic due process norms might also be opposable in those situations when Security Council legislation affects individuals.

The development of Security Council legislation is interesting in view of the traditional approach to the idea of "international legislation." In the broad tradition of international law, the term, "international legislation" generally referred only to treaties and conventions. It was commonly said that none of the principal organs of the UN was truly a legislative body, and their resolutions were not considered international legislation.[18]

And indeed, it is certainly true that none of the UN principal organs is broadly representative of the world's population, in the way that a legitimate

---

15. S.C. Res. 1373, ¶ 1(c), U.N. Doc. S/RES/1373 (Sept. 28, 2001).

16. *See generally, e.g.*, José E. Alvarez, *Hegemonic International Law Revisited*, 97 Am. J. Int'l L. 873 (2003); Talmon, *supra* note 13.

17. Talmon, *supra* note 13, at 184.

18. *E.g.*, Oscar Schachter, *The UN Legal Order: An Overview*, in *The United Nations and International Law* 3, 3 (Christopher C. Joyner, ed. 1997) [hereinafter *The UN and International Law*] ("Neither the United Nations nor any of its specialized agencies was conceived as a legislative body.").

legislature of a domestic state would normally be.[19] Nevertheless, it was always understood that resolutions of the Security Council and General Assembly could still state or indirectly affect binding rules of international law, as noted above. This was the case even though the resolutions weren't traditionally viewed as "international legislation." Now, with the Security Council taking actions that are viewed as legislative, jurisprudential limits such as the due process and proportionality principles mentioned above are becoming important to help assure the legitimacy of those of its actions that could be called "legislative."

These limitations are worth noting as a doctrinal matter, and are therefore mentioned here. However, the general rule should remain clear: When acting within its sphere of authority and within appropriate jurisprudential limits for its legislative acts, the Security Council has the legal capacity to issue resolutions that are binding on the Member states to which they are addressed.

B. General Assembly Resolutions

1. General Rule

As noted in chapter 3 of this book, as a general rule resolutions issued by the General Assembly do not constitute binding rules of international law.[20] The UN Charter does not require Member states to "accept and carry out" the decisions of the General Assembly, as it does for decisions of the Security Council.[21]

In spite of this general lack of direct obligatory character, General Assembly resolutions have had a formative effect on international law rules in a variety of ways.[22]

---

19. Recall that the General Assembly, although it provides representation for every UN Member state, gives equal voting strength to all states, whether very large or very small. It is not really majoritarian at all, and could not be called democratic in a majoritarian sense. Even more baldly, the Security Council at any given time comprises representatives from only a minority of states, and gives the veto power only to its five permanent members.

20. This was stated in part IV.A of chapter 3. *See also* Christopher C. Joyner, *Conclusion: The United Nations as International Law-Giver, in The UN and International Law, supra* note 18, at 432, 443 ("The General Assembly may draft, approve, and recommend international instruments for multilateral agreement. That body can not, however, compel them as binding obligations upon member states.").

21. *Cf.* U.N. Charter art. 25.

22. *See* Joyner, *supra* note 20, at 440 (referencing the "quasi-legislative" capability of the General Assembly to "influence the nature and substance of contemporary international law in a number of ways").

2. Possible Effect on Rules of Customary International Law

First, General Assembly resolutions can be cited as evidencing either or both of the general practice or *opinio juris* components necessary to establish customary international law. Statements made by national representatives during General Assembly discussion and debate may provide evidence of either component. In particular, resolutions that are adopted with a unanimous, or nearly unanimous, vote can in some cases be more likely than rules adopted with less complete approval to furnish authority for a rule of customary international law.[23]

Note that this does not mean that all General Assembly resolutions adopted by a unanimous vote are legally binding. Rather, the unanimity just makes it marginally more likely that there is *opinio juris* for a customary rule. (For a complete discussion of *opinio juris* and the formation of rules of customary international law, refer to chapter 8 of this book.)

Furthermore, an assertion that any particular General Assembly resolution has this effect is often open to challenge, since the generality of state practice and the existence of *opinio juris* are complex factors that can generally be analyzed in a variety of ways.[24]

3. Promulgation of Declarations

It is also relatively common for the General Assembly to adopt "declarations" that broadly indicate international social or political values in certain areas, particularly human rights. The most famous example is probably the Universal Declaration of Human Rights, from 1948.[25] Another key example would be the 1970 Declaration on Principles of International Law Concerning Friendly Relations and Co-operation among States.[26]

---

23. *See* Simon Chesterman, Thomas M. Franck & David M. Malone, *Law and Practice of the United Nations* 118 (2008) [hereinafter *UN Law & Practice*] (referencing General Assembly Resolution 2131(XX) (1965), and describing the view of some that its principles are recognized as customary international law, in part because of the nearly unanimous vote by which it was adopted).

24. *E.g.*, *UN Law & Practice*, *supra* note 23, at 118 (referencing other authority challenging the legal character of the resolution).

25. G.A. Res. 217 (III), U.N. Doc. A/810 (Dec. 10, 1948).

26. G.A. Res. 2625 (XXVI), U.N. Doc. A/8028 (Oct. 24, 1970). *See* John F. Murphy, *Force and Arms, in The UN and International Law*, *supra* note 18, at 97, 97 (stating that this Declaration is of the kind that has "restated, amplified, and clarified the meaning" of certain provisions of the UN Charter and is "generally regarded as an authoritative interpretation of broad principles of international law expressed in the Charter").

Sometimes declarations like this are provided within the text of the resolution, and sometimes they are added as annexes. Such declarations often state principles that are so well respected and so characteristic of enlightened views that most states are reluctant to disparage them by refusing to sign them or by admitting derogation from them. Accordingly, it is possible for these declarations to serve as evidence for general principles of law or help form customary international law rules. Again, we discuss this phenomenon in more detail in chapter 8 of this book.

4. Promulgation of "Norm-Creating" Treaties

The General Assembly also has a role in the creation of new binding multilateral conventions. In particular, two General Assembly entities are engaged in this work.

First, the General Assembly has created a prestigious body known as the International Law Commission (or the "ILC"). The General Assembly created this body in view of its obligation under the UN Charter to "encourage the progressive development of international law and its codification."[27] The ILC consists of 34 prominent authorities on international law elected by the General Assembly.[28] Its primary role is the preparation of draft multilateral conventions for signature and ratification by states.

When the ILC has finished a draft convention, it proposes the draft to the General Assembly, which would usually approve the draft, perhaps with modifications. Then the General Assembly will often adopt the draft convention as part of a resolution, thereby releasing the convention for signature by states. Many international conventions have been promulgated in this way, including the Vienna Convention on the Law of Treaties[29] (discussed at length in chapter 5) and the Vienna Convention on Diplomatic Relations.[30]

Second, one of the standing committees of the General Assembly (the so-called "Sixth Committee") is its "Legal Committee." Its responsibility is to deal with legal matters of concern to the General Assembly. It is usually involved with the development of draft conventions by the ILC. But it can often be involved with draft conventions prepared by other General Assembly bodies, such as the UN Commission on International Trade Law (also called "UNCITRAL"). Among the more significant of the treaties prepared by UNCITRAL have been

---

27. U.N. Charter art. 13(1)(a).

28. The current size of the ILC was fixed through a 1981 General Assembly resolution. G.A. Res. 36/39, ¶ 1, U.N. Doc. A/RES/36/39 (Nov. 18, 1981).

29. May 23, 1969, 1155 U.N.T.S. 331, 8 I.L.M. 679.

30. April 18, 1961, 23 U.S.T. 3227, 500 U.N.T.S. 95.

the UN Convention on Contracts for the International Sale of Goods[31] and the UN Convention on the Carriage of Goods by Sea.[32]

The General Assembly's Sixth Committee is instrumental in the encouragement and promulgation of new conventions prepared through the work of the ILC and UNCITRAL, and through other means.

IV. Researching Resolutions

A. UN Document Symbols for Security Council and General Assembly Resolutions

One of the first steps in learning to work with UN resolutions is familiarizing one's self with the UN "document symbol" system. Most documents published by the UN are given these "document symbols," which are usually a series of capital letters and numerals separated at various intervals by forward slashes. Each new forward slash generally signifies that the information following it is more specific than the information preceding it. We will look at the document symbol system in more detail in chapter 9. In this chapter we need to focus only on document symbols for resolutions of the Security Council and the General Assembly.

1. UN Document Symbols for Security Council Resolutions

For Security Council resolutions, the first component of the document symbol is always the capital letter "S," signifying the Security Council. After a forward slash, the next component is always the capitalized abbreviation, "RES," to signify a resolution. After another forward slash, the third component is the sequential number of the resolution. All Security Council resolutions have been numbered sequentially since the Security Council's inception in 1945. The fourth component is the year in which the resolution was adopted, expressed in full with four digits, with no forward slash preceding it, but enclosed by parentheses.

For example, on October 24, 2002, the Security Council adopted its 1440th resolution, which condemned the taking of hostages at a theater in Moscow. The UN document symbol for this resolution is:

S/RES/1440 (2002).

---

31. Apr. 11, 1980, 1489 U.N.T.S. 3, 19 I.L.M. 668.
32. Mar. 31, 1978, 1695 U.N.T.S. 3.

The UN document symbols for all other Security Council resolutions follow the same pattern.

However, note that the UN document symbol for any resolution is simply a unique identifier for that resolution, useful when retrieving and dealing with documents in the UN's various information systems. A resolution's UN document symbol is not necessarily the same thing as the approved citation form for that resolution, under the *Bluebook* or any other applicable citation protocol. For example, the applicable *Bluebook* citation rule requires a different treatment for the date of Security Council resolutions than that prescribed for the UN document symbol. Citation form for Security Council resolutions is discussed in part V of this chapter.

2. UN Document Symbols for General Assembly Resolutions

The formulation of UN Document Symbols for General Assembly resolutions is complicated by the fact that the system changed from the end of its 30th Session, in the spring of 1976, to the beginning of its 31st session, in September of 1976. Before the change, the General Assembly numbered its resolutions sequentially, formulated from the first resolutions adopted at the first Session in 1945. (Accordingly, before the change, the General Assembly was numbering its resolutions in the same way that the Security Council has always been numbering its resolutions.) After the change, the General Assembly began numbering its resolutions serially, with the numbering sequence newly restarting at the beginning of each new regular session.

a. *Through the end of its 30th session.*

During this period, UN document symbols for General Assembly resolutions are constructed as follows. The first component is the capital letter, "A," signifying the General Assembly. After a forward slash, the next component is the capitalized abbreviation, "RES." After another forward slash, the next component is the sequential number of the resolution, formulated as from the inception of the General Assembly in 1945. The final component, not preceded by a forward slash but in parentheses, is the number of the General Assembly session during which the resolution was adopted, expressed in capitalized roman numerals.

For example, on September 28, 1950, shortly after the start of its fifth session, the General Assembly passed its 491st resolution, pursuant to which it admitted Indonesia as a member of the UN. The UN document symbol for this resolution is:

A/RES/491 (V).

The UN document symbols for all General Assembly resolutions during this period follow this same pattern.

The special sessions and emergency sessions of the General Assembly have been numbered sequentially since the inception of the General Assembly. Special sessions and emergency sessions before September 1976 are indicated by adjusting the normal format as follows: a parenthetical phrase is added following the resolution number, containing first the abbreviations "S" or "ES," followed by a hyphen and a roman numeral indicating the sequential number of that special or emergency session.

For example, the General Assembly convened its third special session from August 21 to August 25, 1961. On the last day of the special session, it issued General Assembly resolution 1622, which was the final resolution of the special session. The resolution was titled "Consideration of the grave situation in Tunisia obtaining since 19 July 1961." The UN document symbol for this resolution is:

A/RES/1622 (S-III).

b. *Beginning with its 31st session in September of 1976.*

During this period, through to the present day, the first two components of UN document symbols for General Assembly resolutions are constructed in the same way as before. However, the third component is the number of the session in which the resolution was adopted (in arabic numerals), and the fourth component is the serial number of the resolution, counting from the first resolution in that particular session.

For example, on July 30, 2010, toward the end of its 64th session, the General Assembly adopted its 293d resolution of the session. Pursuant to this resolution, the General Assembly adopted its "Global Plan of Action to Combat Trafficking of Persons." The UN document symbol for the resolution is:

A/RES/64/293.

Special sessions and emergency sessions during the period beginning in September 1976 are indicated by adjusting the normal format as follows: after the "/RES/" term, the abbreviation "S" or "ES" is added, followed by a hyphen and an arabic numeral indicating the sequential number of that special or emergency session, followed in turn by a forward slash and the sequential number of that resolution within that special or emergency session.

For example, the General Assembly convened its eleventh special session from August 25 through September 15, 1980. On the last day of the special session, it adopted the third resolution of that special session, titled "Suggestions by the Secretary-General to overcome the critical economic situation of many developing countries." The UN document symbol for this resolution is:

A/RES/S-11/3.

B. Finding Resolutions When the UN Document Symbol or Date Is Known

If one knows the UN document symbol for a resolution, or its date of adoption, it is generally easy to find its text at the UN website. We think the easiest approach is simply to go to the sub-site that each principal organ maintains at the UN website. There are links at each organ's sub-site for its resolutions. Some tenacity may be required to locate the links for historical sessions, but they are available for access.

The resolutions are then listed in reverse chronological order, with the UN document symbol for each resolution serving as a link to its text. The textual versions of the current session's resolutions are often still in masthead form, while resolutions from earlier sessions are generally from the Official Records Supplement volume. You can also go to the Official Document System of the United Nations (ODS) at http://documents.un.org/.

The most generally available print source containing the most significant UN resolutions is *International Legal Materials* (or "ILM"), introduced in chapter 5. If one knows the date of the resolution being searched, and it is an especially significant resolution, ILM can be a useful hard-copy alternative source.

Its editors often include, in each bi-monthly issue of ILM, the most significant UN resolutions issued during the time period for that issue. Most law libraries subscribe to the print version of ILM or have it available through HeinOnline. Each annual volume of ILM closes with an annual index issued by the ILM editors. These indexes can be used when searching for resolutions issued during the time periods covered by the bound volumes. More recent significant resolutions are retrievable from the individual paper-bound issues of ILM, before they have been bound. ILM searches will only be productive for those resolutions that the editors have considered to be adequately significant to be included in ILM. Recall that ILM is also available online through Lexis-Nexis, Westlaw, and HeinOnline. Among these electronic sources, HeinOnline provides a searchable pdf version of ILM.

C. Finding Resolutions When the UN Document Symbol and Date Are Not Known

The UN website maintains several electronic research tools. The two most useful for our purposes now are the "Official Document System" (or "ODS") and the "UN Bibliographic Information System Network" (or "UNBISnet").

Each of these research tools has individual web pages on the UN website, and each is reachable through various links throughout the site. One way to get to links for both is to reach the UN home page, and select the link for "Documents." The design of the UN home page may change from time to time, although we believe there should always be a "Documents" link at the home page. At the time of publication, the "Documents" link is in a "Resources and Services" menu box on the home page.

When you get to the "Documents" page of the UN website, there should be various links to assist for document searching. At the time of publication these links are under a caption heading called "Search." Two of the main links provided under this heading are to the ODS and UNBISnet.

1. ODS

The ODS is the UN's electronic repository of official documents. It would be the basic database for UN reports, verbatim records of meetings, resolutions, and other materials that would normally be included in the Official Records. At the time of publication, most UN official documents are available on ODS only if they were published from 1993 on. The UN is gradually adding pre-1993 documents. However, the UN also takes the position that, in the special case of resolutions, availability exists on ODS for all resolutions issued by most of the principal organs back to 1946.

At the time of publication, there are two versions of ODS operating on the UN website, the "previous" version and the current version. Both versions provide a standard "search" format and an "advanced search" format. The "previous" version follows a far more detailed initial format than the current version, with the option to narrow the search in many more ways while formulating the initial search. The current version has fewer restrictions available while formulating the initial search, but allows for further searching refinements after the initial search results are retrieved.

The advanced search format of both ODS versions allows full-text searching for resolutions. (For the "previous" version's advanced search format, one needs to specify "Resolutions 1946–1993" from a special drop-down menu if one is searching for a resolution issued before 1993.)

2. UNBISnet

UNBISnet provides a bibliographic search engine that allows access to the bibliographic entries for all material at the UN Library, professionally known as the Dag Hammarskjöld Library. Accordingly, the UNBISnet database has bibliographic entries for an extremely broad collection of documents. However, the database also includes bibliographic entries for UN official documents, and these entries for UN documents often include links to the documents' full-text versions.

UNBISnet also provides an advanced search function (called simply a "keyword search"), but only bibliographic information is searchable. Accordingly, no full text search on UNBISnet will be possible covering the content of the full documents sought. One advantage to UNBISnet is that its advanced search format allows for a very broad variety of searching fields. Note that when entering a UN document symbol into a UNBISnet search, one must delete all the punctuation marks (forward slashes, periods, hyphens, etc.), and enter only the capital letters and arabic numerals.

Also, given the vagaries of electronic data entry at large institutions such as the UN, in our experience a resolution can sometimes be more easily located on UNBISnet than on the ODS. This can be the case even though it is the ODS that is supposed to be the repository of official UN documents, and even though UNBISnet only provides searching of bibliographic entries. So if a search on one of these databases proves unsuccessful, researchers are always encouraged to try the other.

D. Voting Records for Resolutions

There are many different methods for finding voting records for UN resolutions. However, if one is concerned only with the numerical totals involved with each vote, UNBISnet is often the most direct route to the information. UNBISnet maintains a separate search capacity for voting records on resolutions. However, one generally needs to know the resolution's UN document symbol, or analogous information, to execute the search.

If one needs to know which countries voted which way on a particular resolution, by country name, the UNBISnet information may be less useful for some older resolutions. (The UNBISnet voting record lists vote totals for some older resolutions, rather than roll call votes.) The resolution charts for the General Assembly database at the UN website presently contain links to press releases providing roll-call voting (where roll-call votes were taken), beginning with the General Assembly's 52d session starting in 1997. This is thus an easy way to get roll-call information for General Assembly resolutions within this date range. (Note also that many resolutions are passed by acclamation, without out a roll-call vote at all; these are so indicated here.)

The link on the Security Council home page for "Voting" simply directs a researcher to the UNBISnet voting file, and the UNBISnet voting file entries for Security Council resolutions contain roll-call votes. The ILM records of resolutions will also often note roll-call tallies for resolutions.

V. Citations for Resolutions

A. General Assembly

The 19th edition of the *Bluebook* provides for two different options in citing General Assembly resolutions. These are the "Official Records" format and the ODS format.

1. Official Records Format

This format envisions the placement of the resolution within the General Assembly Official Records, or "GAOR." (The "Official Records" of the various UN bodies, and the Supplements published with them, were discussed in segment II.C of this chapter.) We recommend that this format of citation be used, if at all, only for resolutions passed before the beginning of its 31st session in September 1976. The UN's publication practices after this time make the use of this format somewhat more involved for certain types of resolutions passed in later years.

Using this format for resolutions passed before September 1976, the citation to a General Assembly resolution is constructed by the following elements in order: the designation "G.A. Res." and the resolution's sequential number, a capital roman numeral in parenthesis indicating the session during which it was passed, the designation, "U.N. GAOR", a designation of the session number using an arabic numeral in ordinal form ("-th", etc.), a designation of the Supplement number in which the resolution was published, the UN document number for that Supplement, and a parenthetical containing the adoption date of the resolution.

For example, on December 7, 1951, during its sixth session, the UN General Assembly passed its 597th resolution, postponing consideration of its "Draft Declaration on Rights and Duties of States." This 1951 resolution was published in Supplement 20 to the General Assembly Official Records for its sixth session, which has UN document number A/2119. The citation to this resolution using the Official Records format is:

G.A. Res. 597 (VI), U.N. GAOR 6th Sess., Supp. No. 20, U.N. Doc. A/2119 (Dec. 7, 1951).

The Supplement number and UN document number for any General Assembly resolution are generally retrievable from the UNBISnet entry for that resolution.

2. ODS Format

This format envisions the placement of the resolution in the UN's electronic Official Document System ("ODS"), described in segment IV.C of this chapter. This is a more streamlined method of citation, and we recommend it for General Assembly resolutions passed from September 1976 to the present. It does not require reference to published Supplements. Also, it relies on the UN document symbols described in segment IV.A.2 of this chapter, which tend to be simpler to use than Official Records references.

Using this format for resolutions passed during or after September 1976, the citation to a General Assembly resolution is constructed by the following elements in order: the designation "G.A. Res."; the session number; a forward slash; the number of the individual resolution; the designation "U.N. Doc."; the resolution's UN document symbol; and then a parenthetical indicating the adoption date.

For example, on May 22, 1992, during its 46th session, the General Assembly passed the 236th resolution of that session, deciding to admit the Republic of Slovenia as a member of the UN. The citation to this resolution using the ODS format is:

G.A. Res. 46/236, U.N. Doc. A/RES/46/236 (May 22, 1992).

With respect to either of these formats, a pinpoint citation to a particular provision of the resolution would be provided after the first term of the citation (that is, after the first comma in either of these formats). For example, a citation to the first operative paragraph of the postponement resolution for the Draft Declaration on Rights and Duties of States would be:

G.A. Res. 597 (VI), ¶ 1, U.N. GAOR, 6th Sess., Supp. No. 20, U.N. Doc. A/2119 (Dec. 7, 1951).

B. Security Council

We recommend that citations to Security Council resolutions be stated in the ODS format. Using this format, the citation to a Security Council resolution is constructed by the following elements in order: the designation "S.C. Res."; the resolution number; the designation "U.N. Doc."; the resolution's UN document symbol (without the year component); and then a parenthetical indicating the adoption date.

For example, on November 4, 1956, the Security Council passed its 120th resolution, deciding to call an emergency session of the General Assembly to address the Soviet invasion of Hungary earlier that year. The citation to this resolution in the ODS format is:

S.C. Res. 120, U.N. Doc. S/RES/120 (Nov. 4, 1956).

As with General Assembly resolutions, a pinpoint citation would be provided after the first comma in the citation. For example, on June 19, 1967, the Security Council passed its 238th resolution, regarding the UN peacekeeping force in Cyprus. In paragraph 3 of the resolution, it extended the operations of the force for an additional six months. A citation to this resolution, including a pinpoint cite to this operative paragraph, would be:

S.C. Res. 238, ¶ 3, U.N. Doc. S/RES/238 (June 19, 1967).

C. Annexes

In segment II.B of this chapter, we emphasized the importance of annexes to Security Council and General Assembly resolutions. We noted that researchers should be careful in indicating whether they are referring to the text of a resolution or a document annexed to the resolution. Accordingly, a citation should also precisely indicate when the citation is to an annex rather than the resolution itself.

The *Bluebook* indicates that, when the citation is to a document annexed to a resolution, the phrase "Annex" should appear immediately after the first comma in the citation (prior to the addition of any pinpoint citations).

For example, on December 21, 2010, during its 65th session, the General Assembly passed its 229th resolution of that session, in which it adopted the UN Rules for the Treatment of Women Prisoners and Non-custodial Measures for Women Offenders. In the first three numbered paragraphs in the operative part of the resolution, the General Assembly noted that an "expert group" operating on the General Assembly's behalf met in Bangkok to develop the rules, that the Thai government provided financial support for the meetings, and that the rules should be known as "the Bangkok Rules."

We know from our discussions earlier in this chapter that the Bangkok Rules cannot themselves be binding rules of international law. Nevertheless, they could well be important in developing a growing consensus among states regarding their subject matter, and they might furnish a basis for rules of customary international law. Regardless of how significant they might be, however, the Bangkok Rules do not appear in the text of the resolution itself; they are appended as an annex to the resolution. A citation to the Bangkok Rules themselves would accordingly read:

G.A. Res. 65/229, Annex, U.N. Doc. A/RES/65/229 (Dec. 21, 2010).

With this, as with any other General Assembly resolutions known by a popular name, the *Bluebook* directs that the title of the resolution be placed at the beginning of the citation. Accordingly, a more complete citation would be:

> U.N. Rules for the Treatment of Women Prisoners and Non-custodial Measures for Women Offenders (the "Bangkok Rules"), G.A. Res. 65/229, Annex, U.N. Doc. A/RES/65/229 (Dec. 21, 2010).

VI. Chapter Summary

Resolutions of the Security Council and General Assembly usually consist of two parts: the preamble and the operative part. The preamble states historical and background material serving as a foundation for the resolution. The operative part contains the paragraphs of the resolution that are intended to have substantive effect.

Resolutions of the Security Council and General Assembly frequently attach one or more annexes. These can be important. Documents annexed to a binding Security Council resolution can sometimes contain the most detailed and salient terms of the legal obligations stated in the resolution.

Resolutions of the Security Council and General Assembly first appear as masthead documents, which are the first public pronouncements of the resolutions' full text. The masthead document leads off with the UN logo, and may be issued with an imprint date that is different from the adoption date of the resolution. In due course, resolutions are then published in the Official Records of the UN organ that has adopted them, without the UN logo and without imprint dates. The accumulated printed General Assembly resolutions appear in Supplements to the General Assembly Official Records.

The General Assembly meets in a series of consecutively numbered annual sessions, beginning in September of each year. The session during which the General Assembly adopts a resolution is important for determining the resolution's UN document symbol and citation. The Security Council does not operate in annual sessions. Rather, pursuant to the UN Charter, it is organized so as to function continuously.

All UN Member states are required to carry out the decisions of the Security Council in accordance with the Charter. Accordingly, the terms of Security Council resolutions connoting obligation (such as those stating that the Security Council "decides that" a certain action is to be taken, or "authorizes" a certain action) are legally binding on all Member states affected by them. Other terms of Security Council resolutions are not necessarily legally binding. Binding Security Council resolutions may be considered as a kind of secondary treaty law.

A modern trend has developed in which the Security Council is increasingly adopting resolutions that have effects on individual persons. Such resolutions can be referred to as "Security Council legislation." The consequences of this trend are still being explored. Limits such as due process and proportionality principles are becoming more important in assuring the legitimacy of Security Council legislation.

As a rule, General Assembly resolutions do not constitute binding rules of international law. Nevertheless, some kinds of General Assembly resolutions can have a formative effect on international law. Statements made during General Assembly debates can support recognition of rules of customary international law. General Assembly resolutions sometimes state international social or political values, either within the resolutions or as annexed declarations. Under appropriate circumstances, these values can become so well respected that they can serve as evidence for general principles of law or rules of customary international law.

Also, the General Assembly can have a role in the creation of new binding multilateral conventions. This is usually through the work of subsidiary bodies of the General Assembly, such as the International Law Commission ("ILC") or the UN Commission on International Trade Law ("UNCITRAL"). The General Assembly often proposes conventions prepared by such bodies by means of the adoption of a General Assembly resolution attaching the proposed conventions as annexes.

Each resolution adopted by a UN principal organ has a unique UN document symbol. For Security Council resolutions, this symbol always begins with the capital letter "S," and then the phrase, "RES," and the number of the resolution, each separated by forward slashes. The year of adoption is then added in parentheses. An example would be: S/RES/1440 (2002).

The document symbol for a General Assembly resolution adopted before September 1976 begins with the capital letter "A," and then continues with the phrase, "RES," and the number of the resolution, each separated by forward slashes. A roman numeral indicating the number of the session during which the resolution was adopted is then added in parentheses. An example would be: A/RES/491(V).

The document symbol for a General Assembly resolution adopted during September 1976 or later begins with the capital letter "A," and then continues with the phrase, "RES," the number of the session during which the resolution was passed, and the number of the resolution, each separated by forward slashes. An example would be: A/RES/64/293.

If one knows the UN document symbol or date of a resolution, it is generally easy to find the resolution on the UN website. It can be retrieved using the lists of resolutions appearing at the home pages for the Security Council and General Assembly. Many resolutions are also available through print or electronic versions of *International Legal Materials* ("ILM").

To find resolutions when the UN document symbol or date is not known, it is generally best to use the UN's online Official Document System ("ODS") or its online UN Bibliographic Information System Network ("UNBISnet"). The UNBISnet maintains a separate search capacity for voting records on resolutions, although its data for older resolutions may simply show vote totals rather than roll calls.

VII. Chapter Review Questions

1. What are the two parts of a Security Council resolution or a General Assembly resolution?

2. Why might documents annexed to a binding Security Council resolution be important?

3. Before being published in the Official Records of the Security Council or General Assembly, resolutions first appear as masthead documents. What are the differences between the format of resolutions as masthead documents and their format in the Official Records?

4. As between the Security Council and the General Assembly, which principal organ meets in annual sessions, and which does not?

5. As between the Security Council and the General Assembly, which principal organ has the capacity to adopt decisions that all UN Member states are required to carry out?

6. What is meant by the phrase, "Security Council legislation"?

7. What are two ways in which General Assembly resolutions can have a formative effect on international law?

8. How is the UN document symbol for a General Assembly resolution adopted before September 1976 constructed?

9. How is the UN document symbol for a General Assembly resolution adopted during or after September 1976 constructed?

10. How is the UN document symbol for a Security Council resolution constructed?

11. What is an easy way to find a Security Council resolution or General Assembly resolution at the UN website, if one knows the document symbol or date for the resolution?

12. If one does not know the document symbol or date of a resolution, what are the two search functions on the UN website that are most apt to be useful in finding the resolution?

VIII. Additional Resources and General Bibliographic References

Jorge Castañeda, *Legal Effects of United Nations Resolutions* (Columbia University Press 1969).

D.H.N. Johnson, *The Effect of Resolutions of the General Assembly of the United Nations*, 32 Brit. Y.B. Int'l L. 97 (1955–1956).

Christopher C. Joyner, *U.N. General Assembly Resolutions and International Law: Rethinking the Contemporary Dynamics of Norm-Creation*, 11 Cal. W. Int'l L.J. 445 (1981).

Rainer Lagoni, "Resolution, Declaration, Decision," in 2 *United Nations: Law, Policies, and Practice* 1081 (Rüdiger Wolfrum & Christine Philipp eds., Martinus Nijhoff Publishers 1995).

James A.R. Nafziger & Edward M. Wise, *The Status in United States Law of Security Council Resolutions Under Chapter VII of the United Nations Charter*, 46 Am. J. Comp. L. Supp. 421 (1998).

Marko Divac Öberg, *The Legal Effects of Resolutions of the UN Security Council and General Assembly in the Jurisprudence of the ICJ*, 16 Eur. J. Int'l L. 879 (2005).

Marko Divac Öberg, *The Legal Effects of United Nations Resolutions in the Kosovo Advisory Opinion*, 105 Am. J. Int'l L. 81 (2011).

Dietrich Rauschning, Katja Wiesbrock & Martin Lailach, *Key Resolutions of the United Nations General Assembly, 1946–1996* (Cambridge University Press 1997).

Blaine Sloan, *United Nations General Assembly Resolutions in Our Changing World* (Transnational Publishers 1991).

Renata Sonnenfeld, *Resolutions of the United Nations Security Council* (Martinus Nijhoff Publishers 1988).

United Nations, *Index to Resolutions of the Security Council: 1946–1996* (1997).

United Nations, *The United Nations and Human Rights: 1945–1995* (1995).

Karel C. Wellens, *Resolutions and Statements of the United Nations Security Council (1946–2000): A Thematic Guide* (Kluwer Law International 2001).

Chapter 8

Customary International Law

I. What Is Customary International Law?

While most people would be generally familiar with the idea of an international treaty or convention, the idea of customary international law probably is less common. As we noted, treaties can be compared to statutes and contracts in domestic legal systems. But many domestic legal systems do not have anything comparable to customary international law. For that reason it may seem unfamiliar.

Customary international law is a body of legal rules restricting the activities of states which is not, as a whole, written down or codified in any particular source. States are generally aware of these rules as they engage in international relations. Commentators write about these rules in treatises and other commentaries. Courts and tribunals occasionally identify and apply particular customary rules in their judgments. Accordingly, one can find discussions of these rules in treatises and other commentary, and in some court and arbitration judgments. But there is no universal written source where all the rules of customary international law are set forth.

Customary rules may well be especially characteristic of primitive or less sophisticated legal systems.[1] As one example, the rules regarding war and peace among the city states of classical Greece can be said to have developed from common usages and behaviors.[2] Such rules arise out of social interactions over gen-

---

1. Malcolm N. Shaw, *International Law* 72 (6th ed. 2008) ("In any primitive society certain rules of behavior emerge and prescribe what is permitted and what is not.").
2. *Starke's International Law* 32 (I.A. Shearer ed., 11th ed. 1994).

erations that establish behaviors that are first thought acceptable or advisable and then become viewed as obligatory.[3] In this type of social setting, such rules would probably not be written down in any organized way, at least at first.[4] Public international law partakes of this kind of primitiveness, since there is still no universal legislature or executive.[5] It should thus not be surprising that custom is still playing a role in international law.

Article 38(1)(b) of the ICJ Statute lists, as one of the sources of international law: "international custom, as evidence of a general practice accepted as law." As discussed in chapter 4, this is a reference to customary international law. Even though all the rules of customary international law are not codified anywhere, customary international law exists, is binding, and is one of the sources of public international law.

II. A Definition of Customary International Law

A rule of customary international law arises whenever a significant number of states consistently engages in a pattern of behavior, and the conviction has developed among the states that this behavior is required by international law. So most authorities agree that there are two criteria for determining whether a particular pattern of state behavior reflects a rule of customary international law.[6] One of these is the "material" criterion — the element of state practice.[7] The other criterion is the "psychological" criterion[8] — the element requiring a conviction by states that the behavior is legally required. This second ele-

---

3. Shaw, *supra* note 1, at 72 ("Such rules develop almost subconsciously within the group and are maintained by the members of the group by social pressures.").

4. *Id.* ("They are not, at least in the early stages, written down or codified, and survive ultimately because of what can be called an aura of historical legitimacy.").

5. Rebecca M.M. Wallace & Olga Martin-Ortega, *International Law* 9 (6th ed. 2009) (emphasizing "the absence of an international executive and legislature" when assessing the current role of customary international law).

6. *Starke's International Law*, *supra* note 2, at 33 ("[B]efore a usage may be considered as amounting to a customary rule of international law, two tests must be satisfied."). *See also* Shaw, *supra* note 1, at 74 ("[I]t is possible to detect two basic elements in the make-up of a custom.").

7. *Starke's International Law*, *supra* note 2, at 33 (referring to the first of the two tests as the "material" test); Shaw, *supra* note 1, at 74 (referring to "the material facts, that is, the actual behavior of states").

8. *Starke's International Law*, *supra* note 2, at 33 (referring to the second of the two tests as the "psychological" test); Shaw, *supra* note 1, at 74.

ment is often referred to by the Latin phrase, *opinio juris*.[9] We will now look at these two elements a little more closely.

A. The "Material" Criterion — State Practice

This "material" criterion refers to the actual practice of states. It refers to how states actually behave in the real world, not some idealized notion of how they should behave.[10] There are two major features of this criterion: the number of states that behave in accordance with the practice (generality), and the length of time over which they behave in accordance with the practice (consistency).

Notionally, a large number of states must behave in accordance with the practice in order for the behavioral pattern to reflect a customary rule.[11] But the actual number of states whose behavior must be conforming in any particular situation cannot be precisely determined.[12]

Some decisions of the ICJ have tended to indicate that state behavior must be nearly universal in order to qualify as the degree of "state practice" necessary for a rule of customary international law. In the *Asylum* case of 1950, the Court seemed to require "a constant and uniform usage."[13] In the Court's *North Sea Continental Shelf* case nineteen years later, it seemed to require that state practice be "extensive and virtually uniform."[14]

On the other hand, authorities have also stated that "[c]omplete uniformity of practice is not required,"[15] and that "state practice need not be absolutely

---

9. *Starke's International Law*, *supra* note 2, at 33 ("The psychological aspect is better known as the *opinio juris sive necessitatis*, or as one authority has termed it 'the mutual conviction that the recurrence . . . is the result of a compulsory rule.'").

10. Shaw, *supra* note 1, at 74 (referring to "the actual behavior of states" in describing "evidence of a general practice").

11. Shaw, *supra* note 1, at 79 (referring, in the context of the "material fact," to the "perceptions of the majority of the states"); *Starke's International Law*, *supra* note 2, at 33 ("there must in general be a recurrence or repetition of the acts which give birth to the customary rule"). *See also* Fisheries Case (U.K. v. Nor.), 1951 I.C.J. 116, 131 (Dec. 18) (discounting the possibility of a customary international law rule in the circumstances of that case, since "other states have adopted a different" practice apart from that being advanced).

12. Shaw, *supra* note 1, at 78 ("The threshold that needs to be attained before a legally binding custom can be created will depend both upon the nature of the alleged rule and the opposition it arouses.").

13. Asylum Case (Colom./Peru), 1950 I.C.J. 266, 276 (Nov. 20).

14. North Sea Continental Shelf (Fed. Rep. Ger./Den.; Fed. Rep. Ger./Neth.), 1969 I.C.J. 3, 44 (Feb. 20).

15. *Brownlie's Principles of Public International Law* 24 (James Crawford ed., 8th ed. 2012)[hereinafter Brownlie].

uniform."[16] These views are also supported by the ICJ in its 1986 *Nicaragua* case. In that case, the Court stated that: "It is not to be expected that in the practice of States the application of the rules in question should have been perfect."[17] It added that it "does not consider that, for a rule to be established as customary, the corresponding practice must be in absolutely rigorous conformity with the rule."[18]

Accordingly, the extent to which state practice must be uniform or general among states is quite subjective. The degree of uniformity or generality will depend on the particular circumstances. For example, it has been said that the behavior of more influential and powerful states may be more useful in establishing the requisite extent of state practice.[19] Also, if a dispute implicates a particular subject matter that involves some types of states more than others, the practices of those states might be more significant than the practices of other states.[20]

On the other major feature of state practice, the length of time over which the common behavior has developed, the authorities are just as equivocal. On the one hand, the common state practice should generally have been consistent over a significant period of time. It is insisted that there be a "recurrence or repetition" of the state practice, and that "conduct to be creative of customary law must be regular and repeated."[21] It is observed that "most countries specify a recognized time-scale for the acceptance of a practice as a customary rule."[22] In its *North Sea Continental Shelf* case, the ICJ determined that under the circumstances of that case, a period of less than one year, and even a period of somewhat less than three years, were insufficiently substantial to support a claim that a customary rule had developed.[23]

On the other hand, the authorities and the ICJ often point out that there is no fixed or mandatory time period applicable to all cases. The extent of the re-

---

16. Antonio Cassese, *International Law* 157 (2d ed. 2005).

17. Military and Paramilitary Activities in and Against Nicaragua (Nicar. v. U.S.), Merits, 1986 I.C.J. 14, 98 (June 27) [hereinafter Nicaragua Merits].

18. *Id.*

19. Shaw, *supra* note 1, at 79 ("[I]t is inescapable that some states are more influential and powerful than others and that their activities should be regarded as of greater significance.").

20. Shaw, *supra* note 1, at 80 ("[F]or a custom to be accepted and recognized it must have the concurrence of the major powers in that particular field."). Shaw uses the example of certain maritime issues affecting maritime states more than others.

21. *Starke's International Law, supra* note 2, at 33.

22. Shaw, *supra* note 1, at 76.

23. North Sea Continental Shelf, 1969 I.C.J. at 43.

quired duration may decrease to the extent that the practice is general among states, for example. It has been flatly said that "no particular duration" is required.[24] More moderately, it is admitted that "even a short time may be enough where the state practice has been extensive and . . . uniform."[25] Most generally, we can say simply that "there is no rigid time element and it will depend upon the circumstances of the case."[26]

B. The "Psychological" Criterion — *Opinio Juris*

To show that a rule of customary international law has formed, it is also necessary to show that there is a general belief among states that the observed state practices are legally obligatory.[27] This general belief is also referred to as the *opinio juris sive necessitatis*, or "*opinio juris*," for short.[28] There are many different reasons that states might engage in a common set of behaviors; they might act out of mutual courtesy, economic necessity, or strategic considerations, for example.[29] As long as states engage in common behaviors out of practical concerns such as these, it can be said that their common behavior is a mere "usage."[30] But once a belief crystallizes among states that a long-observed state practice is legally required, the usage becomes a rule of customary international law.[31]

The ICJ has emphasized the *opinio juris* requirement in some of its decisions. In the *North Sea Continental Shelf* case noted above, the Court said that settled state practices must be "carried out in such a way, as to evidence a belief that this practice is rendered obligatory by the existence of a rule of law requiring it."[32] The Court repeated this requirement in its *Nicaragua* decision, also noted above. There the Court specified that "not only must the acts concerned amount to a settled state practice, but they must be accompanied by the *opinio juris sive necessitatis*."[33]

---

24. Brownlie, *supra* note 15, at 24.

25. *Starke's International Law*, *supra* note 2, at 33.

26. Shaw, *supra* note 1, at 76.

27. *Id.* at 84.

28. *Starke's International Law*, *supra* note 2, at 33.

29. Cassese, *supra* note 16, at 157 (noting that states might conform to a common practice out of "economic, political or military considerations").

30. *See Starke's International Law*, *supra* note 2, at 31 ("Usage represents the initial stage of custom. Custom begins where usage becomes general.").

31. Shaw, *supra* note 1, at 84.

32. North Sea Continental Shelf, 1969 I.C.J. at 44.

33. Nicaragua Merits, 1986 I.C.J. at 108–09.

It may seem that this *opinio juris* requirement is circular: a behavior pattern cannot become a rule of international law until states start to believe that it is already a rule of international law.[34] This problem is more or less openly acknowledged. Some authorities simply note that the formation of customary international law is a continuous process, implying that any continuous process will involve some degree of uncertainty.[35] Another view is that a state should be excused from acting in a way that departs slightly from established customary rules as long as the new action "contains the germ of a new law."[36] However this is resolved, it is often admitted that the most difficult aspect of establishing a rule of customary international law is proving the existence of *opinio juris*.[37]

It may be most reasonable to say that customary rules are most usefully employed only after they have clearly been established. It may be less satisfactory to try to use customary rules as a basis for prospectively determining the legality of new state actions that are at "the cutting edge" of international relations.[38]

III. Variations on Customary International Law

For the most part, those arguing for the existence of a rule of customary international law want the rule to be as broadly applicable as possible. Since general and consistent state practice must be shown in order to establish the rule, most advocates would try to show that a large number of states have followed the practice for a long period of time. In some exceptional cases, however, the doctrine of customary international law allows for variations on the general approach.

---

34. *Accord*, Shaw, *supra* note 1, at 86–87 ("The great problem connected with the *opinio juris* is that if it calls for behavior in accordance with law, how can new customary rules be created . . . ?").

35. Cassese, *supra* note 16, at 157–58 (acknowledging that the "moment" at which "States begin to believe that they must conform to the practice" is "difficult to pinpoint exactly, since it is the result of a continuous process").

36. Shaw, *supra* note 1, at 87.

37. *Id.* at 88 (noting "the difficulty in practice of proving the existence of the *opinio juris*"); Wallace & Martin-Ortega, *supra* note 5, at 17 ("The problem with *opinio juris* is one of proof.").

38. Even this cautionary observation may be less valid, however, in connection with possible areas of "instant custom," noted in segment III.B of this chapter.

A. Local Custom

Sometimes it can be argued that a customary rule has developed in a particular geographic region, rather than throughout the world.[39] In that event, the assertion would be that the rule is binding, not on all the states of the world, but rather only on the states in the relevant region. One of the most frequently cited authorities on this is the ICJ's opinion in the *Asylum* case,[40] involving a diplomatic skirmish between Colombia and Peru. There Colombia asserted what the Court called "an alleged regional or local custom peculiar to Latin-American States."[41] Although the Court did not find that this particularly asserted custom in fact was a rule of local customary international law in that case,[42] the Court seemed clearly to acquiesce in the possibility of local custom.

Sometimes the "region" involved can be as small as two states. The most famous example of this is the ICJ's *Right of Passage over Indian Territory* case.[43] In that case, the Court reviewed a long-term course of dealing between India and Portugal, and determined that the "practice was accepted as law by the Parties and has given rise to a right and a correlative obligation."[44]

Another geographic variation would be a rule developing from a state practice pertaining to states in a particular geographic position, such as island states, land-locked states, mountainous states, or states with substantial seacoasts. The ICJ has (at least arguably) shown itself receptive to the possibility of such a rule,[45] even though it would apply to states with certain characteristics, rather than states in a particular region.

---

39. *E.g.,* Shaw, *supra* note 1, at 92–93 (discussing "regional and local custom" at length); Cassese, *supra* note 16, at 163–65 (discussing "local customary rules" at length).

40. 1950 I.C.J. 266. *See supra* note 13. Both Shaw and Cassese cite the *Asylum* case when discussing local custom. Shaw, *supra* note 1, at 92; Cassese, *supra* note 16, at 163–64.

41. 1950 I.C.J. at 276.

42. *Id.* at 277 ("[I]t is not possible to discern . . . any constant and uniform usage, accepted as law, with regard to the alleged rule.").

43. (Port. v. India) (Merits), 1960 I.C.J. 6 (Apr. 12).

44. *Id.* at 40.

45. North Sea Continental Shelf, 1969 I.C.J. at 43 (referencing the suitability to the development of customary rules of "state practice, including that of States whose interests are specially affected").

B. No Formally Established Minimum Time; "Instant Custom"

As noted earlier, there is no fixed minimum time period over which a state practice must develop to establish a rule of customary international law.[46] The length of time required may depend on the facts of the particular situation.[47] Authorities have been explicit that in some circumstances even a very short period of time may be adequate.[48]

Indeed, in some situations, it might be possible to argue that an "instant customary international law rule" has arisen.[49] If a proposed rule involves conduct in outer space,[50] for example, or some other context where only a small number of states can possibly be involved, or where the issue owes its existence only to very recent technology,[51] a very short time may be sufficient to support a customary rule. This, however, could be viewed as an aggressive approach[52] and might be best used only with caution.

---

46. Shaw, *supra* note 1, at 76 ("In international law there is no rigid time element and it will depend upon the circumstances of the case . . . .").

47. Cassese, *supra* note 16, at 158 ("[T]he *time element* in the formation of customary rules may vary, depending on the circumstances of the case and the States' interest at stake.").

48. *Starke's International Law, supra* note 2, at 33 ("even a short time may be enough where the state practice has been extensive and for all practical purposes uniform"). The ICJ echoed this view when, in the circumstances of the *North Sea Continental Shelf* case, it noted that "the passage of only a short period of time is not necessarily, or of itself, a bar to the formation of a new rule of customary international law." (North Sea Continental Shelf, 1969 I.C.J. at 44).

49. *See* Shaw, *supra* note 1, at 78 (declaring that, "instant customary law is possible" (internal quotations omitted), and noting further that: "In a society constantly faced with new situations because of the dynamics of progress, there is a clear need for a reasonably speedy method of responding to such changes . . . .").

50. *See* Cassese, *supra* note 16, at 158 (specifically using the example of conduct in outer space as a possible sphere for the development of "instant custom," since "only two Great Powers (the Soviet Union and the USA) had the technological resources for using that portion of the air").

51. *See* Wallace & Martin-Ortega, *supra* note 5, at 18 (commenting that the doctrine of the Exclusive Economic Zone off coastal waters "became established customary international law in the 1970s," and noting that while "mining of the continental shelf was [initially] neither technologically nor economically feasible," the situation quickly changed "given advancing technology").

52. *E.g., id.* at 19 (warning that " 'instant custom' is an exception to the norm").

C. Persistent Objector Doctrine

The weight of authority holds that if, during the development of a rule of customary international law, a state consistently represents that it does not acquiesce in the developing rule, the rule will not apply to that state even after the rule has become clearly established.[53] This is often referenced as "the persistent objector" doctrine.[54] The ICJ seemed to acknowledge the persistent objector doctrine in its *Fisheries* decision from 1951.[55]

Although some prominent authorities clearly acknowledge the persistent objector doctrine,[56] some modern authorities disapprove of it.[57] Modern researchers working on a particular argument can probably use the doctrine in their work, but need to be careful as to the receptivity of particular audiences to it. The more traditional an audience is, perhaps the more likely that audience will be to accept the doctrine.

D. Relative Importance of the Two Elements

The relationship between the two elements defining a rule of customary international law bears a brief discussion. The simplest approach is to view the two elements, state practice and *opinio juris*, as of more or less equal importance. Some of the more venerable writers seem to imply a rough equality of importance,[58] and the relevant opinions of the ICJ also seem to treat them as of basically equal significance.[59]

---

53. *E.g.,* Shaw, *supra* note 1, at 90 ("a state opposing the existence of a custom from its inception would not be bound by it").

54. *E.g.,* Brownlie, *supra* note 15, at 28 (specifically emphasizing "the persistent objector" doctrine).

55. 1951 I.C.J. at 131 (refusing to apply to Norway an asserted 10-mile limit to its internal waters, "inasmuch as she [Norway] has always opposed any attempt to apply it to the Norwegian coast"). (*See supra* note 11.)

56. *See also* Fisheries Case, 1951 I.C.J. at 131 ("Given the majoritarian tendency of international relations the principle is likely to have increased prominence.").

57. *See especially* Cassese, *supra* note 16, at 163 (insisting, contrary to other authorities cited in notes 53–55 *supra*, that "there is no firm support in State practice and international case law for a rule on the 'persistent objector'").

58. *Brierly's Law of Nations* (Andrew Clapham ed., 7th ed. 2012) ("Custom in its legal sense means something more than mere habit or usage; it is a usage felt by those who follow it as obligatory."); Shaw, *supra* note 1, at 74 (The "two basic elements in the make-up of a custom . . . are the material facts, that is, the actual behavior of states, and the psychological or subjective belief that the behavior is 'law.'").

59. *E.g.,* Continental Shelf (Libya/Malta), 1985 I.C.J. 13, 29 (June 3) ("It is of course

However, some authors take the position that *opinio juris* is more significant than state practice,[60] while others have taken the contrary view.[61] Somewhat recently, an influential commentary[62] maintained that the two elements of custom should be viewed on a "sliding scale." Under this approach, as the strength of the evidence of state practice declined, a greater showing of *opinio juris* should be required, and vice versa.[63] Another commentator suggests that the material element is more important "whenever there exist at the outset conflicting (economic or political) interests," while *opinio juris* would be more important for such traditionally disfavored acts as "genocide, slavery, and torture."[64]

These variations can be borne in mind in pursuing research, although the safest approach for a junior researcher may be to proceed with the idea that the two elements are equally important.

IV. Research for Customary International Law

Researching customary international law is perhaps the most laborious aspect of international law research. The most rigorous approach would be to first find real-world evidence of state practice, and then separately find evidence of *opinio juris* supporting that practice. This work would involve review of the primary sources we describe in segments C through D of this part IV.

However, a preliminary step often used by researchers is to consult secondary sources, such as treatises, law review articles, monographs, and other commentators' works. These publications often contain declarations as to the existence of customary rules. The best of them also contain detailed information as to the primary sources from which the rules were derived. The researcher can then

---

axiomatic that the material of customary international law is to be looked for primarily in the actual practice and *opinio juris* of States."); Asylum Case, 1950 I.C.J. at 276; North Sea Continental Shelf, 1969 I.C.J. at 44–45.

60. *See* Shaw, *supra* note 1, at 75 ("[T]he relative importance of the two factors, the overt action and the subjective conviction, is disputed by various writers. Positivists . . . stress the paramount importance of the psychological element.")

61. *Id.* at 75–76 ("Other writers have taken precisely the opposite line and maintain that *opinio juris* is impossible to prove and therefore of no tremendous consequence."); *see also Starke's International Law*, *supra* note 2, at 34 (asserting that "the *opinio juris* is not an essential element of custom").

62. Frederic L. Kirgis, Jr., *Custom on a Sliding Scale*, 81 Am. J. Int'l L. 146 (1987).

63. *Id.* at 149.

64. Cassese, *supra* note 16, at 158.

work backwards, so to speak, from the secondary source to the primary sources in building a case for a given rule of customary law. This preliminary step, involving the initial use of secondary sources, is described in segment A of this part IV.

A small number of primary sources are of such prominence and are so widely accepted that they directly state rules of customary international law. These primary sources are discussed in segment B of this part IV. Examples would include some multilateral conventions with broad acquiescence and some UN resolutions with acknowledged customary stature. Rules stated in these primary sources can often be considered customary rules without further reference to state practice or *opinio juris*. These primary sources will usually provide more authoritative evidence of custom than secondary sources. But even their use can be complemented, if a researcher wants to be especially rigorous, by other primary sources that provide independent evidence of state practice and *opinio juris*.

As noted, we will address first the use of secondary sources in segment A, then the small number of primary sources that directly state customary rules in segment B, and then finally sources for the distinct elements of state practice and *opinio juris* in segments C and D, respectively.

A. Secondary Sources Stating Customary Rules

As noted above, many academic writers will make declarations in their treatises, articles, monographs, or other commentary as to the existence of rules of customary international law. Such declarations may or may not be authoritative (depending on the prominence of the author and, where an article is involved, the quality of the article and the prominence of the law review or journal in which it appears). As a general matter, the more prominent the journal or treatise is, the more likely that it will contain helpful statements of customary rules.

1. Treatises and Articles in Law Reviews and Law Journals

Some of the most prominent English-language treatises are listed in chapter 10 of this book. One of the most influential law reviews for public international law is the *American Journal of International Law*, published by the American Society of International Law. It is available in hard-copy in every comprehensive law library, and it is available online through Westlaw, Lexis-Nexis, and HeinOnline. In the United States, law reviews specifically devoted to international law published at the most prominent law schools would also be most likely to contain useful discussions of rules of customary international law. These sources can be electronically searched for international topics in the same way they would be searched for domestic legal topics.

A researcher might begin searching for a rule of customary international law by consulting secondary sources. For a broad-brush approach, finding a set of relevant customary rules in secondary sources might be adequate. However, for a rigorous approach, the researcher would then investigate the primary sources referenced in the secondary sources as bases for the rule.

2. The Work of the International Law Commission (the "ILC")

The International Law Commission (or "ILC") is a body established by the UN General Assembly.[65] Its work can be a powerful secondary source for customary international law rules. The ILC is also discussed in greater detail later in this book, in chapter 9 and, especially, in chapter 10.

For present purposes, we can note that the ILC is an esteemed body of experts that works on a continuous basis toward the development of international law. It has a dual role: to both "codify" existing international law and promote the "progressive development" of new rules of international law.[66] The ILC's role to "codify" international law means that the ILC is to collect, clarify, systematize, and restate existing rules, which are usually in the form of customary international law.[67] The ILC's role to promote the "progressive development" of international law means that the ILC is to draft new legal rules, not in effect beforehand, to respond to new technological developments, scientific insights, or even newly prevailing social norms.[68]

---

65. Establishment of an International Law Commission, G.A. Res. 174(II), U.N. Doc. A/519 (Nov. 21, 1947). The "Statute of the International Law Commission" was attached as an annex to this resolution.

66. Statute of the International Law Commission, art. 1(1) ("The International Law Commission shall have for its subject the promotion of the progressive development of international law and its codification."). G.A. Res. 174(II), Annex, U.N. Doc. A/519 (Nov. 21, 1947).

67. *See, e.g.,* Paul C. Szasz, *General Law-Making Processes, in The United Nations and International Law* 27, 30 (Christopher C. Joyner ed., 1997) (characterizing "codification" as "the process of collecting, clarifying, systematizing, and restating existing law," and noting that while such existing law can be in the form of existing treaties, it "more often is customary international law").

68. *Id.* (noting that "progressive development" means "the creation of new law as required by the world community—which may be old needs not previously addressed legislatively, but more often constitute new demands arising from technological developments, scientific insights, or merely the ever-increasing number and complexity of international interactions").

To the extent the ILC engages in "codification," it is generally codifying what it perceives to be rules of customary international law that have already crystallized.[69] Since the ILC is very prestigious and its members highly regarded,[70] its views as to which patterns of state behavior have crystallized into rules of customary international law are greatly respected.[71]

From time to time the ILC produces draft agreements, which upon approval by the General Assembly are then submitted to states for ratification as binding conventions and treaties. Among the agreements drafted by the ILC that have been ratified as conventions are the Vienna Convention on the Law of Treaties[72] (discussed at length in chapter 5 of this book), the Vienna Convention on Diplomatic Relations,[73] and many others.

In addition to draft treaties, the ILC also produces draft "articles" and "principles." Among these have been the ILC Draft Articles on State Responsibility, issued in 2001, and the Principles of International Law Recognized in the Charter of the Nürnberg Tribunal and in the Judgment of the Tribunal, issued in 1950.[74]

To the extent they represent codification of already-crystallized rules, the ILC's draft treaties, draft articles, or draft principles can be very strong evidence of rules of customary international law.[75] This is not to say that all material issued by the ILC is evidence of customary international law. After all, to the extent the ILC engages in "progressive development," its work would not necessarily reflect customary law at all.

To determine when the ILC is performing which function, one can sometimes rely on its own texts, which will often include commentaries providing guidance on this point. Otherwise, a beginning researcher can (and should) investigate other secondary sources (such as treatises and law review and jour-

---

69. *See supra* note 67 and accompanying text.

70. *E.g.,* Szasz, *supra* note 67, at 39 (noting that the ILC is "the preeminent master" of codification).

71. *Id.* (In his general description of the codification process, Szasz prominently refers to studies undertaken by bodies such as the ILC and notes: "Because of the reliability of the person or body that prepared them . . . , these studies are often accepted as authoritative statements of the existing law.").

72. May 23, 1969, 1155 U.N.T.S. 331, 8 I.L.M. 679 (entered into force Jan. 27, 1980).

73. Apr. 18, 1961, 23 U.S.T. 3227, 500 U.N.T.S. 95 (entered into force Apr. 24, 1964).

74. Links to these two examples, and many others can currently be found at the "Texts, Instruments and Final Reports" page of the ILC website.

75. Shaw, *supra* note 1, at 121 ("Its drafts [i.e., drafts by the ILC] may constitute evidence of custom, contribute to the corpus of usages which may create new law and evidence the *opinio juris.*").

nal articles) to acquire additional background and familiarity with the subject being researched. Familiarity with these additional secondary sources usually makes it easier to determine which aspects of ILC documents state rules of customary international law. The website of the ILC (http://www.un.org/law/ilc/) provides an exhaustive record of its work over the years, including detailed commentary.

3. The Third Restatement

In U.S. law practice, discussions about customary international law often reference the *Third Restatement on Foreign Relations Law of the United States*.[76] Especially among U.S. researchers, this is sometimes called "the *Third Restatement*," or even simply "the *Restatement*." It was issued by the American Law Institute (the "ALI"), which is also responsible for the *Restatements* on Contracts, Torts, and other matters with which most U.S. law students and lawyers are familiar. There is a more complete discussion of the ALI in chapter 10.

The *Third Restatement* is a helpful source of basic consensus views of customary international law held by U.S. commentators. It certainly does not cover all substantive areas of public international law. Its issuance is also not especially recent. But its treatment of most subjects it does cover would, in a U.S. practice, be authoritative as to any customary rules it identified or described.[77] The exceptions would be subjects, such as the law of the sea, that the *Third Restatement* covers and that may have been pre-empted to some degree by subsequent treaties or conventions.[78]

The *Third Restatement* is available in print form with pocket part updates, and can be found in many law libraries. The *Third Restatement* is also available on both Westlaw and LexisNexis. At the publication time for this book, for

---

76. Restatement of the Law (Third), The Foreign Relations Law of the United States (1986) [hereinafter Third Restatement].

77. For example, the *Third Restatement* contains extensive treatment of the immunities of diplomats, consuls and international organizations. Third Restatement §§ 464–470. While there are broadly subscribed conventions on diplomatic and consular immunities, the *Third Restatement* could be a useful source of information in U.S. practice regarding customary law apart from the conventions. The two conventions are the Vienna Convention on Diplomatic Relations, *supra* note 73, and the Vienna Convention on Consular Relations, Apr. 24, 1963, 21 U.S.T. 77, 596 U.N.T.S. 261.

78. *See* Third Restatement §§ 501–523. Since the issuance of the *Third Restatement*, the 1982 UN Law of the Sea Convention has come into effect. United Nations Convention on the Law of the Sea, Dec. 10, 1982, 1833 U.N.T.S. 3 (entered into force Nov. 16, 1994). The United States, however, is not yet a party to this treaty.

Westlaw it was in the American Law Institute database, filed under the "Treatises, CLEs and other Practice Material" heading. For LexisNexis it was located with other Restatements under the "Jurisprudences, Restatements and Principles of the Law" heading.

The use of treatises, law review articles, ILC documents, and the *Third Restatement* as authority for the existence of a customary rule can, in less formal contexts, give the researcher a source for the rule without requiring the researcher to separately investigate sources for state practice and *opinio juris*. However, the optimal research procedure would then involve using the information obtained from these sources to locate specific authority for state practice and *opinio juris* as outlined in segments B through D of this part IV.

B. Certain Primary Sources Directly Stating Customary Rules

A limited number of primary sources have such stature that they are usually viewed as directly stating customary rules themselves. For the rules stated in these sources, it would generally not be necessary to do additional investigation to uncover separate evidence of state practice and *opinio juris*. These kinds of primary sources tend to be especially prominent and very widely accepted.

Generally, there are three groups of these especially prominent and widely accepted sources. The first of these are certain law-making treaties (or conventions), in whose content virtually all states have broadly acquiesced. The second group is a small set of General Assembly resolutions that are widely acknowledged to have taken on customary stature. The third group is composed of rules stated in, or referenced in, judicial decisions issued by especially prominent international tribunals. Such tribunals would include the ICJ or the international criminal tribunals established by treaty or Security Council resolutions.

1. Major Multilateral Conventions with Broad Acquiescence

As noted in chapter 5, usually treaties bind only the states that are parties to them. That chapter also notes that some treaties are intended to set forth regimes of broadly applicable legal rules for an indefinite duration. These treaties are usually multilateral and are often called "law-making treaties," or "conventions." Conventions, no less than other treaties, generally bind only the states that are parties to them.

However, some conventions embody rules that have been accepted by a large majority of states and authorities around the world. The rules stated in these conventions have become so broadly respected that virtually all states would acquiesce in the idea that they are rules of customary international law.

There are basically two types of such conventions. The first consists of those that have acquired extremely great moral authority over time. That is, their provisions (or most of them) have come to be extremely widely valued and admired for their moral weight. The rules in these conventions have attained the stature of customary international law, and thus would bind all states, even those few who are not parties to them.

Among these conventions would be:

- The General Treaty for the Renunciation of War, also called the "Kellogg-Briand Pact" or the "Pact of Paris"[79]
- The Genocide Convention[80]
- The Geneva Conventions of 1949[81]

The second group consists of conventions stating rules that are valued not so much for moral impact, but for their effectiveness in establishing uniform standards of state behavior. In these cases, states view adherence to uniform standards to be especially important. So the conventions stating these standards have attained great respect among states. Many, but not all, of these conventions were initially drafted by the UN's ILC, discussed earlier in this chapter.

Among these conventions would be:

- The Vienna Convention on Diplomatic Relations[82]
- The Vienna Convention on Consular Relations[83]
- The Vienna Convention on the Law of Treaties[84]
- The 1982 UN Convention on the Law of the Sea[85]

---

79. Aug. 27, 1928, 46 Stat. 2343, 94 L.N.T.S. 57.

80. Dec. 9, 1948, 78 U.N.T.S. 277 (entered into force Jan. 12, 1951).

81. Convention (No. I) for the Amelioration of the Condition of the Wounded and Sick in Armed Forces in the Field, Aug. 12, 1949, 75 U.N.T.S. 31; Convention (No. II) for the Amelioration of the Condition of Wounded, Sick and Shipwrecked Members of Armed Forces at Sea, Aug. 12, 1949, 75 U.N.T.S. 85; Convention (No. III) Relative to the Treatment of Prisoners of War, Aug. 12, 1949, 75 U.N.T.S. 135; Convention (No. IV) Relative to the Protection of Civilian Persons in Time of War, Aug. 12, 1949, 75 U.N.T.S. 287 (all entered into force Oct. 21, 1950).

82. Apr. 18, 1961, 23 U.S.T. 3227, 500 U.N.T.S. 95 (entered into force Apr. 24, 1964).

83. Apr. 24, 1963, 21 U.S.T. 77, 596 U.N.T.S. 261 (entered into force Mar. 19, 1967).

84. May 23, 1969, 1155 U.N.T.S. 331, 8 I.L.M. 679 (entered into force Jan. 27, 1980).

85. Dec. 10, 1982, 1833 U.N.T.S. 3, 21 I.L.M. 1261 (entered into force Nov. 16, 1994).

The conventions in both categories are relatively small in number. The only way for a researcher without substantial expertise to know which conventions qualify as stating customary international law is to consult the types of secondary sources described in segment A above.

There may be particular provisions, even in some of these conventions, in which not all states acquiesce. This is mostly the case with conventions in the second category above. In these situations, even the objecting states will usually recognize the remaining provisions of the convention as customary international law. The United States, for example, has not become a party to either the Vienna Convention on the Law of Treaties or the 1982 UN Convention on the Law of the Sea. The United States has resisted some of the provisions in these conventions, but has nevertheless acquiesced in the proposition that most of the provisions of these conventions state customary international law.

2. General Assembly Resolutions with Acknowledged Customary Stature

As noted in chapter 7, UN General Assembly resolutions generally do not state rules of international law. They are not included, either explicitly or implicitly, in the list of sources of public international law in Article 38 of the ICJ Statute. However, some General Assembly resolutions can result in the creation of binding international law.[86]

One way this can happen is if the resolution, or an annex to the resolution, is in the form of an international agreement. In that case, upon adoption by the General Assembly, a significant number of sovereign states may vote to ratify the propagated agreement as an international treaty. If that happens, then the agreement propagated by the General Assembly resolution essentially and ultimately can become binding as a treaty.[87] Two of the best known examples of this pattern are the International Covenant on Civil and Political Rights[88] and the International Covenant on Economic, Social and Cultural

---

86. Brownlie, *supra* note 15, at 42 (including "resolutions of the United Nations General Assembly" among those sources that "can provide a basis for the progressive development of the law"); *Starke's International Law*, *supra* note 2, (emphasizing a special role for "General Assembly Resolutions ... framed in the form of a Declaration").

87. *Starke's International Law*, *supra* note 2, at 46 ("A significant number of such General Assembly Resolutions have been framed in the form of a Declaration or of a Charter ... , and these have contributed in due course to the adoption of conventions on the same subject matter.").

88. It can accordingly be cited both as a General Assembly resolution (G.A. Res. 2200 (XXI), Annex, U.N. GAOR, 21st Sess., Supp. No. 16, U.N. Doc. A/6316 (Dec. 16, 1966))

Rights.[89] To the extent such treaties become treaties of the types described in segment B.1 above, they become rules of customary international law.

And in rare instances, depending on the circumstances involved, General Assembly resolutions are stated in the form of legal declarations that can also come to be viewed as stating customary law,[90] even without state ratification. One needs to exercise caution here, though, since clearly most General Assembly resolutions are not supposed to have binding legal effect. If a General Assembly declaration is part of a large series of General Assembly resolutions expressing a consistent position on a particular issue over a significant time period, then it or the series may sometimes be viewed as evidence of state practice.[91] Alternatively, factual statements expressed in the declaration, or in statements made by national representatives during debate on a resolution, may reflect state practice. And similarly, if there is additional evidence of an *opinio juris* for the rules stated in the declaration, then the psychological component for a customary rule will be present.[92] Resolutions possessing both these features can then become rules of customary international law.

Examples of UN General Assembly resolutions that have been credibly viewed[93] as stating customary international law rules are:

---

and a treaty (International Covenant on Civil and Political Rights, Dec. 16, 1966, 999 U.N.T.S. 171, 6 I.L.M. 368 (entered into force Mar. 23, 1976)).

89. Similarly, it can be cited as a General Assembly resolution (G.A. Res. 2200 (XXI), Annex, U.N. GAOR, 21st Sess., Supp. No. 16, U.N. Doc. No. A/6316 (Dec. 16, 1966)) and a treaty (International Covenant on Economic, Social and Cultural Rights, Dec. 16, 1966, 993 U.N.T.S. 3, 6 I.L.M. 360 (entered into force Jan. 3, 1976)).

90. *Starke's International Law, supra* note 2, at 46 ("Resolutions in the form of Declarations may be relevant as . . . being declaratory of, or as authentic evidence of, existing customary law.").

91. Shaw, *supra* note 1, at 115 ("Where the vast majority of states consistently vote for resolutions and declarations on a topic, that amounts to a state practice . . . .").

92. *Id.* (noting that, where a General Assembly resolution or set of resolutions can establish state practice, "a binding rule may very well emerge provided that the requisite *opinio juris* can be proved").

93. Brownlie and Crawford view all of these resolutions as "important 'law-making' resolutions." Brownlie, *supra* note 15, at 42. Shaw views the "Granting of Independence to Colonial Countries and Peoples" declaration as binding, as it was "adopted with no opposition and only nine abstentions and followed a series of resolutions in general and specific terms attacking colonialism," and particularly as in the light of later developments it has "marked the transmutation of the concept of self-determination from a political and moral principle to a legal right and consequent obligation." Shaw, *supra* note 1, at 115–16. Shaw also repeatedly discerns binding effect for the outer space declaration. *Id.* at 116 & 544.

- Declaration on the Granting of Independence to Colonial Countries and Peoples[94]
- Declaration on the Rights of Indigenous Peoples[95]
- Declaration of Legal Principles Governing Activities of States in the Exploration and Use of Outer Space[96]

Again, a researcher without substantial experience in the area will generally only be able to know which UN General Assembly resolutions state customary law by consulting secondary sources.

3. Opinions of Judicial Tribunals Stating Customary International Law Rules

Judicial decisions also sometimes declare rules of customary international law. When the tribunal issuing such decisions has an appropriately prominent status, such statements can be authoritative evidence of such rules.

For example, in its *Arrest Warrant*[97] decision, the ICJ determined that there is a rule of customary international law to the effect that an incumbent minister of foreign affairs for a sovereign state has immunity from the criminal jurisdiction in the domestic courts of other states.[98] Another example is the ICJ's judgment in *Military and Paramilitary Activities in and Against Nicaragua*.[99] In that case, the Court determined that the "principle of the non-use of force [by one state against another] may . . . be regarded as a principle of customary international law."[100]

High-ranking domestic courts, particularly those of last resort, can also furnish persuasive authority for the existence of rules of customary international law. Here the most famous example is the ruling of the U.S. Supreme Court in the *Paquete Habana*[101] case from 1900. There the Court held, in effect, that there was a rule of customary international law providing that "coast

---

94. G.A. Res. 1514 (XV), U.N. Doc. A/4684 (Dec. 14, 1960).

95. G.A. Res. 61/295, U.N. Doc. A/61/295 (Sept. 13, 2007).

96. G.A. Res. 1962 (XVIII), U.N. Doc. A/5515 (Dec. 13, 1963).

97. Arrest Warrant of April 11, 2000 (Dem. Rep. Congo v. Belg.), 2002 I.C.J. 4 (Feb. 14).

98. *Id.* at 23. The Court stated the proposition in the negative, but this still confirmed the Court's view of the existence of the rule as a rule of customary international law. ("The Court . . . has been unable to deduce . . . that there exists under customary international law any exception to the rule according immunity from criminal jurisdiction . . . to incumbent Ministers for Foreign Affairs.")

99. 1986 I.C.J. 14; *see supra* note 17.

100. 1986 I.C.J. at 100.

101. The Paquete Habana, 175 U.S. 677 (1900).

fishing vessels, . . . catching and bringing in fresh fish, have been recognized as exempt . . . from capture as prize of war."[102]

In situations such as these, and depending on the circumstances, it can be sufficient to cite to the ICJ opinion(s) or other high court opinion(s) for the proposition that the rule of customary international law exists. One judicial opinion standing on its own might not be enough (unless it was from the ICJ, say, under very clear circumstances). But if there is a judicial statement of this kind, and other authorities are supportive, it may not be necessary to provide separate evidence of state practice and *opinio juris*. The point can be fortified by also referencing secondary authorities, such as any treatises and law journals that may be in accord. And of course, if the researcher desires to be especially thorough, any additional evidence of state practice or *opinio juris* would also be appropriate.

C. Sources of Evidence for State Practice

As noted above, to determine the existence of a rule of customary international law, the preliminary steps are usually to check secondary sources and the types of primary sources that can state rules of customary international law. The next and definitive step is to investigate sources for the purposes of independently determining the existence of state practice and *opinio juris*.

Of course, one indication of state practice is normal news reports, from newspapers, news magazines, and weekly and quarterly news journals.[103] In the modern era, electronic news reports should also be considered, as long as they are reliable. All these materials certainly contain indications of how states behave. The disadvantage is that, to build a convincing pattern of state practice "from scratch" so to speak, one would generally need a large number of such reports all supporting the same pattern of behavior.

Other types of material indicating state practice over time are diplomatic records.[104] Regarding U.S. diplomacy, chapter 10 of this book discusses the series, *The Foreign Relations of the United States*, compiled by the U.S. State

---

102. *Id.* at 686.

103. *E.g.*, Shaw, *supra* note 1, at 82 ("The obvious way to find out how countries are behaving is to read the newspapers, consult historical records, listen to what governmental authorities are saying and peruse the many official publications.").

104. *See id.* ("There are also memoirs of various past leaders, official manuals on legal questions, diplomatic interchanges and the opinions of national legal advisors."); *see also* Brownlie, *supra* note 15, at 24 (referencing "diplomatic correspondence, policy statements [and] press releases").

Department. This would be one source of diplomatic correspondence and other diplomatic material. Chapter 10 also discusses *The Public Papers of Presidents of the United States,* another series published by the government that can furnish evidence of state practice. Authorities also suggest military, air force and naval manuals, historical memoirs of prominent leaders, opinions of national legal advisors, and correspondence between other governmental officials.[105] Similarly, as described in chapter 10, some yearbooks may also contain officially generated information indicating the practice of the individual states from which the yearbooks are published.

In addition, many of the materials already discussed in this chapter can also furnish evidence of state practice. For example, General Assembly resolutions, even if they do not usually state binding legal rules, often contain lengthy preambles.[106] The preambles can include detailed factual recitations that attest to state behavior. Other provisions of General Assembly and Security Council resolutions can also contain evidence of state practice. Similarly, statements in judicial opinions and materials produced by the ILC can evidence the behavior of states.[107] The existence of treaties in certain areas, whether or not the states involved are parties, and the behavior of international organizations, can also evidence state practice.[108]

Research techniques regarding each of these types of materials are covered in the chapters of this book devoted to each type of material. (For example, treaties are covered in chapter 5 and judicial opinions in chapter 6.) When looking for state practice, one is generally simply seeking evidence of how

---

105. *See Starke's International Law, supra* note 2, at 33 (referencing "military, naval and air force manuals, or the internal regulations of each state's diplomatic and consular services"); *see also* Brownlie, *supra* note 15, at 24 (referencing "the opinions of government legal advisers [and] official manuals on legal questions, e.g. manuals of military law, executive decisions and practices and orders to military forces").

106. *See also* Shaw, *supra* note 1, at 115 ("Where the vast majority of states consistently vote for resolutions and declarations on a topic, that amounts to a state practice and a binding rule may very well emerge provided that the requisite *opinio juris* can be proved.").

107. *See* Shaw, *supra* note 1, at 82 ("In addition, one may note resolutions in the General Assembly, comments made by governments on drafts produced by the ILC, decisions of the international judicial institutions, decisions of national courts, treaties and the general practice of international organizations."); *see also* Brownlie, *supra* note 15, at 6 (referencing "international and national judicial decisions, recitals in treaties and other international instruments[,] an extensive pattern of treaties in the same terms, the practice of international organs, and resolutions relating to legal questions in UN organs, notably the General Assembly").

108. *See supra* note 107.

states behave in the real world, rather than determining the facial content of the source.

D. Sources for *Opinio Juris*

Most of the sources described above for state practice can also be sources of *opinio juris*. The question is not so much the kind of source used, as what type of evidence is presented by the source. Material contained within the source document that relates to state behavior can be used to show state practice, while material within the source document regarding state views on legality can be used to show *opinio juris*.

The authors of treatises, articles in law reviews and law journals, monographs, and other academic materials often comment on the *opinio juris* of states. Their opinions, although a "subsidiary means" of discerning international law under Article 38(1)(d) of the ICJ Statute, are still legitimate points of reference. Similarly, as in the discussion of state practice, diplomatic correspondence, the legal opinions of state officials, military manuals, documents produced by and concerning the ILC, and international and national judicial opinions, can all be indicative of *opinio juris* as well as state practice. The question is simply whether the source material indicates or references a common opinion of states.

One of the primary topics of discussion in this regard is the extent to which UN General Assembly resolutions can furnish *opinio juris*. The ICJ addressed this point in its advisory opinion on the *Legality of the Threat or Use of Nuclear Weapons*.[109] The relevant passage reads:

> The Court notes that General Assembly resolutions, even if they are not binding, may sometimes have normative value. They can, in certain circumstances, provide evidence important for establishing the existence of an *opinio juris*. To establish whether this is true of a given General Assembly resolution, it is necessary to look at its content and the conditions of its adoption; it is also necessary to see whether an *opinio juris* exists as to its normative character. Or a series of resolutions may show the gradual evolution of the *opinio juris* required for the establishment of a new rule.[110]

Accordingly, some General Assembly resolutions can contain statements of *opinio juris*, depending on the intent of the Assembly, on whether there is a pattern of similar resolutions containing such statements over time, and other fac-

---

109. 1996 I.C.J. 226 (July 8).
110. *Id.* at 254–55.

tors suggested by the Court in this passage. In the *Nuclear Weapons* opinion itself, the Court noted that, even though some General Assembly resolutions could have been read to establish an *opinio juris* for a nuclear weapons prohibition, other evidence tended to counteract that result.

The counter-evidence included the fact that the General Assembly resolutions in question had been adopted over "substantial numbers of negative votes and abstentions," that earlier resolutions on the same subject seemed much more equivocal in their outlook, and that binding international treaties contained provisions that also seemed to undercut such an *opinio juris*.[111] Accordingly, the extent to which General Assembly resolutions can constitute *opinio juris* can be affected by a broad variety of related and external circumstances. Attention should thus be paid to the degree of support a resolution has in the Assembly, the extent to which it is part of a pattern, and the potential impact of prior treaties and other legal rules.

As suggested by the above discussion of the *Nuclear Weapons* opinion, treaty provisions can also sometimes help to furnish an *opinio juris*. For example, in the *Nicaragua* case,[112] the ICJ agreed that, due to reservations taken by one of the parties, provisions of the UN Charter could not be used directly to resolve the dispute.[113] Nevertheless, the Court determined that the UN Charter provisions in question provided evidence of an *opinio juris* that supported the existence of a rule of customary international law.[114] The Court then combined the evidence provided by the Charter with evidence provided by an earlier General Assembly resolution to find an *opinio juris*.[115]

It is to be recalled, however, that these cases (the *Nuclear Weapons* opinion and the *Nicaragua* case) were decided in particularly dramatic circumstances. For junior researchers, a very careful and cautious attitude is appropriate, and there should be ample evidence of an *opinio juris* before an argument asserting its existence will be persuasive.[116]

---

111. *Id.* at 255.

112. 1986 I.C.J. 14. *See supra* notes 17 & 18 and accompanying text.

113. 1986 I.C.J. at 97 (proceeding to consider the action on the merits "notwithstanding the exclusion from [the Court's] jurisdiction of disputes 'arising under' " the UN Charter).

114. *Id.* at 99 (stating that both parties in the case "take the view that the fundamental principle" involved was expressed in the UN Charter, notwithstanding its technical inapplicability to the case).

115. *Id.* at 100 (the resolution being the Declaration on Principles of International Law concerning Friendly Relations and Co-operation among States in accordance with the Charter of the United Nations, G.A. Res. 2625 (XXV), U.N. Doc. A/8028 (Oct. 24, 1970)).

116. *See especially* Nicaragua Merits, 1986 I.C.J. at 99–100 (seeming to admonish that *opinio juris* be deduced from General Assembly resolutions "with all due caution").

E. Other Important Concepts

At this point we discuss three other concepts of public international law that can be useful to research. They are technically not about customary international law *per se*. However, it is often useful to research them in much the same way that one researches customary international law.

1. Jus Cogens

Article 53 of the Vienna Convention on the Law of Treaties,[117] also called the "VCLT," was briefly introduced earlier in this chapter.[118] Article 53 of the VCLT provides that a treaty is void if it "conflicts with a peremptory norm of general international law." Any such "peremptory norm" would also be called a rule of "*jus cogens*." These *jus cogens* rules are viewed as being especially important and fundamental, usually in a humanitarian sense.[119] They are so important and fundamental that any treaty provision that runs counter to any of them is void.[120]

Among the *jus cogens* rules most frequently cited are the prohibitions of genocide, slavery, the slave trade, piracy, and the unlawful use of force by one state against another.[121]

Proving the existence of a *jus cogens* rule can be a powerful strategy, since *jus cogens* rules can invalidate treaty provisions. However, the assertion of the existence of a *jus cogens* rule (other than one of the commonly acknowledged rules of the type noted above) should not be undertaken lightly. Treatise authors clearly believe that there is a very high bar to cross in order to state persuasively that a *jus cogens* rule exists.[122]

---

117. May 23, 1969, 1155 U.N.T.S. 331, 8 I.L.M. 679 (1969) (entered into force Jan. 27, 1980). There is a detailed discussion of this convention in chapter 5 of this book.

118. *See supra* note 72 and accompanying text.

119. Article 53 of the VCLT also defines a *jus cogens* norm as "a norm accepted and recognized by the international community of States as a whole as a norm from which no derogation is permitted and which can be modified only by a subsequent norm of general international law having the same character." *See also* Shaw, *supra* note 1, at 125 ("The concept of *jus cogens* is based upon an acceptance of fundamental and superior values . . . akin to the notion of public order or public policy in domestic legal orders.").

120. Article 64 of the VCLT also provides that if a new *jus cogens* norm emerges, "any existing treaty which is in conflict with that norm becomes void and terminates."

121. *E.g.,* Shaw, *supra* note 1, at 126 ("Various examples of rules of *jus cogens* have been provided, . . . such as unlawful use of force, genocide, slave trading and piracy."); *accord*, Brownlie, *supra* note 15, at 595 ("The least controversial members of this class are the prohibition of the use of force [and] of genocide, . . . and the rules prohibiting trade in slaves.").

122. *E.g.,* Shaw, *supra* note 1, at 126 ("a stringent process is involved, and rightly so, for the establishment of a higher level of binding rules has serious implications for the inter-

One author suggests that discerning a *jus cogens* rule involves two steps. The first is that one needs to show "the establishment of the proposition as a rule of general international law." The second would be that one needs to show "the acceptance of that rule as a peremptory norm by the international law community of states as a whole."[123]

Because *jus cogens* rules (also called *jus cogens* "norms") can overrule treaties, so to speak, textbooks often discuss them in connection with treaties. However, we discuss them in connection with customary international law. One reason we do this is that some authorities view *jus cogens* norms as an aspect of, or a special kind of, customary international law.[124] Another reason is that we think that usually one would do research about *jus cogens* rules in much the way one would do research on customary international law rules.

Authorities supporting the existence of a *jus cogens* rule would most usually be secondary sources (such as treatises, law journals, or law review articles), and the decisions of international tribunals. Many law journal or law review articles address issues of *jus cogens*, and at least some could be expected to argue for or against the existence of particular *jus cogens* rules in particular circumstances. General Assembly resolutions and other UN resolutions can also make statements as to the existence of *jus cogens* norms, as can materials in yearbooks and governmental sources.

2. Soft Law

In recent years a new feature of the international legal community has appeared. This is the development of "soft law."[125] Generally, "soft law" refers to standards, commitments, principles, or other statements[126] that are not intended to be legally binding, but which are nevertheless intended to in-

---

national community"); *accord,* Brownlie, *supra* note 15, at 595–96 (repeatedly referencing the controversy associated with *jus cogens* rules, and warning that "[m]ore authority exists for the concept of peremptory norms than for its particular consequences").

123. Shaw, *supra* note 1, at 126.

124. *E.g.,* Brownlie, *supra* note 15, at 510 ("They [*jus cogens* rules] are rules of customary law that cannot be set aside by treaty or acquiescence but only through the formation of a subsequent customary rule of the same character.").

125. Cassese, *supra* note 16, at 196 ("In recent years a new phenomenon has taken shape in the international community: the formation of what has come to be termed 'soft law.' ").

126. *Id.* (referring to "soft law" as: "A body of standards, commitments, joint statements, declarations of policy or intention, . . . resolutions," etc.).

fluence the behavior of states, in constructive ways.[127] Sometimes soft law documents are in the form of non-binding international agreements among states,[128] sometimes they are in the form of standards or other documents published by international organizations,[129] and sometimes they are in the form of resolutions of the UN General Assembly or other prominent international bodies.[130]

Soft law is not law, per se, but its promotion can be influential.[131] Major examples of soft law documents are:

- The Universal Declaration of Human Rights,[132] passed by the UN General Assembly in 1948. Although itself non-binding, it helped pave the way for a set of significant binding international treaties on human rights, including the International Covenant on Civil and Political Rights[133] and the International Covenant on Economic, Social and Cultural Rights.[134]
- The "Helsinki Final Act" of 1975,[135] a non-binding agreement among the United States, Canada, and many European states. It set forth basic understandings about human rights and mutual security, and may well have helped precipitate, in the long run, the end of the Cold War.

---

127. *E.g.,* Shaw, *supra* note 1, at 117–18 ("[A] document . . . does not need to constitute a binding treaty before it can exercise an influence in international politics.").

128. Anthony Aust, *Handbook of International Law* 11 (2d ed. 2010) ("Generally, [the phrase, 'soft law,'] is used to describe international instruments that their makers recognize are *not* treaties, but have as their purpose the promotion of 'norms' which are believed to be good and therefore should have general or universal application. . . . Because the subject matter is usually not yet well developed, or there is a lack of consensus on the content, it cannot be embodied in a treaty.").

129. Cassese, *supra* note 16, at 196 ("Normally 'soft law' is created within international organizations or is at any rate promoted by them.").

130. *E.g., id.* (referencing, as a possible source of soft law, UN General Assembly resolutions).

131. Shaw, *supra* note 1, at 117 ("Soft law is not law.") & 118 ("The propositions of 'soft law' are important and influential, but do not in themselves constitute legal norms.").

132. G.A. Res. 217 (III), U.N. Doc. A/810 (Dec. 10, 1948), referenced as an example of soft law in Aust, *supra* note 128, at 11.

133. Dec. 16, 1966, 999 U.N.T.S. 171, 6 I.L.M. 368 (entered into force Mar. 23, 1976).

134. Dec. 16, 1966, 993 U.N.T.S. 3, 6 I.L.M. 360 (entered into force Jan. 3, 1976).

135. Conference on Security and Cooperation in Europe, Final Act, 14 I.L.M. 1292 (1975), referenced as an example of soft law in Shaw, *supra* note 1, at 118 and in Cassese, *supra* note 16, at 196. The agreements subsumed within the Helsinki Final Act are often referred to as the "Helsinki Accords."

- The Rio Declaration on Environment and Development, from 1992.[136] It was issued at the end of an international conference and helped raise consciousness around the world about the ecological interdependence of states and the effects of pollution on economic development.

Soft law is not necessarily an aspect of customary international law. However, as with *jus cogens*, soft law would often be researched in much the same way that one begins to research questions of customary international law. For example, one might well begin one's investigation as to the possible existence of soft law in a particular subject area by consulting secondary authorities, like treatises and journal articles. This is similar to the initial methods we reviewed above for customary international law.

Also similarly, note that soft law rules in any particular subject area could be evidenced by international agreements that are not (or not yet) binding or in force, UN resolutions, standards issued by international organizations, and other similar documents. These can also be used to help establish either a rule of customary international law itself, or at least the *opinio juris* for such a rule.[137]

Soft law remains controversial, and some authorities may still maintain that it does not really exist.[138] However, a thorough job of research will nevertheless consider the possible application of soft law.

3. General Principles of Law

In chapter 4 we saw that the third category of international law sources, as listed in Article 38(1)(c) of the ICJ Statute, is "general principles of law recognized by civilized nations." In chapter 4 we also noted that there are various ways to view this category. However, we determined that the most common meaning of the phrase entails basic underpinning legal ideas that are so general that they transcend all national borders. We noted among possible examples the principle of proportionality and the idea that a legal wrong must occasion a legal means of redressing that wrong.

---

136. U.N. Conf. on Env't & Dev., Rio Decl. on Env't & Dev., A/CONF.151/5/Rev. 1 (June 13, 1992), 31 I.L.M. 874 (1992), referenced as an example of soft law in Aust, *supra* note 128, at 11.

137. *See, e.g.,* Shaw, *supra* note 1, at 118 ("The use of such [soft law] documents, whether termed, for example, recommendations, guidelines, codes of practice or standards, is significant in signaling the evolution and establishment of guidelines, which may ultimately be converted into legally binding rules.").

138. *E.g.,* Aust, *supra* note 128, at 11 ("There is no agreement about what is 'soft law,' or indeed if it really exists.").

For most researchers using this book, the most helpful sources of general principles of law are likely to be articles in law reviews and law journals, treatises, monographs, or other commentaries. Authors of these works on occasion assert that particular principles are general principles of law for purposes of Article 38(1). Such statements can be authoritative, depending more or less on the prominence of the source(s) involved. In this respect, researching general principles of law resembles the early stages of much research into customary international law. Nevertheless, also as noted in chapter 4, the requirements for state practice and *opinio juris* do not directly apply to general principles of law.

Such prominent secondary sources as ILC materials and the *Third Restatement*, where relevant, can also furnish bases for the assertion of general principles of law. These, of course, were also discussed above in conjunction with research for customary international law. Judges, courts, and authorities in general are not always receptive to the idea of newly-asserted general principles. Junior researches should therefore exercise caution when arguing for the existence of general principles that do not have ample authority in secondary sources.

V. Chapter Summary

Customary international law is a body of legal rules restricting the activities of states which is not, as a whole, written down in any particular source. States are aware of these rules, and commentators write about them in treatises and other commentaries. Courts and tribunals occasionally identify and apply particular customary rules in their judgments. Accordingly, one can find discussions of some of these rules in treatises and other commentary, and in some court and arbitration judgments. But there is no universal written source where all the rules of customary international law are set forth.

There are two criteria for determining whether a particular pattern of state behavior reflects a rule of customary international law. One of these is the "material" criterion—the element of state practice. The other criterion is the "psychological" criterion—the element requiring a conviction by states that the behavior is legally required. This second element is often referred to by the Latin phrase, *opinio juris*.

The "material" criterion refers to the actual practice of states. There are two major features of this criterion: the number of states that behave in accordance with the practice (generality), and the length of time over which they behave in accordance with the practice (consistency).

Notionally, a large number of states must behave in accordance with the practice in order for the behavioral pattern to reflect a customary rule. But the actual number of states whose behavior must be conforming in any particular situation cannot be precisely determined. Some decisions of the ICJ have tended to indicate that state behavior must be nearly universal in order to qualify as the degree of "state practice" necessary for a rule of customary international law.

On the other hand, authorities have also stated that complete uniformity is not required, and that state practice need not be absolutely uniform. The ICJ has also supported these views on occasion. Accordingly, the degree of uniformity or generality will depend on the particular circumstances.

On the other major feature of state practice, the length of time over which the common behavior has developed, the authorities are just as equivocal. On the one hand, the common state practice should generally have been consistent over a significant period of time. On the other hand, the authorities and the ICJ often point out that there is no fixed or mandatory time period applicable to all cases. Most generally, we can say simply that there is no rigid time element and it will depend upon the circumstances of the case.

To show that the "psychological" criterion has been satisfied, it must be shown that there is a general belief among states that the observed state practices are legally obligatory. While the ICJ has emphasized this *opinio juris* requirement in some of its decisions, establishing an *opinio juris* is often the most difficult aspect of establishing a rule of customary international law.

Certain variations on the general doctrine of customary international law are worth noting. First, sometimes it can be argued that a customary rule has developed in a particular geographic region, rather than throughout the world. In that event, the rule would be binding, not on all the states of the world, but rather only on the states in the relevant region. In several types of situations, the ICJ has seemed clearly to acquiesce in this possibility of "local custom."

Also, in some situations, it might be possible to argue that an "instant customary international law rule" has arisen. If a proposed rule involves conduct in outer space, for example, or some other context where only a small number of states can possibly be involved, or where the issue owes its existence only to very recent technology, a very short time may be sufficient to support a customary rule.

Another, somewhat controversial, variation is the "persistent objector" doctrine. This doctrine holds that if, during the development of a rule of customary international law, a state consistently represents that it does not acquiesce in the developing rule, the rule will not apply to that state even after the rule has become clearly established. The ICJ has seemed to acknowledge the doctrine, but some academic authorities are hostile to it.

There is an additional set of issues regarding the relative importance of the two elements, state practice and *opinio juris*, in establishing a rule of customary international law. The most conventional view is to treat them as having more or less equal importance. However, some authors take the position that *opinio juris* is more significant than state practice, while others have taken the contrary view. Somewhat recently, an influential commentary maintained that the two elements of custom should be viewed on a "sliding scale."

Researching customary international law is perhaps the most laborious aspect of international law research. The most rigorous approach would be to first find real-world evidence of state practice, and then separately find evidence of *opinio juris* supporting that practice. However, a preliminary step often used by researchers is to consult secondary sources, such as law review articles, treatises, monographs, and other commentators' works. The treatises listed in chapter 10 and cited throughout this book in footnotes would be among the most prominent English-language treatises for this purpose. One of the most influential law reviews for public international law is the *American Journal of International Law*, published by the American Society of International Law.

For a broad-brush approach, finding a set of relevant customary rules in secondary sources might be adequate. However, for a rigorous approach, the researcher would then investigate primary sources referenced in the secondary sources as bases for the rule.

Apart from treatises and articles in law reviews and law journals, the work of the International Law Commission (or "ILC") is also a valuable secondary source for possible customary international law rules. It was established by the UN General Assembly to both "codify" and promote the "progressive development" of international law. It issues draft treaties, articles, and principles, and to the extent these materials are meant to "codify" international law, they can be respected authority as to which patterns of state behavior have crystallized into rules of customary international law.

In U.S. law practice, an often helpful secondary source of evidence of customary international law rules is the *Third Restatement on Foreign Relations Law of the United States*. The *Third Restatement* certainly does not cover all substantive areas of public international law. But its treatment of most subjects it does cover would, in a U.S. practice, be authoritative as to any customary rules it identified.

The optimal research procedure would involve using primary resources to locate specific authority for state practice and *opinio juris*. A limited number of primary sources have such stature that they are usually viewed as directly stating customary rules themselves. For the rules stated in these sources, it would generally not be necessary to do additional investigation to uncover separate evidence of state practice and *opinio juris*.

Generally, there are three groups of these especially prominent and widely accepted sources. The first of these are certain law-making treaties (or conventions), in whose content virtually all states have broadly acquiesced. The second group is a small set of General Assembly resolutions that are widely acknowledged to have taken on customary stature. The third consists of some of the decisions of especially prominent international and national tribunals.

Some conventions embody rules that have been accepted by a very large majority of states and authorities around the world. The rules stated in these conventions have become so broadly respected that virtually all states would acquiesce in the idea that they are rules of customary international law.

There are basically two types of such conventions. The first consists of those that have acquired extremely great moral stature over time.

The second group consists of conventions stating rules that are valued not so much for moral impact, but for their effectiveness in establishing uniform standards of state behavior. In these cases, states have come to view adherence to uniform standards to be especially important. There may be particular provisions, even in some of these conventions, in which not all states acquiesce. This is mostly the case with conventions in the second category above. In these situations, even the objecting states will usually recognize the remaining provisions of the convention as customary international law.

Some General Assembly resolutions, or annexes to resolutions, are drafted as international agreements. Such agreements can attain legally binding status. One way this can happen is if, upon adoption by the General Assembly, a significant number of sovereign states votes to ratify the agreement as an international treaty. If that happens, then the agreement propagated by the General Assembly essentially and ultimately becomes binding as a treaty. To the extent such a treaty attains broad acquiescence, it can become a rule of customary international law.

But in rare instances, depending on the circumstances involved, General Assembly resolutions in the form of legal declarations can also come to be viewed as stating customary law.

Opinions of judicial tribunals can also state customary international law. Such opinions can be issued by established international courts, such as the ICJ; by domestic courts of last resort; or by other tribunals having appropriately prominent status.

Once secondary and primary sources have been checked, the next step is to investigate sources for independently determining the existence of state practice and *opinio juris*. Such sources would include news reports, diplomatic records, military manuals, historical memoirs, opinions of national legal advisors, and correspondence between other governmental officials. General Assembly resolutions, even though not generally binding in themselves, can sometimes include evidence of state practice or *opinio juris*. The state practice can sometimes be discerned from factual material in the preambles for the resolutions. *Opinio juris* can sometimes be determined on the basis of a combination of factors, such as the degree of support for the resolution in the General Assembly and whether it is part of a pattern of other resolutions to the same or similar effect. Also potentially relevant are the prevalence of prior treaties and other legal rules on the same subject.

While not technically the same thing as customary international law, researchers need to keep in mind the possible relevance of *jus cogens* rules. These are "peremptory norms" that are so important and fundamental that any treaty provision that runs counter to them is void. Among *jus cogens* rules are those against genocide, slavery, the slave trade, piracy, and the unlawful use of force by one state against another. *Jus cogens* rules are researched in much the same way as early-stage research for rules of customary international law.

The phrase, "soft law," refers to standards, commitments, principles, or other statements that are not intended to be legally binding, but which are nevertheless intended to influence the behavior of states. Sometimes soft law documents are in the form of international agreements, sometimes they are in the form of standards published by international organizations, and sometimes they are in the form of resolutions of international bodies. They are also researched in much the same way as early-stage research for rules of customary international law.

The third category of sources for international law, as listed in Article 38(1)(c) of the ICJ Statute, is "general principles of law." These general principles are, for our purposes, most likely to be found in secondary sources. They are accordingly also researched in much the same way as early-stage research for rules of customary international law.

VI. Chapter Review Questions

1. Are the rules of customary international law, as a whole, written down in any particular source?

2. How would you generally describe the "material" criterion for determining whether a pattern of state behavior reflects a rule of customary international law?

3. How would you generally describe the "psychological" criterion for determining whether a pattern of state behavior reflects a rule of customary international law?

4. What are the two major features of the "material" criterion?

5. When deciding whether the "material" criterion has been satisfied, can the number of states whose behavior must be conforming be precisely determined?

6. Also, when deciding whether the "material" criterion has been satisfied, is there a rigid required time period over which the common behavior must have developed?

7. What is the Latin phrase used to describe the "psychological" criterion?

8. What is meant by the phrase, "local custom"?

9. What are some of the types of circumstances in which it might be possible to argue that an "instant customary international law rule" has arisen?

10. How would you describe the "persistent objector doctrine"?

11. What is the conventional view regarding the relative importance of the two criteria for determining whether a pattern of state behavior reflects a rule of customary international law?

12. As a preliminary step in researching customary international law, do researchers sometimes consult secondary sources? If so, what would some of these secondary sources be?

13. What are the two roles of the International Law Commission? Which of the two is more helpful in establishing which patterns of state behavior have crystallized into rules of customary international law?

14. Does the *Third Restatement* cover all substantive areas of public international law?

15. What three groups of primary sources can be viewed as directly stating customary rules themselves?

16. How would you generally describe the two types of conventions that have become so broadly respected that they would be acquiesced in as rules of customary international law?

17. Can agreements contained within, or annexed to, General Assembly resolutions, be ratified by sovereign states, so as to ultimately become binding as treaties?

18. What are some of the circumstances in which General Assembly resolutions drafted as legal declarations can come to be viewed as customary law?

19. Do the opinions of judicial tribunals have a role in providing evidence for rules of customary international law?

20. What are some of the sources for independently determining the existence of state practice and *opinio juris*? ·

21. What is the Latin phrase for "peremptory norms" that are so important and fundamental that any treaty provision that runs counter to them is void?

22. What is the phrase that describes standards, commitments, principles, or other statements that are not intended to be legally binding, but which are nevertheless intended to influence the behavior of states?

23. What is the third category of international law sources listed in Article 38(1) of the ICJ Statute, and which kinds of sources are generally most helpful for researching this category?

VII. Additional Resources and General Bibliographic References

Michael Akehurst, *Custom as a Source of International Law*, 47 Brit. Y.B. Int'l L. 1 (1974–75).

T. Alexander Aleinikoff, *Agora: International Law, Sovereignty and American Constitutionalism: Reflections on the Customary International Law Debate*, 98 Am. J. Int'l L. 91 (2004).

Jason Beckett, "Customary International Law," in *International Law for International Relations* 122 (Başak Çali ed., Oxford University Press 2010).

David J. Bederman, "Public International Law: Custom Among Nations," in *Custom as a Source of Law* 135 (Cambridge University Press 2010).

Curtis A. Bradley & Jack L. Goldsmith, *Customary International Law as Federal Common Law: A Critique of the Modern Position*, 110 Harv. L. Rev. 815 (1997).

Enzo Cannizzaro & Paolo Palchetti, *Customary International Law on the Use of Force: A Methodological Approach* (Martinus Nijhoff Publishers 2005).

Anthony A. D'Amato, *The Concept of Custom in International Law* (Cornell University Press 1971).

G.M. Danilenko, *Law-Making in the International Community* (Martinus Nijhoff Publishers 1993).

Digest of International Law (Francis Wharton, 1886 ((as *A Digest of the International Law of the United States*)); John Bassett Moore, 1906; Green Haywood Hackworth, 1940–1944; Marjorie M. Whiteman, 1963–1973; *Cumulative Digest of United States Practice in International Law*, 1981–1988; *Digest of United States Practice in International Law*, 1974–2010 (U.S. G.P.O.)).

Foreign Relations of the United States (U.S. Department of State) (published periodically since 1861), *available at* http://history.state.gov/historical documents/volume-title-search.

Ralph Gaebler & Maria Smolka-Day, *Sources of State Practice in International Law* (Transnational Publishers 2002).

Jack L. Goldsmith & Eric A. Posner, *A Theory of Customary International Law*, 66 U. Chi. L. Rev. 1113 (1999).

Jack L. Goldsmith & Eric A. Posner, *The Limits of International Law* 1 (Oxford University Press 2005).

Jean-Marie Henckaerts & Louise Doswald-Beck, *Customary International Humanitarian Law* (Cambridge University Press 2005)(3 volumes), *available at* http://www.icrc.org/customary-ihl/eng/docs/home.

Chapter 9

Other UN Materials

I. Introduction

Some of the most visible UN operations are not conducted directly by the Security Council or the General Assembly, but rather by other bodies that are subsidiary to one or the other of them. These are often called "subsidiary organs" because they are created by the principal organs, and are generally funded by, and responsible to, the principal organs that created them.[1] Examples here would be UNDP (the United Nations Development Program) and the Office of the UN High Commissioner for Refugees, both subsidiary organs of the General Assembly.

There are also UN entities, not subsidiary to any principal organ, that perform very important and sometimes controversial roles. Examples would be the International Monetary Fund (or "IMF") and UNESCO (the United Nations Educational, Scientific and Cultural Organization). These are called "specialized agencies," and are created by the states that are members of them, rather than by the Security Council or General Assembly. They are designed to operate with more independence from the principal organs than the subsidiary organs have.

Finally, there are also "related organizations" that have a very high degree of independence from the UN framework, such as the World Trade Organization

---

1. Articles 22 and 29 of the UN Charter specifically authorize the General Assembly and the Security Council, respectively, to "establish such subsidiary organs as [each] deems necessary for the performance of its functions." Article 69 of the Charter also directs ECOSOC to "set up commissions in economic and social fields," and in other areas, but these are generally less significant from the standpoint of international law.

(the "WTO") and the Organization for the Prohibition of Chemical Weapons (the "OPCW").

All of these kinds of bodies can have very dramatic effects "on the ground" throughout the world. They are part of, or affiliated with, the UN organization, but are not themselves principal organs of it. In general, these bodies have less of a specifically law-creating role than the Security Council, but they are still significant to the field of international law. First, their work can still have substantial indirect effects on the development of international law, in ways that will be discussed below. Second, their work takes place pursuant to legal structures and procedures that are themselves examples of international law in action. Given the significance of these bodies, we will study their basic functions and structures, and discuss methods for researching their work products that can have legal implications.

II. Specialized Agencies

A. Specifications in the UN Charter

We will begin by looking at the specialized agencies. These are established by multilateral treaties entered into by the states that thereby compose their membership. The specialized agencies are governed by bodies created by the treaties that establish the agencies. Accordingly, neither the Security Council nor the General Assembly has a direct role in their creation or governance. In addition to the IMF and UNESCO, named above, prominent specialized agencies include the World Health Organization (the "WHO"), the World Bank (formally, the "International Bank for Reconstruction and Development," or "IBRD"), the International Civil Aviation Organization (the "ICAO"), and the World Intellectual Property Organization ("WIPO").

The use of specialized agencies helps to, among other things, decentralize operations and decrease politicization.[2] The UN Charter also implies that the specialized agencies should be repositories of expertise in their areas of activ-

---

2. Robert Kolb, *An Introduction to the Law of the United Nations* 157–58 (Katherine Del Mar trans., 2010). Kolb also suggests that the experience of the League of Nations, under which League member states valued the ability to work with separate agencies, and also a desire to facilitate contributions by states that might not be members of the UN itself, were additional reasons for establishing the framework for specialized agencies.

ity.[3] Notwithstanding their somewhat independent character, the UN Charter enthusiastically acknowledges their existence.[4] The UN Charter also directs ECOSOC (or the "Economic and Social Council," introduced in chapter 3 as one of the six principal organs of the UN) to enter into agreements with them so that they will be "brought into relationship with" the UN.[5]

The Charter requires the UN to make recommendations for the co-ordination of policies and activities of the specialized agencies,[6] and gives ECOSOC the authority to coordinate their activities through consultations and recommendations.[7] The framers of the UN Charter designed ECOSOC to have an important role connecting the specialized agencies to the UN. However, although ECOSOC does fulfill notable administrative tasks, ECOSOC's work in this area is not as prominent as initially contemplated.[8]

Finally, the UN Charter also gives the General Assembly the authority to "examine the administrative budgets" of the specialized agencies "with a view to making recommendations" to them.[9]

The Charter provides for the General Assembly's authority to "consider and approve any financial and budgetary arrangements" of the UN with the specialized agencies.[10] It has been thus asserted that the General Assembly "controls the budgets of the specialized organizations."[11] It has also been explained that "the United Nations collects the financial contributions from member States and distributes them to the affiliated organizations."[12] Nevertheless, in negotiating their relationship agreements with ECOSOC, the specialized agencies can have some degrees of bargaining capacity. For example, it has been suggested that the IMF and the World Bank "were careful to negotiate specialized agency agreements that protected their budgetary independence."[13]

---

3. UN Charter Article 57 refers to the specialized agencies as "having wide international responsibilities" in "economic, social, cultural, educational, health, and related fields."

4. *Id.* art. 57, directing that the specialized agencies "shall be brought into relationship with" the UN.

5. *Id.* art. 63(1).

6. *Id.* art. 58.

7. *Id.* art. 63(2).

8. *See, e.g.,* Kolb, *supra* note 2, at 24 (referring to the "marginalization" of ECOSOC).

9. U.N. Charter, art. 17(3).

10. *Id.*

11. Kolb, *supra* note 2, at 159.

12. *Id.*

13. Stephen Zamora, *Economic Relations and Development, in The United Nations and International Law* 232, 244 (Christopher C. Joyner ed., 1997).

B. General Organizational Plan of Specialized Agencies

Since the specialized agencies are created by treaties, their foundational documents are binding rules of international law. As noted above, this imparts a legal character to the operations of most specialized agencies.[14]

The treaties establishing most specialized agencies provide for three organizational levels. These are a general assembly (in which all states that are members of the agency are represented), an executive board (with a more limited membership), and a secretariat.[15]

An example of this structure is the World Health Organization, or "WHO." Its foundational treaty is called the "Constitution of the World Health Organization." This treaty was signed in 1946 as part of the International Health Conference held that year in New York, and it became effective two years later. According to the treaty, the work of the WHO is carried out by three bodies.[16] The first of these is the World Health Assembly, composed of delegates representing all the WHO Member States.[17] The second is the "Executive Board," which presently consists of delegates from 34 of the Member States.[18] (At the time of publication, the WHO has 193 Member States.) The third body is the WHO Secretariat.[19]

C. Specialized Agencies and International Law; Related Organizations

Specialized agencies undertake a variety of actions that can have direct or indirect legal effects.

---

14. This can be viewed as significant for the influence of international law. *See* Oscar Schachter, *The UN Legal Order: An Overview, in The United Nations and International Law* 3, 8 (Christopher C. Joyner ed., 1997). Others have expressed doubt, on the other hand, that constitutive treaties of the specialized agencies actually partake of the characteristics of international treaties. Benedetto Conforti & Carlo Focarelli, *The Law and Practice of the United Nations* 351 (4th rev. ed. 2010).

15. *E.g.,* Conforti & Focarelli, *supra* note 14, at 349 ("With few exceptions, their structure consists of a plenary organ in which all the Member States are represented, of a Council with a more restricted membership, and a Secretariat.").

16. Constitution of the World Health Organization art. 9, July 22, 1946, 62 Stat. 2679, 14 U.N.T.S. 185 (entered into force Apr. 7, 1948) [hereinafter WHO Constitution].

17. *Id.* art. 10.

18. *Id.* art. 24.

19. *Id.* art. 30.

Some specialized agencies publish codes or standards of conduct, which (even if not by their terms obligatory) can attain sufficient prestige and acceptance to be binding, as a practical matter. One example would be the Codex Alimentarius, a set of international standards for food designed to protect consumer health, and produced by the WHO and the FAO (the Food and Agriculture Organization). Although it is not legally mandatory, it has come to serve as the functional equivalent of binding rules.[20]

Apart from codes or standards, some specialized agencies publish recommendations, either general or directed to particular types of circumstances. These recommendations, due to general acceptance in the international community, can have a normative effect even if not technically binding. A major example here is UNESCO, which frequently issues recommendations on educational, scientific, and cultural matters.[21] One example is a UNESCO Recommendation concerning the Promotion and Use of Multilingualism and Universal Access to Cyberspace.[22]

Similarly, some specialized agencies prepare draft multilateral conventions. One example is the FAO,[23] which promulgated the International Treaty on Plant Genetic Resources for Food and Agriculture.[24] Once they become binding treaties, these conventions owe their obligatory character to their status as treaties, rather than to their character as the agency's work product. Nevertheless, the agencies developing the treaty texts have major effects on the development of international law.

---

20. Schachter, *supra* note 14, at 8.

21. The UNESCO Constitution authorizes the UNESCO "General Conference" to make recommendations. Constitution of the United Nations Educational, Scientific and Cultural Organization art. IV(B)(4), Nov. 16, 1945, 61 Stat. 2495, 4 U.N.T.S. 275 (entered into force Nov. 4, 1946) [hereinafter UNESCO Constitution]. Some recommendations issued by some specialized agencies serve as the functional equivalent of protocols to treaties in force. Frederic L. Kirgis, *Specialized Law-making Processes, in The United Nations and International Law* 65, 90 (Christopher C. Joyner ed., 1997). *See also* Conforti & Focarelli, *supra* note14, at 349.

22. United Nations Educ., Scientific and Cultural Organization [UNESCO], *Recommendation Concerning the Promotion and Use of Multilingualism and Universal Access to Cyberspace*, UNESCO Doc. 32 C/Res. 41 (Oct. 15, 2003), *available at* http://portal.unesco.org /en/ev.php-URL_ID=17717&URL_DO=DO_TOPIC&URL_SECTION=201.html.

23. Christopher C. Joyner, *Conclusion: The United Nations as International Law-Giver, in The United Nations and International Law* 432, 450 (Christopher C. Joyner ed., 1997) ("[T]he FAO has negotiated numerous international agreements and institutional arrangements."). *See generally* Conforti & Focarelli, *supra* note 14, at 349.

24. Nov. 3, 2001, 2400 U.N.T.S. 303 (entered into force June 29, 2004).

Agencies can establish legislative facts through reporting that can be used by other bodies, such as the Security Council, for more binding action.[25] Some agencies engage in contractual or quasi-contractual relations with various states, and thereby become obligors on legally binding obligations. Primarily among these would be the IMF and the World Bank. Still other specialized agencies, as a result of their particular responsibilities, have the authority to issue binding regulations to their member states.

As noted above, the activities of some UN "related organizations" are more independent from General Assembly review than activities of specialized agencies. We saw that these related organizations include the WTO and the OPCW. Another is the International Atomic Energy Agency (the "IAEA").[26] These UN related organizations can often impose binding obligations on states, enforced either through their own judicial mechanisms (in the case of the WTO, for example) or the Security Council (in the case of the IAEA, for example).

III. Operations Responsible to the General Assembly

A. Permanent Main Committees

Within the general administrative umbrella of the General Assembly, there are many subsidiary organs: commissions, committees, sub-committees, programs, and funds of various kinds.[27] However, amid all this variety the General Assembly maintains six permanent main committees, through which it does the bulk of its work. Each of these permanent main committees consists of delegates from all UN Member states, but the particular people representing each state usually change from one committee to the next.

The six permanent main committees have been numbered (1 through 6), and in common parlance the committees are often referred to by their number

---

25. Kirgis, *supra* note 21, at 92. For example, the UNESCO Constitution directs the UNESCO General Conference to report to the UN on specified matters. UNESCO Constitution, *supra* note 21, art. IV(B)(5).

26. *See* Joyner, *supra* note 23, at 454.

27. It has been emphasized that: "Neither the Assembly nor ECOSOC, and consequently, not even their subsidiary organs, have binding powers." Conforti & Focarelli, *supra* note 14, at 340. But it is also asserted that: "The fact that normative acts of the United Nations . . . do not have legally binding force must not lead to discounting their value and their usefulness . . . ." *Id.*

rather than their subject matter. The six permanent main committees, as numbered, are:[28]

- First Committee: disarmament and international security questions
- Second Committee: economic and financial questions
- Third Committee: social, humanitarian and cultural questions
- Fourth Committee: special political and decolonization questions
- Fifth Committee: administrative and budgetary questions
- Sixth Committee: legal questions

There are many other subsidiary organs or bodies working in the General Assembly, at various levels of authority.[29] Our discussion below will focus on the most significant types of subsidiary bodies. There are many other subsidiary bodies at generally lower levels of authority. They may be called working groups, preparatory committees, sub-commissions, and so on. However, our discussion below will focus on those bodies with generally higher levels of authority.

B. Commissions

Some of the subsidiary bodies of the General Assembly take the form of commissions. We will briefly describe two of them, to give an overall impression of the kinds of activities in which commissions engage.

A commission with special significance for international law is UNCITRAL (the UN Commission for International Trade Law). Its mandate is "to further the progressive harmonization and unification of the law of international trade."[30] To that end, it prepares draft conventions and other legal texts for the regulation and development of international trade. The commission has sixty member states, all of which are represented as delegates to the commission at any given time. Perhaps its most major accomplishment is the drafting and completion of the 1980 UN Convention on Contracts for the International

---

28. Conforti & Focarelli, *supra* note 14, at 103. They also note the existence of two permanent committees of a procedural character: the General Committee (consisting of the President of the Assembly, the vice-presidents of the Assembly, and the Chairs of the main committees), and the Credentials Committee.

29. Articles 22 and 29 of the UN Charter refer to "subsidiary organs," while much UN administrative documentation refers to "subsidiary bodies." There does not seem to be an officially-sanctioned or other formal distinction, and we use the two phrases interchangeably.

30. *See Origin, Mandate and Composition of UNCITRAL*, UNCITRAL, http://www.uncitral.org/uncitral/en/about/origin.html (last visited June 19, 2013).

Sale of Goods (or the "CISG Convention"). It is also known for having drafted and completed the 1978 Convention on the Carriage of Goods by Sea.

Another General Assembly Commission significant in the area of international law specifically is the International Law Commission (or the "ILC"). As noted in chapter 8, the General Assembly created the ILC pursuant to Article 13 of the UN Charter, which requires the General Assembly to "initiate studies and make recommendations" for, among other things, "the progressive development of international law and its codification." It currently consists of thirty-four members, all of whom are established legal authorities from various regions of the world.[31] It has prepared many draft conventions that have been formalized and entered into as binding treaties. Among the most prominent is the Vienna Convention on the Law of Treaties.[32]

C. Programs and Funds

It can be said that UN organs and bodies fulfill roles that are either normative or operational in character. Normative functions could be said to consist of the adoption and implementation of legal rules, while operational functions could concern the effectuation of concrete measures on the ground.[33] Usually normative functions would be most closely related to the creation and enforcement of international law. While we have seen that specialized agencies can have an active role in international law, most UN programs and funds would be largely operational, although the activities of several would have normative elements.

For illustrative purposes, we will review a small number of UN programs and funds. The focus is both on those programs and funds that are most well-known, and also on considering the extent to which their activities could have legal effects.

Among the most significant General Assembly programs and funds are:

1. UNCTAD

One of the most active General Assembly programs in recent years has been UNCTAD, which stands for the "UN Conference on Trade and Development."

---

31. Joyner, *supra* note 23, at 442.

32. May 23, 1969, 1155 U.N.T.S. 331, 8 I.L.M. 679 (entered into force Jan. 27, 1980).

33. *See* Conforti & Focarelli, *supra* note 14, at 339 (general discussion of the distinction between normative and operational functions).

It has been described as the "principal forum for the study and discussion of international economic issues of importance to developing countries."[34] It has an indirect influence on creation, amendment, and interpretation of treaties regarding international trade, such as the General Agreement on Tariffs and Trade (or "GATT").[35] In these respects, it would be exercising normative functions. UNCTAD's administrative structure has also led to it being called "an organization within the Organization, since its structure is quite similar to that of the specialized agencies."[36]

2. UNICEF

UNICEF is a primarily operational fund, originally established by the General Assembly in 1946 as the "UN International Children's Emergency Fund." Its original mission was to provide emergency assistance to children in the countries ravaged by World War II. The General Assembly made its status permanent in 1953, and changed its name to the "UN Children's Fund," while retaining the original acronym. UNICEF "focuses on low-cost community-based programs covering early childhood, the primary school years, adolescence, and women's reproductive years."[37] Virtually all of UNICEF's income is derived from voluntary sources, either from governments, private sources, or UN specialized agencies.[38]

While primarily operational in character, UNICEF has significant involvement with the 1989 Convention on the Rights of the Child.[39] Under Article 45 of the Convention, UNICEF is entitled to participate in implementation actions,

---

34. Zamora, *supra* note 13, at 243. *See* Thomas G. Weiss, David P. Forsythe, Roger A. Coate & Kelly-Kate Pease, *The United Nations and Changing World Politics* 261 (6th ed. 2010) ([T]he General Assembly "created UNCTAD as a permanent 'voice' of the Third World within the U.N. system . . . .").

35. Zamora, *supra* note 13, at 243–44. *See also* Conforti & Focarelli, *supra* note 14, at 344 (UNCTAD has been active in "encouraging negotiation of [relevant] multilateral agreements" in ways that have been felt to assist developing countries, referring specifically to "multilateral agreements on some primary products," such as rubber and cocoa).

36. Conforti & Focarelli, *supra* note 14, at 344. *See also* Zamora, *supra* note 13, at 236 (UNCTAD has "largely taken over the task of coordinating policy options concerning trade and development."). *But see* Kolb, *supra* note 2, at 25 (asserting that, in contrast to the "significant hold" on economic and social matters of the World Bank, the IMF, and the WTO, in recent years UNCTAD has "declined").

37. *See generally* Edmund Jan Osmanczyk, *Encyclopedia of the United Nations and International Agreements* 2424 (Anthony Mango ed., 3d ed. 2003).

38. *Id.*

39. Nov. 20, 1989, 1577 U.N.T.S. 3 (entered into force Sept. 2, 1990).

and the Committee on the Rights of the Child may invite UNICEF to provide advice on, and submit reports on, the Convention's further implementation.

3. UNEP

The General Assembly established the UN Environment Program (the "UNEP") in 1972, following the Stockholm Conference on the Human Environment. Like UNICEF, its functions are primarily operational. It states that its mission is "to provide leadership and encourage partnership in caring for the environment by inspiring, informing, and enabling nations and peoples to improve their quality of life without compromising that of future generations."[40]

The UNEP's influence on international law derives in part from its role as a secretariat for conventions entered into among states, including the Convention on the International Trade in Endangered Species (the "CITES") and the Convention on the Conservation of Migratory Species of Wild Animals.

IV. Types of Documents of Potential Significance

We have now reviewed specialized agencies, related organizations, and subsidiary organs or bodies of the UN. We will now discuss how to research documents issued by these bodies that affect international law. We can summarize the types of documents that we would be working with as follows:

- Reports by specialized agencies, related organizations, and subsidiary organs and bodies, either to a general audience or to another organ of the UN;
- Draft or pending treaties and agreements prepared by specialized agencies or subsidiary organs or bodies;
- Standards or criteria issued by specialized agencies or subsidiary organs or bodies;
- Resolutions or recommendations of specialized agencies, related organizations, or subsidiary organs or bodies;
- Regulations, where the issuing entity has the authority to issue them;
- Verbatim records of meetings of primary organs; and

---

40. United Nations Envtl. Program [UNEP], About UNEP: The Organization, http://www .unep.org/Documents.Multilingual/Default.asp?DocumentID=43 (last visited June 19, 2013).

- Letters sent to the primary organs and considered in the issuance of res-olutions and decisions by the primary organs.

V. UN Document Symbols, More Generally

As an initial step, we will expand upon our discussion from chapter 7 regarding UN document symbols. That discussion addressed only document symbols for resolutions. We will now address the system for the broader spectrum of UN documents. This discussion loosely follows an excellent discussion at the UN website on document symbols.[41]

First, note that the system of UN document symbols applies only to documents generated by or for the four currently operating primary non-judicial organs of the UN. That is, the General Assembly, the Security Council, ECOSOC or the Secretariat, or any of their subsidiary bodies, such as committees or commissions.

This discussion will thus not apply to the Trusteeship Council, which sus-pended its operations in 1994,[42] and it does not apply to the ICJ, which main-tains a distinct system of documentation. Furthermore, and most broadly, the system of UN document symbols does not generally apply to the specialized agencies, which operate independently from the UN principal organs.

A. First Component

As before, the first component of any UN document symbol generally indi-cates the principal organ to which the document is submitted or the principle organ that is issuing it. We saw in chapter 8 that these components for the Gen-eral Assembly and the Security Council are "A/-" and "S/-," respectively. These symbols are used for most documents generated by or under the General As-sembly and the Security Council, not just resolutions. The initial components for ECOSOC and the Secretariat are "E/-" and "ST/-," respectively.

Documents issued by some especially significant subsidiary bodies have their own initial components. Examples would be:

UN Development Program ("UNDP")	"DP/-"
UN Conference on Trade and Development ("UNCTAD")	"TD/-"

---

41. *See* Dag Hammarskjöld Library, *UN Documentation: Overview: Document Symbols*, United Nations Research Guides & Resources, http://research.un.org/en/docs/symbols (last visited June 19, 2013).

42. *See supra* chapter 3, segment IV.D.

UN Environment Program ("UNEP")   "UNEP/-"

UN Document Symbols for documents issued by any of these bodies would begin with the components listed above, rather than "A/-," even though they are all subsidiary organs of the General Assembly.

B. Second Component

The second component, following the forward slash after the first, indicates which subsidiary organ or body generated the document, if any. If the document was generated by a principal body itself (such as the General Assembly or Security Council), then the second component will be derived according to the discussion below for the "third component."

For documents generated by subsidiary organs or bodies, the abbreviations for various types of subsidiary bodies are sets of capital letters, such as those indicated below.

Ad hoc committee	"-/AC. . . . /-"
Standing, permanent, or main committee	"-/C. . . . /-"
Commission	"-/CN. . . . /-"
Conference	"-/CONF. . . . /-"
Governing council	"-/GC. . . . /-"
Preparatory committee	"-/PC. . . . /-"
Subcommittee	"-/SC. . . . /-"
Subcommission	"-/Sub. . . . /-"
Working group	"-/WG. . . . /-"

In an actual document symbol, the ellipses in the above abbreviations would be replaced by an arabic numeral (1, 2, 3, etc.). Each subsidiary body has been assigned an arabic numeral for purposes of constructing the document symbols for the documents it issues.

The arabic numerals for the General Assembly's six permanent main committees are simply the numerals that correspond to their names. The document symbol for a document issued by the General Assembly's Third Committee would thus begin "A/C.3/-."

For other subsidiary bodies, the assigned arabic numerals have no necessary connection to the title or function of the body. They are assigned as a mechanical matter by the Secretariat. For example, UNCITRAL has been assigned the code numeral "9." Accordingly, the symbol, "A/CN.9/55" references the 55th document issued in connection with UNCITRAL's work, a report from 1971 regarding international shipping legislation.

Similarly, the ILC has been assigned the code numeral "4." Accordingly, the symbol "A/CN.4/69" references the 69th document issued in connection with the ILC's work, a report from 1953 on the high seas.

Other bodies receive other numerals, and particularly specialized bodies can receive designations of combined letters, numbers, additional slashes, and other punctuation. All the coded numerals and more specialized designations are listed and indexed in a volume released periodically by the Secretariat, the most recent of which was published in 1998. This is the *United Nations Document Series Symbols, 1946–1996*, and it can be downloaded from the "Document Symbols" page of the online UN Documentation Research Guide, noted above.

C. Third Component

With the third component, the document symbol construction moves away from the type of body that issued the document, and begins to reflect the type of document issued. The third component reflects the general nature of the document. Among the more significant abbreviations are:

Information series	"-/INF/-"
Limited distribution (often used for draft resolutions)	"-/L. . . . /-"
Statements by non-governmental organizations	"-/NGO/-"
Petitions	"-/PET/-"
Verbatim records of minutes (also called "proces-verbaux")	"-/PV. . . . /-"
Resolutions	"-/RES/-"
Working papers	"-/WP. . . . /-"

Ellipses in the above abbreviations indicate that in any given session or working period of the issuing body there will be several documents of the type indicated. Accordingly, in the place of the ellipses there would be an arabic numeral indicating which particular document of that type issued by that body is referenced. The numeral will indicate the sequential order of that document in its corresponding series.

For example, A/PV.123 is the document symbol for the verbatim record of the 123d plenary meeting of the General Assembly, which met during the General Assembly's second session on November 21, 1947. At this plenary meeting, among other things, the General Assembly directed the ILC to formulate the "Nuremberg Principles," derived from the Nuremberg Charter under which Nazi war criminals had been tried. (Session numbers were not included in General Assembly document symbols until 1976, so neither the session number nor the year is included in this document symbol. This corresponds to the situation with document symbols for General Assembly resolutions, discussed earlier.[43])

D. Final Component

The final component among those consisting of linguistic abbreviations is not always used, but does appear on occasion. This component indicates changes or modifications to an original document. Examples of the kinds of changes that can be indicated are:

Addendum	"-/Add. . . ."
Alteration or amendment	"-/Amend. . . ."
Revision (replacing the entirety of a text originally issued)	"-/Rev. . . ."
Summarized version	"-/Summary"

Again, the ellipses in these abbreviations indicate that in a given period of time there will be more than one such document issued. (That is, for example, there would be more than one addendum or amendment for a particular document.) In the place of the ellipses above, there would be an arabic numeral indicating sequentially which addendum or amendment, for example, was being referenced.

E. Sequential Numbers

Often, at the end of the chain of most of the components described above for a particular document, there is an arabic numeral. That numeral indicates the sequential order of the referenced document in the relevant documents issued by that issuer. For example, UN Document A/784 is simply the 784th document in sequence considered by the General Assembly. (This was an amendment proposed by the Soviet Union in 1948 to alter the draft of the Univeral Declaration of Human Rights then under consideration.)

The sequential document numeral would appear before the "Final Component" described above, in those cases in which there has been a change or modification to the document.

F. Dates

Originally, years or session numbers (for the General Assembly) were not incorporated in document symbols. However, starting in the late 1970's, the principal organs began to reflect years or session numbers in their document symbols.

---

43. *See supra* chapter 7, segment IV.A.2.

The General Assembly began in 1976, at its 31st session, to include the relevant session number (in arabic numerals), as a separate component set off by forward slashes, after the principal organ component. An illustrative UN document symbol after this change could be: A/60/L.48. This was the 48th limited-distribution document circulated in the General Assembly during its 60th Session (the session for 2005–2006). It was a draft resolution by the president of the General Assembly proposing the establishment of the new Human Rights Council, to replace the former Human Rights Commission. This numbering change in 1976 was also discussed in chapter 7, regarding General Assembly resolutions; we now see that the treatment of resolutions discussed there was merely a special case of the general situation discussed here.

ECOSOC began including designations for the year in its document symbols in 1978, placing them after the principal organ component, set off by forward slashes. The Security Council began this practice in 1994, except that it still does not include a year designation for resolutions and meeting records. (Nevertheless, as noted earlier, general textual references to Security Council resolutions usually include the adoption date in parentheses after the document symbol.)

VI. Locating and Searching UN Documents

A. Specialized Agencies

If one is researching materials produced by a specialized agency, the best place to work from is that agency's website. All of the documents that any specialized agency produces with potential legal significance, such as standards and recommendations, are generally available at its website. Among the specialized agencies that list and describe or reproduce standards or recommendations at their websites, with some representative examples, are:

International Labor Organization ("ILO") at www.ilo.org:

>   Maternity Protection Recommendation

>   Protection of Workers' Health Recommendation

International Civil Aviation Organization ("ICAO") at www.icao.int:

>   Standards and Recommended Procedures

>   Procedures for Air Navigation Services

International Maritime Organization ("IMO") at www.imo.int:

>   International Maritime Solid Bulk Cargoes Code

>   International Safety Management Code

In addition, a specialized agency that serves as a depositary for any treaty or convention will generally maintain detailed information at its website regarding each such treaty or convention. Such information would include lists of signatories and member states, the texts of any reservations, declarations and exceptions, and the text of the treaty or convention itself. This feature of specialized agency operations was alluded to segment X.D of chapter 5, dealing with international organizations as depositaries. In line with that discussion, we note here some of the specialized agencies that serve as depositaries for a significant number of international treaties and conventions, together with some representative examples:

Food and Agriculture Organization of the UN ("FAO") at www.fao.org:

> International Plant Protection Convention (1951)
>
> International Treaty on Plant Genetic Resources for Food and Agriculture (2001)

ILO:

> Equal Remuneration Convention (1951)
>
> Labor Statistics Convention (1985)

UN Educational, Scientific and Cultural Organization ("UNESCO"), at www.unesco.org:

> Convention Concerning the International Exchange of Publications (1958)
>
> Convention Concerning Protection of the World Cultural and Natural Heritage (1972)

The information provided for treaties and conventions on the web pages covering an agency's role as depositary would generally be authoritative, and will also include amendments, protocols, and other ancillary information.

B. Principal Organs and Subsidiary Organs

1. Online Databases

At the time of publication, more recent UN documents are generally available and searchable online, and Security Council documents are currently available and searchable from 1946 onward. The starting year of coverage depends on the database being searched, as noted below. Documents from earlier years will probably come on line at later times. (Again, all resolutions of the principal organs are generally online and searchable from 1946; we are now discussing documents issued by the principal organs other than resolutions.) The primary online search facilities for these documents, as noted in chapter 7, are the Official Document System ("ODS") and the UN Bibliographic Information System ("UNBISnet").

a. ODS.

As noted in chapter 7, the ODS is the UN's electronic repository of official documents. Its general coverage begins with 1993. For the years it covers, it provides access to the full-text versions of all verbatim meeting records, resolutions, and other materials that would normally be included in the UN Official Records. At the time of publication, there are two formats of ODS on the UN website, the "previous" and the current formats. The previous version provides the opportunity to narrow the search terms at the beginning of the search, while the current version incorporates a broader initial search, with the option of using filter terms for narrowing after the initial results have been gathered.

Both the previous and current versions allow a user to choose between a "simple" search and an "advanced" search. The advanced-search option in the previous version allows many more fields for narrowing the search than the advanced-search option in the current version.

b. UNBISnet.

As noted in chapter 7, UNBISnet provides a bibliographic search engine for access to the bibliographic entries for all material at the UN's Dag Hammarskjöld Library. At press time for this book, its general coverage begins in 1979. Searches on UNBISnet most frequently turn up merely bibliographic references, and often do not have links to the full-text version of the documents themselves. (Except that full-text links are the norm for resolutions.) UNBISnet affords keyword searches using a very broad variety of searching fields.

c. UN-I-QUE.

The UN maintains a third general searchable data base, called "UN-I-QUE" (for "United Nations Info Quest"). The database consists not of bibliographic entries or of links to full-text documents, but rather it consists of UN document symbols for a large variety of documents. It can be used, among other things, to find a large range of UN documents that have mentioned or discussed a certain concept or issue since 1946. The concepts or issues that will retrieve results are limited to those that have been entered into the search feature for the database as searchable headings. The UN document symbols obtained from a conceptual or issue search can then be "copied and pasted" into an ODS or UNBISnet search field for further document retrieval.

2. Searches Using Online Databases

If one knows the UN document symbol for which one is searching, it can be entered as a search term in either ODS or UNBISnet. For the previous version of ODS, and for UNBISnet, all forward slashes and other punctuation should be removed from the document symbol when entering it as a search term. The removal of such marks is not required or desirable for a search on the new version of ODS.

When using UNBISnet, one can select "U.N. Document Symbol/Sales No." as a searching field. In the previous version of ODS, there is also an individual searching field for "U.N. Document Symbol." In the current version of ODS, one can enter the document symbol (with punctuation) as a standard search term, then select the body that adopted the document, and other parameters, for further narrowing after the initial search is completed.

If one does not know the UN document symbol for which one is searching, one can use keywords in either version of ODS or in UNBISnet. However, for UNBISnet recall that the database is bibliographic entries, so the keyword would need to appear in the bibliographic entry for it to be retrievable. Similarly, if the date of adoption is known, it can also be used to limit retrievals. UNBISnet and the current ODS allow limitation by year, while the precise date can be a search limitation in the previous version of ODS.

3. Print Versions

All UN Official Records should be accessible in the collection of any UN depository library, although many documents may be on microfiche. Particularly significant documents appear in *International Legal Materials* ("ILM"), initially discussed in chapter 5, and the *United Nations Yearbook* (yearbooks will be discussed in detail in chapter 10). Indexes at the end of each annual volume of ILM, and contents and indexing in each issue of the *United Nations Yearbook*, indicate which documents are included.

VII. Citing UN Documents

As was described in chapter 7, the 19th edition of the *Bluebook* does prescribe reasonably detailed and specific formats for citations to General Assembly and Security Council resolutions. However, once one moves beyond the field of resolutions and into the broad variety of other kinds of UN documents, the use of the *Bluebook* can become somewhat more problematic.

The *Bluebook* does not (and could not) provide precise instructions and examples for the citation of every kind of document issued by every UN principal organ and subsidiary body. Its rules and examples for these documents should be viewed as a general outline of citation practice. It's best to be familiar with what the *Bluebook* prescribes for the sources it does specifically address, and then work on the basis of analogy for sources the *Bluebook* does not specifically address.

Here are the main categories of citation forms the *Bluebook* prescribes for UN documents other than resolutions.

A. Verbatim and Summary Records

The *Bluebook* provides formats for citations to verbatim records of the General Assembly and Security Council (the two main bodies that currently publish verbatim records). These are specified in *Bluebook* rule 21.7.1. The components specified for inclusion in the citation for any verbatim record should not be problematic, since the specifications only require information normally included in the text of the verbatim record itself.

B. UN Reports

The various organs, subsidiary bodies, specialized agencies, and other entities within the UN framework issue numerous reports. The *Bluebook* addresses the citation of UN reports in rule 21.7.3.

1. Reports in General (subsection (a))

Subsection (a) of rule 21.7.3 purports to provide a general approach to citing UN reports, but only discusses reports from UN organs, committees, or the Secretariat. This is a bit ambiguous. For example, the next subsection of rule 21.7.3, subsection (b), applies to reports of subsidiary bodies to parent organizations. And yet, the reports of "committees" referred to in this subsection (a) would often also be reports by committees to their parent organizations. So a particular report by any of several UN committees might be cited according to the format indicated in either subsection (a) or subsection (b). It seems relatively clear that subsection (a) would cover reports by one of the Main Committees of the General Assembly.

In spite of this ambiguity, we suggest that this subsection (a) be used for any report that does not fall into one of the categories specified in subsections (b)-(d), discussed below. Prominently among the reports in this catch-all position would be regular reports issued by specialized agencies to the general public.

This general rule 21.7.3(a) requires that a citation to a report be composed of the following components:

- The name of the body and subcommittee (if any) that authored the report (abbreviate any terms in the body's name according to the abbreviations in rule 15.1(d));
- The title of the report;
- The pinpoint citation, if one is being used;
- The UN document symbol for the report (if any); and
- The date of the report.

Subsection (a) does not specify which "date" is intended. If the report or its accompanying materials reference more than one date, we suggest using the date of original issuance, unless another date is used more prominently by those most concerned with the report.

One example within the possible scope of subsection (a) would be a report issued by one of the Main Committees of the General Assembly. For instance, the report issued on November 14, 2001 (during the General Assembly's 56th session), by the First Committee (disarmament and international security) on the subject of military budgets. This report was the 526th document issued in connection with the General Assembly's work during its 56th session. A citation to it could read:

> U.N. Gen. Assembly, First Committee, Rep. of Military Budgets, U.N. Doc. A/56/526 (Nov. 14, 2001).

2. Reports of Subsidiary Bodies to Parent Organizations (subsection (b))

Examples here would be from a UN fund or program (such as UNICEF or UNEP) to the General Assembly. Also included would be reports by General Assembly commissions, such as the ILC, to the General Assembly. The examples also indicate that this rule is followed for reports authored by sub-units of larger bodies other than a principal organ, such as a committee, to the larger body or one of its officers. On the other hand, this subsection would not seem to include reports from the specialized agencies, since the specialized agencies are not subsidiary bodies, and since no principal organ of the UN is a "parent" of a specialized agency.

The *Bluebook*, taking into account the examples used in subsection (b), prescribes these components for these kinds of reports:

- The title of the report;
- The name of the issuing body;
- The session number of the reporting body and the dates of the session;

- The pinpoint citation, if one is being used;
- The UN document symbol for the report;
- An Official Records abbreviation specifying the parent organ receiving the report (when appropriate), followed by the session number (if any) and Official Records supplement number (if any) for the publication of the report by the receiving body; and
- The date of publication.

The examples in *Bluebook* rule 21.7.3(b) are somewhat inconsistent as to whether the title of the report or the name of the authoring body comes first. Apparently this is left to individual judgment.

One example would be the report of the ILC to the General Assembly regarding the ILC's work from May through August, 2007. Although this work constituted the ILC's 59th session, the report was delivered to the General Assembly during the General Assembly's 62d session, and was included in the 10th supplement imprinted by the General Assembly for its 62d session.

> Rep. of the Int'l Law Comm'n, 59th Sess., May 7–June 5, July 10–Aug. 10, 2007, U.N. Doc. A/62/10; GAOR, 62d Sess., Supp. No. 10 (2007).

3. *Reports from the Secretary-General or Other Officials* (subsection (c))

This rule is clear enough when a report's authorship by an individual official is prominently stated. However, some reports can appear to be issued corporately by UN bodies, such as committees, working groups, or task forces, that are actually authored by the individual officials who lead them. A certain amount of diligent inspection of a report is thus called for when constructing a citation to such a report.

The *Bluebook* specifies these components for these kinds of reports:

- The author of the report;
- The title of the report;
- The pinpoint citation, if one is being used;
- The body to which the report is being delivered, if needed;
- The UN document symbol; and
- The date.

Regarding the author's name, the subsection directs that only the official title should be used, unless the official author's name is given as part of the report. In that event, the subsection requires that the author's given name be included in a parenthetical at the end of the citation. We also note that none of the examples for *Bluebook* rule 21.7.3(c) includes "the body to which the document is delivered," so this is apparently not generally considered "needed."

Again, reports by specialized agencies are sometimes issued to the general public, and not by any particular officer of the specialized agency. Such a report would probably not be included in this subsection, which is one reason we suggested above that such reports be cited according to subsection 21.7.3(a).

An example here would be the 2002 annual budget report from the Secretary-General to the General Assembly for peacekeeping forces in Cyprus. Since the report was delivered in December 2002, it was delivered to the 57th session of the General Assembly, and was the 667th document imprinted by the General Assembly for that Session.

> U.N. Secretary-General, *Performance Rep. on the Budget of the U.N. Peacekeeping Force in Cyprus for the Period from July 1, 2001 to June 30, 2002*, U.N. Doc. A/57/667 (Dec. 18, 2002).

4. Reports from Conferences (subsection (d))

Often reports will be issued as the culmination of multilateral conferences; some are very high-profile and closely-followed, and some less so. These conference reports are generally distinct from annual and other regular reports that specialized agencies, subsidiary bodies, and others issue more as a matter of course from their usual work. The more regular reports would generally not be included in this subsection.

The *Bluebook* requires that conference reports be cited using the following components:

- The conference name;
- The name of this particular meeting of the conference, if it is in a series;
- The place of the conference, unless it is at the headquarters of the organizing agency;
- The dates of the conference;
- The report title;
- The pinpoint citation, if one is being used;
- The UN document symbol, if applicable; and
- The official document date, if different from the conference date.

Note as well that under subsection 21.7.3(e), reports with very long names must still be cited in full the first time they are cited, but a shorter form can be used in subsequent citations. Remember, however, to introduce the short form that will be used in a square-bracketed expression as part of the first citation.

An example would be:

World Conference against Racism, Racial Discrimination, Xenophobia and Related Intolerance, Durban, South Africa, Aug. 31- Sept. 8, 2001, *Rep. of the World Conference against Racism, Racial Discrimination, Xenophobia and Related Intolerance,* U.N. Doc. A/CONF.189/12 (Jan. 10, 2002)[hereinafter *Report of the World Conference against Racism*].

C. Masthead Documents

We saw in chapter 7 that virtually all General Assembly and Security Council resolutions are published first as masthead documents before they are included in the Official Records. We also noted that resolutions that have been published in the Official Records can be cited to their Official Records version, while resolutions that are too new to be in the Official Records can be cited using the document-symbol format.

Some documents are issued on the UN masthead that never appear in the Official Records. Most prominently among such documents are many letters sent to a UN principal organ or subsidiary body by states or their representatives, and many memoranda among such parties or UN bodies. These masthead documents will often receive UN document symbols, and when they do, they will be cited using a document-symbol format, similar to that for newer resolutions.

Bluebook rule 21.7.4 applies to these kinds of masthead documents, and requires the following components:

- The name of the institutional author, if any;
- The title of the document;
- The pinpoint citation, if one is being used;
- The UN document symbol; and
- The date of publication.

An example would be a letter sent by the Permanent Representative of Iran to the UN on December 29, 1994, complaining about Iraqi violations of the cease-fire agreement then in effect between the two countries. The letter was the 1460th document imprinted by the Security Council in 1994, and was issued as a masthead document on December 31 of that year. A citation to the letter would be:

Permanent Representative of the Islamic Republic of Iran, Letter dated Dec. 29, 1994 from the Permanent Representative of the Islamic Republic of Iran to the UN Addressed to the Secretary-General, U.N. Doc. S/1994/1460 (Dec. 31, 1994).

D. Adjudicatory Bodies Established by the UN

In recent years the Security Council has established tribunals for the trial of war criminals and other defendants in particular regions of the world. Among these are the International Criminal Tribunal for the Former Yugoslavia ("ICTY") and the International Criminal Tribunal for Rwanda ("ICTR"). There are also so-called "hybrid" tribunals, such as the Special Court for Sierra Leone or the Special Tribunal for Lebanon, and others. These hybrid tribunals have some characteristics of international courts, and some characteristics of domestic courts.

The *Bluebook* provides guidance for citing materials from these tribunals in rule 21.7.6.

E. UN Press Releases and Sales Publications

These types of documents will usually have content less directly related to specifically legal rules. But they can nevertheless be significant for background. In some circumstances, press releases may lead researchers to information that provides evidence for a rule of customary international law, for example. As for sales documents, the usefulness of the material will depend on the nature of the document. Some sales documents can be particularly helpful tools for international legal research. The *Bluebook* provides formats to cite press releases and sales publications in rules 21.7.5 and 21.7.7.

F. Yearbooks and Periodicals

These will be discussed in more detail chapter 10. The *Bluebook* prescribes citation forms for these sources in rules 21.7.8 and 21.14.

G. Intergovernmental Organizations

The *Bluebook* has a rule specifically addressing intergovernmental organizations, which are international membership entities formed by governments, of which states themselves are generally members. Among these would be the North Atlantic Treaty Organization (often called "NATO"), and the Organization of Oil Exporting Countries (often called "OPEC"). Intergovernmental organizations can be distinguished from non-governmental organizations ("NGO's") and multinational corporations, for example. The *Bluebook* rule for citing documents issued by intergovernmental organizations is rule 21.12.

The examples in rule 21.12 indicate that the *Bluebook* editors consider UN specialized agencies to be intergovernmental organizations. Accordingly, this rule nominally covers citations of reports and other documents issued by UN specialized agencies. Nevertheless, we have not emphasized rule 21.12 in this chapter. That is because the rule principally directs that documents of inter-governmental organizations merely be cited "by analogy" to the citation rules for UN documents we have already covered. The examples in rule 21.12 provide some additional indications of the intended citation patterns, but no additional detailed instructions regarding any particular kinds of documents.

VIII. Chapter Summary

Some of the most visible UN operations are not conducted by its principal organs, such as the Security Council or General Assembly. There are various other organs and bodies that can have very dramatic effects for UN operations "on the ground" throughout the world. There are three main types of these other organs and bodies. The first type consists of "subsidiary" organs or bodies. Each of the subsidiary organs or bodies has been created by one of the UN principal organs, and is responsible to, and generally funded by, the principal organ that created it. Prominent examples are the UNDP (the United Nations Development Program) and the Office of the UN High Commissioner for Refugees.

A second type would be "specialized agencies," which are created pursuant to treaties entered into by the states that create them. They have more independence from the principal organs than subsidiary organs and bodies. Prominent examples are the IMF (the International Monetary Fund) and UNESCO (the United Nations Educational, Scientific and Cultural Organization). Within the third type are "related organizations," which have a very high degree of independence from the principal organs. The most famous example is the WTO (the World Trade Organization).

We first took a closer look at specialized agencies. They can help to decentralize operations, decrease politicization and channel expertise. The UN Charter authorizes ECOSOC to coordinate their activities. The Charter also authorizes the General Assembly to examine their budgets, and approve budgetary arrangements with them. Although the General Assembly thus has some measure of control over the specialized agencies, each specialized agency negotiates a separate relationship agreement with ECOSOC, giving the specialized agencies a potential degree of bargaining capacity.

Each of the specialized agencies has a structure involving three operational levels. These are a general assembly (in which all states that are members of the agency are represented), an executive board (with a more limited membership), and a secretariat.

Specialized agencies can affect international law in a variety of ways. Some specialized agencies issue standards of conduct that, although not legally binding, have nearly binding effects as a practical matter. Some specialized agencies publish recommendations or prepare draft multilateral conventions. In addition, some agencies (such as the IMF and the World Bank) engage in legally binding contractual relations with particular states.

We next looked at different types of operations that are responsible to the General Assembly. We first observed that the General Assembly maintains six permanent main committees, that in common parlance are referenced by the number (1 through 6) that has been assigned to each. The Sixth Committee is the committee on "legal questions."

Other subsidiary bodies of the General Assembly take the form of commissions. Among the two most prominent are UNCITRAL (the United Nations Commission on International Trade Law) and the ILC (the International Law Commission). Both UNCITRAL and the ILC have been very active over many years in preparing draft conventions that have later been formalized and entered into as binding treaties.

Still other subsidiary bodies of the General Assembly take the form of programs and funds. Among these are UNCTAD (the United Nations Conference on Trade and Development), UNICEF (the United Nations Children's Fund), and UNEP (the United Nations Environment Program). These bodies have primarily operational impact, although some of their activities can have normative significance. For example, UNICEF has significant involvement with the UN Convention on the Rights of the Child.

Documents issued by or for the Security Council, the General Assembly, the Secretariat, or ECOSOC, or any of their subsidiary bodies or organs, are assigned UN document symbols. Each UN document symbol consists of a number of components, separated by forward slashes. The first component is a capital letter or letters indicating the principal organ from which the document derives. For example, "S" denotes the Security Council, and "A" denotes the General Assembly.

The second component indicates which subsidiary organ or body generated the document. Generic capital letters indicate which type of organ or body is involved; for example, "C" most prominently denotes one of the six main committees, and "CN" denotes a commission. Most subsidiary organs or bodies are assigned arabic numerals for identification. So, "C.6" denotes the Sixth Committee and "CN.4" denotes the ILC. The third component indicates the type of document involved. For example, "PET" denotes a petition, and "PV" denotes verbatim records of minutes (also called "proces-verbaux"). The final component is not always used, but can indicate changes or modifications to an original document. For example, "Add." denotes an addendum to an original document.

Each document with a UN document symbol is assigned a unique sequential number for that document symbol, which appears either at the end of the chain of components described above, or before the final component, when it exists. Also, in the 1970's the principal organs began to designate calendar years or (for the General Assembly) session numbers in their document symbols. These designations normally appear as a separate component after the principal organ component.

To locate materials produced by a specialized agency, the best place to work from is that agency's website. The website of a specialized agency generally contains any standards or recommendations issued by the agency. In addition, a specialized agency that serves as a depositary for any conventions will maintain detailed status information at its website concerning all such conventions. Information provided in an agency's role as depositary would generally be authoritative.

The UN maintains three major online databases through which UN documents can be searched and retrieved. These are ODS (the Official Document System), UNBISnet (the UN Bibliographic Information System Network) and UN-I-QUE (UN Info Quest).

IX. Chapter Review Questions

1. What are some examples of UN subsidiary organs or bodies? What are the general features of the relationship between the UN principal organs and UN "subsidiary organs or bodies"?

2. What are some examples of UN specialized agencies? How are UN "specialized agencies" created?

3. What is an example of a UN "related organization"?

4. Which UN principal organ coordinates the activities of the specialized agencies?

5. Which UN principal organ is authorized to examine the budgets of the specialized agencies?

6. What are the three structural levels of each specialized agency?

7. What are some ways in which specialized agencies can affect international law?

8. How many "main committees" are maintained by the General Assembly?

9. What are some examples of commissions responsible to the General Assembly?

10. What are some examples of programs and funds responsible to the General Assembly?

11. Which UN principal organs are the bodies whose documents, whether prepared by or for them, are assigned UN document symbols?

12. Try to describe each of the four components of a typical UN document symbol.

13. How are sequential numbers for documents, and document dates, reflected in UN document symbols?

14. What is generally the best method of retrieving documents issued by UN specialized agencies?

15. What are the three major online searchable databases maintained by the UN for retrieving UN documents?

X. Additional Resources and General Bibliographic References

Charles Henry Alexandrowicz, *The Law-Making Functions of the Specialised Agencies of the United Nations* (Sydney: Angus and Robertson, in association with the Australian Institute of International Affairs 1973).

José E. Alvarez, *International Organizations as Law-Makers* (New York: Oxford University Press 2005).

Niels M. Blokker & Ramses A. Wessel, *International Organizations Law Review* (Leiden: Martinus Nijhoff Publishers) (published periodically since 2004), *available at* http://www.brill.nl/international-organizations-law-review.

Lyonette Louis-Jacques & Jeanne S. Korman, *Introduction to International Organizations* (New York: Oceana Publications 1996).

Edmund Jan Osmanczyk, *Encyclopedia of the United Nations and International Agreements* (Anthony Mango ed., 3d ed. New York: Routledge 2003).

Jon Pevehouse, *International Organization* (Boston: World Peace Foundation) (published periodically from 1947), *available at* http://journals.cambridge.org/action/displayJournal?jid=INO.

Philippe Sands & Pierre Klein, *Bowett's Law of International Institutions* (6th ed., London: Sweet & Maxwell 2009).

Michael P. Scharf & Paul R. Williams, *The Law of International Organizations: Problems and Materials* (3d ed. 2013).

Union International Association, *Yearbook of International Organizations* (Munich: K.G. Saur) (published yearly since 1948), *available at* http://www.uia.be/yearbook-international-organizations-online.

Chapter 10

Academic, Professional, and Diplomatic Sources

I. Introduction

As we saw in chapter 4, Article 38(1)(d) of the ICJ Statute directs the ICJ to apply, among other sources, "the teachings of the most highly qualified publicists of the various nations." This mostly means treatises published by established commentators on international law. Such commentators are usually prominent university professors of international law, or high-ranking judges with experience in international law.[1]

But practitioners, commentators, and courts treat this provision of the ICJ Statute as encompassing a broader variety of sources, apart from only the published treatises of distinguished commentators. In this chapter we review the leading types of sources that would be broadly acknowledged as falling within Article 38(1)(d). In addition to the published treatises of distinguished commentators, these also include reference works and codifications prepared by academic and professional societies, periodicals published by such societies, draft treaties and other materials prepared by the International Law Commission (the

---

1. *See, e.g.*, Malcolm N. Shaw, *International Law* 112–13 (6th ed. 2008) (referencing in this context "academic writers," "textbook writers," and "the writings of the leading juristic authorities"). *See also* James R. Fox, *Dictionary of International and Comparative Law* 268 (3d ed. 2003) (defining "publicists" as "scholars writing on the subject of international law," and noting that "their work is a source which the International Court of Justice may consult in finding international law," citing Article 38 of the ICJ Statute).

"ILC"), online commentaries provided by multilateral organizations, and certain other types of sources.[2]

On the one hand, Article 38(1)(d) is thus seen to encompass a broad variety of materials. These materials can be a rich source for researchers, because they address a wide spectrum of topics and encapsulate much investigation and analysis that has already been performed by reputable authorities. Much argumentation on international law, in both publications and litigation, references these kinds of materials.[3]

On the other hand, the authorization in Article 38(1)(d) for the use of these kinds of materials has certain limitations. One limitation is the reference in Article 38(1)(d) to "the most *highly qualified* publicists," which suggests that only the work of those with a notable degree of accomplishment is eligible for consideration. All the materials we will cover in this chapter are from sufficiently accomplished sources to qualify.

Another limitation is the language of Article 38(1)(d) indicating that these kinds of materials are to be used as "a *subsidiary* means" for determining international law rules. Accordingly, these kinds of materials are technically viewed not as sources in their own right, but merely as evidence of what the law, derived from other sources, is.[4] Additionally, the use of the qualifier "subsidiary" suggests that these kinds of materials are to be accorded less weight than treaties, conventions, and customary international law,[5] for example, in the event of any tension between these materials and the more direct sources.[6]

---

2. *See, e.g., Brownlie's Principles of Public International Law* 43 (James Crawford ed., 8th ed. 2013) (referencing "the work of the ILC [and] the reports and resolutions of the Institute of International Law and other expert bodies"). *See also* Restatement (Third) of the Foreign Relations Law of the U.S. § 103 reporters' note 1 (1987) [hereinafter Third Restatement] ("Such writings include treatises and other writings of authors of standing; resolutions of scholarly bodies such as the Institute of International Law (Institut de droit international) and the International Law Association; draft texts and reports of the International Law Commission, and systematic scholarly presentations of international law . . . .").

3. *E.g.,* Shaw, *supra* note 1, at 113 (asserting that states, national law officials, international judicial and arbitral bodies, and municipal judges "all consult and quote the writings of the leading juristic authorities").

4. Third Restatement, *supra* note 2, § 103 cmt. a (referring to these kinds of materials as "secondary evidence indicating what the law has been found to be" as opposed to primary evidence, such as treaties, conventions, or customary international law).

5. *E.g.,* Shaw, *supra* note 1, at 113 ("the general influence of textbook writers has somewhat declined").

6. *E.g.,* Third Restatement, *supra* note 2, § 103 cmt. a ("Such evidence [the writings of scholars] may be negated by primary evidence, for example, as to customary law . . . .").

While all authorities recognize these limitations in Article 38(1)(d), there is not always an express acknowledgment, when such works are discussed and cited, that they have this indirect and subsidiary character referenced in Article 38(1)(d). When these kinds of materials are especially helpful to an advocate's cause, we think it is fair for the advocate to make full use of them. However, the advocate needs to be aware that opponents or decision-makers may minimize, to a degree, the weight of these materials as a result of these limitations in Article 38(1)(d).

There is another use for the kinds of materials covered in this chapter. Many of the materials can be used to try to establish an *opinio juris* for a rule of customary international law. This would be especially the case for draft conventions prepared by the ILC, in view of its prominence and prestige. The other kinds of materials covered in this chapter (such as treatises and reference works published by academic and professional societies) can also be used for establishing an *opinio juris*. Indeed, to the extent treatises and other works discuss historical facts, they might also be used to establish state practice.

In view of the relevance of these materials for customary international law, this chapter also addresses the use of diplomatic sources and other materials as possible sources of state practice and *opinio juris*. Some can also furnish background support for general principles of law.

II. Treatises

As suggested in chapter 2, academic treatises formed the basis of the original Law of Nations. Even today, the writings of Gentili, Grotius, Vattel, and others can still be cited in arguments regarding international law. However, it is more usual for current international law discourse to reference more modern treatise writers. Among the most useful English-language treatises for present-day researchers are:

Anthony Aust, *Handbook of International Law* (2d ed. 2010).

Brierly's Law of Nations (Andrew Clapham ed., 7th ed. 2012).

Brownlie's Principles of Public International Law (James Crawford ed., 8th ed. 2012).

Antonio Cassese, *International Law* (2d ed. 2005).

Malcolm N. Shaw, *International Law* (6th ed. 2008).

Starke's International Law (I.A. Shearer ed., 11th ed. 1994).

Rebecca M.M. Wallace & Olga Martin-Ortega, *International Law* (6th ed. 2009).

The above list is far from exhaustive. There are many other useful published academic discussions of international law. This short list, however, reflects a focus on the encyclopedic character of the works, the comprehensiveness of their discussions, the international repute of their authors in English-speaking practice settings, their general availability, the currency of their most recent editions, the generality of their approach, and the need to keep the list succinct.

There are many works on particular subjects that are encyclopedic, recent and complete, but relate only to particular subjects, such as the Law of the Sea or the Law of Armed Conflict. This list concentrates on those treatises that address international law in general.

Many readers will probably note that many of the sources listed above have been used as authorities for this book. Many of the sources discussed in the remainder of this chapter can also be found in the footnotes and bibliographies of this book. We intend this to be an illustration of the generally authoritative character of these works.

Since treatises are "books" within the meaning of the *Bluebook*, citations to treatises or portions of them should follow rule 15 of the *Bluebook* on "Books, Reports and Other Nonperiodic Materials." Using this rule should not present many problems for most readers.

III. Academic and Professional Organizations

A. The ALI and the Third Restatement

The American Law Institute (or the "ALI") is a private organization, unaffiliated with any governmental entity, composed of about 4000 lawyers, judges, and law professors in the United States. The ALI is responsible for the preparation and promulgation of the "*Restatements*" with which most American lawyers are familiar. Among these are the *Restatement of the Law (Second) of Contracts* and the *Restatement of the Law (Third) of Torts*, that U.S. law students usually encounter in the first year of study.

Most of the ALI's work has historically related to the law of the states of the United States. Indeed, part of the value of its *Restatements* has been the unified perspective they bring to subjects that can vary in their particulars from one U.S. state to the next. However, some of the ALI's projects also take on a more international dimension.

Foremost among these is the *Restatement of the Law (Third): The Foreign Relations Law of the United States*, which in the context of international law is often simply called the "*Third Restatement*." While this is nominally a treatment of the U.S. federal approach to the legal aspects of foreign relations, it can be read as a summation of many topics within the field of public international law. Accordingly, it is cited in many U.S. casebooks, and some U.S. treatises, as a general authority on public international law, especially with regard to customary international law. Like the other *Restatements*, the *Third Restatement* is a compendium of rules, drawn from a variety of sources, that is designed to present a unified and coherent exposition of the relevant body of legal rules. Also like the other *Restatements*, it is not itself law in any jurisdiction. Nevertheless, it can be viewed as carrying authoritative weight by virtue of the prestige and background of the ALI and its members, and of the ALI's past accomplishments.

Reference to the *Third Restatement* may be more frequent in discussions of international law within and by legal institutions in the United States. (In one of its more influential decisions of recent years touching on international law, the U.S. Supreme Court referred to the *Third Restatement* repeatedly.[7]) For institutions operating outside the United States, reference to or reliance on the *Third Restatement* may not be as common. But still its legitimacy as a source of authority is recognized in some contexts well beyond the borders of the United States.

Editions of the *Bluebook* generally prescribe a specific format for citations to the ALI's *Restatements*. In the 19th edition, specific forms for citing these *Restatements*, which would include the *Third Restatement*, are found in rules B5.1.3 and 12.9.5.

B. The Institut de droit international (the "IDI")

The *Institut de droit international* (the "IDI"), or the International Law Institute,[8] is a private membership organization, as is the ALI. However, unlike the ALI, it has an exclusive focus on international law, and its membership consists of international law specialists from countries throughout the world. It was

---

7. Medellín v. Texas, 552 U.S. 491, 506 n.3 & 522 (2008).

8. Although "International Law Institute" is probably the best translation for "Institut de droit international," this translation could create confusion with another organization. As noted in the text, the Institute discussed there is based in Europe, dates to 1873, and is designed through its deliberations to influence the development of rules of public international law. There is another organization, based in Washington, D.C., called the "International Law Institute." It was founded in 1955 and predominantly assists public officials from countries around the world in developing their domestic legal regimes to reflect the rule of law. While its activities are eminently worthwhile, we don't think they are as apt to have an instrumental effect on the development of public international law rules as the Institute discussed in the text.

founded in 1873 in the Belgian city of Ghent by eleven individuals who were then prominent in international affairs. Most of them were from Western Europe, although some were from the Americas. Today, the IDI's members (about a hundred full members and about thirty associate members) are broadly representative of most all general regions of the world.[9]

The IDI conducts a formal session every two years, and the sessions take place in various cities throughout the world. The members of the IDI are divided among various "commissions," according to subject matter. The two operational languages are English and French.

In between the formal session meetings, the commissions work on preparing draft resolutions that are designed to state current rules of international law, or suggest appropriate paths of progressive development for international law. These resolutions by themselves are not law in any jurisdiction. Indeed, they are generally issued in the form of deliberative resolutions, such as a debating society might publish after detailed discussions and interchanges. They are not issued in the form of draft legislation, as are some documents issued by the ALI, or in the form of draft treaties, as are many documents issued by ILC.[10] But they are communicated to governments, international organizations, and other members of the international academic community. Accordingly, they can have some weight in the determination of the status of customary international law from time to time.

Like the ALI, the IDI is very prestigious in the academic world. Additionally, in the field of international law, the IDI's reputation benefits from its exclusive focus on public international law, its independence from any organized governments, and the broadly international provenance and renown of its members.

As noted above, the primary work products of the IDI are resolutions prepared by its commissions. The *Bluebook* does not contain a precise form for citing IDI resolutions. Recent editions of the *Bluebook* have provided guidance on the citation of resolutions by intergovernmental organizations. Although the IDI is not an intergovernmental organization, we believe it would be appropriate to follow the *Bluebook*'s format for resolutions of intergovernmental organizations when citing IDI resolutions. In the 19th edition of the *Bluebook* this format is given in rule 21.12.

---

9. At the time of publication, a complete listing of the IDI's members can be found at its website. *Members*, Institut de droit international, http://www.idi-iil.org/idiE/navig _members.html (last modified Oct. 4, 2012).

10. The ALI is represented on the Permanent Editorial Board of the Uniform Commercial Code, and thus has a role in the formulation of some materials ultimately adopted as state legislation. Regarding the ILC, *see infra* segment III.F of this chapter 10.

C. The Hague Academy of International Law

Unlike the ALI and the IDI, which are primarily membership associations, The Hague Academy of International Law is an operating educational institution. The Academy conducts six weeks of advanced educational courses in international law every summer; three weeks in public international law topics, and three weeks in private international law topics. The speakers invited to deliver the courses produce monographs memorializing their lectures, and these monographs are published in an annual series of volumes going back to 1923. (A "monograph" is a learned treatise-type discussion on a specifically defined subject. A monograph is longer than an essay, has a more specific focus than a complete treatise, and does not have the implication that the author is being tested, as is the case with a dissertation. However, in other respects, monographs resemble all three of these types of documents.)

This published series, the *Recueil des cours*, is one of the best known, and one of the more prestigious, regularly published academic periodicals in international law. (Its title could be translated into English as the "Collected Courses.") The course monographs are indexed every ten years or so in separate non-cumulative index volumes, published serially as the series progresses. Monographs appearing in the series are either in English or in French.

The Hague Academy is located in the Peace Palace in The Hague, along with the ICJ and the Bureau of the Permanent Court of Arbitration. The Academy also maintains a Centre for Research, which is open during the summer instructional period. However, for most working in international law, it is through the *Recueil des cours* that The Hague Academy makes its most serviceable contribution. Reference to the *Recueil des cours* can often be appropriate in determining the status of customary international law.

Since the *Recueil des cours* is an academically-oriented legal periodical, it should be cited under the *Bluebook*'s rule 16 on periodic materials. Since it is published annually with numbered volumes attributable to each year, a monograph in it should be cited as an "article in a consecutively paginated journal," as provided in rule 16.4.

D. UNIDROIT (The International Institute for the Unification of Private Law)

Alone among the institutions discussed in this chapter, UNIDROIT is a free-standing inter-governmental organization, rather than a private body or a subsidiary body of a larger organization. It was originally an outgrowth of the League of Nations, but now operates independently of the United Nations. It currently has sixty-three states parties, including almost all the most developed countries of the world, and representing all the inhabited continents. It is headquartered in Rome, and its two operating languages are English and French.

UNIDROIT is also unique among the bodies discussed in this chapter because it is devoted, more or less exclusively, to private international law. Although the primary focus of this book is on public international law, UNIDROIT is included in this discussion due to its prominence and prestige. Also, some of the documents it has produced have ramifications for public international law.

The mission of UNIDROIT is to "examine ways of harmonizing and coordinating the private law of States and of groups of States, and to prepare gradually for the adoption by the various States of uniform rules of private law."[11] It issues draft international conventions for adoption by states,[12] and also on occasion issues "principles" that, while not provided in the form of international agreements, are meant to guide the behavior of states and other international actors in their relations.

In academic or judicial discussions of international commercial transactions, there can be references to, for example, the UNIDROIT Principles of International Commercial Contracts. These principles address such usual contractual issues as offer and acceptance, contract validity, modes of performance, consequences of breach, and so on. They do so for a broad variety of commercial contracts, and thus have a potentially wider sphere of application than existing international conventions specifically focusing on the international sale of goods,[13] for example.

The best citation format for UNIDROIT materials depends on the type of material involved. UNIDROIT conventions that have come into effect can be cited as other conventions would be cited. At this writing, several are included in the electronic version of the United Nations Treaty Collection. All currently effective UNIDROIT conventions are available at its website. Accordingly, as a default, *Bluebook* rule 18 on "The Internet, Electronic Media, and Other Nonprint Resources" would be an appropriate guide for any UNIDROIT conventions that are readily available only at the UNIDROIT website.

---

11. Charter of the International Institute for the Unification of Private Law art. 1, Mar. 15, 1940, 15 U.S.T. 2494 (entered into force July 15, 1955).

12. *See id.* art. 1(a)&(b) (directing the organization to "prepare drafts of laws and conventions with the object of establishing uniform internal law; and prepare drafts of agreements with a view to facilitating international relations in the field of private law").

13. *E.g.,* UN Convention on Contracts for the International Sale of Goods, Apr. 11, 1980, 1489 U.N.T.S. 3. 19 I.L.M. 668 (entered into force Jan. 1, 1988).

UNIDROIT's model laws and principles can be cited according to *Bluebook* rule 12.9.5 on "Model Codes, Restatements, Standards, and Sentencing Guidelines."

E. The American Society of International Law (the "ASIL")

The American Society of International Law (the "ASIL") is headquartered at Tillar House, a stately colonial-revival mansion in Washington, D.C. It is a private membership organization with an extremely large membership, both in the United States and internationally. It is one of the primary private international law associations in the world. It publishes two flagship periodicals, with which virtually all U.S. international-law practitioners would be familiar. The first is ILM, or *International Legal Materials*, which was introduced in chapter 5. It is a bi-monthly compendium of significant new treaties, decisions, resolutions, and other primary sources in international law. The other is the *American Journal of International Law*, an especially prestigious law journal, containing academically-oriented articles on public international law.

The ASIL also publishes periodic updates of various kinds regarding current issues and developments in international law. These are sent on a regular basis to its members electronically. At the time of publication, among the most notable of these are transmittals called "ASIL Insights." These function similarly to short law-review essays prepared by scholars of public international law on subjects of current importance.

Also important to note are several electronic databases maintained at the ASIL's website. One of these is the Electronic Information System for International Law (or "EISIL"). This database contains links for many of the conventions, decisions, and organizations already covered in this book. Also helpful can be the ASIL's Electronic Resource Guide (or "eRG"), which contains expository essays on resources for public international law. Additionally, the ASIL maintains a search tool for retrieving U.S. cases and other materials referencing or dealing with international law issues (called "i-LEX").

F. The International Law Commission (the "ILC")

We have mentioned the International Law Commission (or "ILC") in earlier parts of this book, in view of its role in preparing draft treaties (chapter 5), its significance for the codification of customary international law (chapter 8), and its status as a subsidiary organ or body of the UN General Assembly (chapter 9). However, those mentions have been a bit fleeting, and this discussion is meant to be somewhat more thorough.

The General Assembly's authority for establishing the ILC derives from Article 13 of the UN Charter, which requires the General Assembly to "initiate studies and make recommendations for the purpose of . . . encouraging the progressive development of international law and its codification."[14] Pursuant to this mandate, the General Assembly created the ILC in 1948.[15] As currently constituted, the ILC consists of 34 members.[16] According to the Statute of the ILC, these members must be "persons of recognized competence in international law."[17] They are elected by the General Assembly from a list of candidates nominated by the governments of the UN Member states,[18] serve five-year terms, and can be re-elected.[19]

In 1981, the General Assembly fixed[20] the geographic provenance of the 34 members according to the following pattern:

8 members to be nationals from African States;

7 members to be nationals from Asian States;

3 members to be nationals from Eastern European States;

6 members to be nationals from Latin American and Caribbean States;

8 members to be nationals from Western European and Other States:

1 member to be, in rotation, from an African or Eastern European State; and

1 member to be, in rotation, from an Asian or Latin American / Caribbean State.

A significant portion of the ILC's work has consisted of preparing draft multilateral treaties for signature and ratification by states. The ILC Statute authorizes it to prepare draft treaty provisions that can have either or both of the functions of progressive development and codification.[21] Draft treaty provi-

---

14. U.N. Charter art. 13(1)(a).

15. G.A. Res. 174(II), U.N. Doc. A/519 (Nov. 21, 1947) (establishing the International Law Commission and approving its Statute).

16. The current size of the ILC was fixed through a 1981 General Assembly resolution, expanding the number of members to 34. G.A. Res. 36/39, ¶ 1, U.N. Doc. A/RES/36/39 (Nov. 18, 1981).

17. Statute of the International Law Commission, G.A. Res. 174(II), *supra* note 15, Annex art. 2(1) [hereinafter ILC Statute].

18. ILC Statute, *supra* note 17, art. 3.

19. The current length of the terms for ILC members was fixed through a 1955 General Assembly resolution, increasing the length of each term to 5 years. G.A. Res. 985(X), U.N. Doc. A/3116 (Dec. 3, 1955).

20. *See* G.A. Res. 36/39, *supra* note 16, ¶ 3.

21. ILC Statute, *supra* note 17, arts. 15–24.

sions, even before they have been finalized and adopted as treaties among states, can also contribute to progressive development and codification. The ILC also sometimes (pursuant to General Assembly request) produces draft "principles" or "articles" that can be very influential in these respects,[22] even without being stated in the terms of treaties or conventions.

In the early years of the UN organization, the ILC turned its attention to codifying some of the most basic structures of international law, structures that had previously been chiefly the realm of customary law or piecemeal bilateral treaties. Among the ILC's earliest projects were the broadly-subscribed Convention on the Continental Shelf,[23] signed in 1958, and related maritime treaties.[24]

With the arrival of the 1960's, the ILC was preparing a set of draft treaties directed to diplomatic relations and other aspects of the relationships between states. The most prominent of these was probably the Vienna Convention on Diplomatic Relations,[25] signed in 1961. It was and remains the basic framework document setting forth the legal rules under which the activities of ambassadors, embassies, and their staffs are conducted. The Vienna Convention on Consular Relations[26] followed, and then in 1969 another signal ILC achievement, the Vienna Convention on the Law of Treaties (the "VCLT"),[27] was signed. (The VCLT was discussed at great length in chapter 5.) The foundational character of all of these treaties was an important stabilizing influence in view of the anxiety surrounding the height of the Cold War.

The ILC has continued on its work through to the present day, and remains one of the most influential bodies in the formulation and advancement of potential rules of international law.

G. The International Committee of the Red Cross (the "ICRC")

The International Committee of the Red Cross (or the "ICRC"), headquartered in Geneva, plays a dominant role in monitoring the development

---

22. A very influential and current example is the ILC's draft articles on state responsibility. *E.g.,* James Crawford, *The International Law Commission's Articles on State Responsibility* (2005).

23. Apr. 29, 1958, 15 U.S.T. 471, 499 U.N.T.S. 311 (entered into force June 10, 1964).

24. *E.g.,* Convention on the Territorial Sea and the Contiguous Zone, Apr. 29, 1958, 15 U.S.T. 1606, 516 U.N.T.S. 205 (entered into force Sept. 10, 1964); Convention on the High Seas, Apr. 29, 1958, 13 U.S.T. 2312, 450 U.N.T.S. 82 (entered into force Sept. 30, 1962).

25. Apr. 18, 1961, 23 U.S.T. 3227, 500 U.N.T.S. 95 (entered into force Apr. 24, 1964).

26. Apr. 24, 1963, 21 U.S.T. 77, 596 U.N.T.S. 261 (entered into force Mar. 19, 1967).

27. May 23, 1969, 1155 U.N.T.S. 331, 8 I.L.M. 679 (entered into force Jan. 27, 1980).

of international humanitarian law. The phrase, "international humanitarian law," describes the set of international law rules regulating the conduct of armed hostilities involving states.[28] These rules address, for example, the treatment of prisoners of war and civilians in occupied territory. Much of the basis of modern international humanitarian law is rooted in the four Geneva Conventions from 1949.[29]

These four basic Geneva Conventions are the Geneva Convention (No. I) for the Amelioration of the Condition of the Wounded and Sick in Armed Forces in the Field, the Geneva Convention (No. II) for the Amelioration of the Condition of Wounded, Sick and Shipwrecked Members of Armed Forces at Sea, the Geneva Convention (No. III) Relative to the Treatment of Prisoners of War, and the Geneva Convention (No. IV) Relative to the Protection of Civilian Persons in Time of War.[30]

The ICRC's role is largely limited to international humanitarian law, and this book is addressed to international law more generally. However, we discuss the ICRC in this chapter because its activities are so pervasive in this particular area, and its work is authoritative. In addition, international humanitarian law in general, and the four Geneva Conventions in particular, play an especially significant part within public international law as a whole.

The depositary for the Geneva Conventions is the government of Switzerland.[31] However, the ICRC maintains a detailed database pertaining to all four

---

28. *E.g.*, Shaw, *supra* note 1, at 1167 (noting that "international law . . . seeks to regulate the conduct of hostilities," adding that such principles "cover, for example, the treatment of prisoners of war, civilians in occupied territory, sick and wounded personnel," etc. and advising that, while this subject area had formerly been referenced as "the laws of war," "[m]ore recently, it has been called international humanitarian law").

29. Some authorities note different historical traditions underlying distinct aspects of international humanitarian law. Two of the most primary examples would be a "Law of The Hague" (referencing legal rules restricting particular classes of weapons and practices) and a "Law of Geneva" (referencing legal rules protecting defined classes of persons). *E.g.*, Frits Kalshoven and Liesbeth Zegveld, *Constraints on the Waging of War* 19–29 (3d ed. 2001). However, later developments with the Geneva Conventions, especially the adoption of their subsequent protocols, have transposed some of the "Law of The Hague," as well as other traditions, into the context of the Geneva documents. *See id.* at 32–34 (noting the "confluence" of the various traditions associated with the development of the protocols).

30. Aug. 12, 1949, 75 U.N.T.S. 31, 75 U.N.T.S. 85, 75 U.N.T.S. 135; 75 U.N.T.S. 287 (all entered into force Oct. 21, 1950).

31. Geneva Convention (I) arts. 55–64; Geneva Convention (II) arts. 54–63; Geneva Convention (III) arts. 133–43; and Geneva Convention (IV) arts. 150–59 (each ascribing detailed responsibilities to the Swiss Federal Council normally undertaken by depositaries in the modern era).

conventions, the three Protocols that have developed pursuant to them,[32] and a large group of related treaties involving international humanitarian law. Also included are codes and secondary materials, such as the 1863 Lieber Code, enforced by the Union Army during the U.S. Civil War. Reference to the ICRC website can be fundamental for researching international humanitarian law.

The ICRC undertakes studies and drafting projects regarding international humanitarian law. A prominent example was its encyclopedic three-volume work, *Customary International Humanitarian Law,* published in 2005.[33] Another example of a publication for interpretive guidance is *Direct Participation in Hostilities,* published in 2009.[34] Such studies and interpretations, given the ICRC's prominence in this area, should certainly qualify as suitable sources for most purposes under Article 38(1)(d).

The 19th edition of the *Bluebook,* in rule 21.13, purports to address citations to ICRC materials. However, the guidance given there is very general and for the most part suggests that citations to ICRC materials be structured analogously to citations for UN materials.

IV. Diplomatic Sources

Diplomatic sources can be useful for establishing either a state practice or *opinio juris* for a potential rule of customary international law. If diplomats of various countries say, for example, in their diplomatic correspondence, that states generally behave in a certain way, this can be evidence for a general state practice. Even more to the point, if diplomats say in their documentary correspondence that international law constrains them in a certain way, that can provide evidence of *opinio juris.* We discuss just some of the most readily available materials.

---

32. Protocol Additional (No. I) to the Geneva Conventions of 12 August 1949, and relating to the Protection of Victims of International Armed Conflicts, June 8, 1977, 1125 U.N.T.S. 3 (entered into force Dec. 7, 1978); Protocol Additional (No. II) to the Geneva Conventions of 12 August 1949, and relating to the Protection of Victims of Non-International Armed Conflicts, June 8, 1977, 1125 U.N.T.S. 609 (entered into force Dec. 7, 1978); Protocol Additional (No. III) to the Geneva Conventions of 12 August 1949, and relating to the Adoption of an Additional Distinctive Emblem, Dec. 8, 2005, 2404 U.N.T.S. 261 (entered into force Jan. 14, 2007).

33. Int'l Comm. of the Red Cross, *Customary International Humanitarian Law* (2005–2009) (by Jean-Marie Henckaerts & Louise Doswald-Beck).

34. Int'l Comm. of the Red Cross, *Direct Participation in Hostilities* (Feb. 2009) (by Nils Melzer).

A. *The Foreign Relations of the United States*

The Foreign Relations of the United States is a series of volumes containing important U.S. diplomatic materials, compiled by the Public Affairs Historian of the Department of State. It is designed to include "all records needed to provide comprehensive documentation of major foreign policy decisions and actions of the United States Government."[35] For the most part it consists of diplomatic correspondence among U.S. embassies, between U.S. embassies and the State Department, among various officers of the State Department, and between U.S. diplomatic officials and diplomatic officials of other countries. The compilation of U.S. diplomatic documents in this form began in 1861, but the series was published under various names until 1947, when the current name was adopted as its primary title. The entire series from 1861 to the present is available on HeinOnline, but many law libraries would carry at least the modern series from 1947 onward.

The State Department Historian chooses successive periods of years into which to divide the coverage of the series. Sometimes there is a rough correspondence between coverage periods and presidential administrations, but not always. The most recent coverage period was 1969–1976, and the most recent coverage period before that was 1964–1968. The first coverage period in the modern series was the single year 1947. Then, for each coverage period, the Historian's staff produces a set of volumes, each volume devoted to a particular foreign-relations issue that was significant during that coverage period. For the 1969–1976 coverage period, there are forty numbered volumes, the fortieth volume being devoted to "Germany and Berlin, 1969–1972." For the 1964–1968 coverage period, there were thirty-four volumes, the first volume being devoted to "Vietnam, 1964," and the thirty-fourth volume being devoted to "Energy Diplomacy and Global Issues."

According to federal law since 1991, and according to the Department's own policies before that, preparation of the series is guided by "the principles of historical objectivity and accuracy; records should not be altered or deletions made without indicating in the published text that a deletion has been made; the published record should omit no facts that were of major importance in reaching a decision; and nothing should be omitted for the purpose of concealing a defect in policy."[36]

Each volume in the modern series begins with a preface describing the issues covered in the volume, a table of contents, an introductory discussion

---

35. 1969–1976, 40 Foreign Relations of the U.S. iii (2007).

36. *Id.; see also* 1947, 1 Foreign Relations of the U.S. iv (1973) (stating virtually the same criteria, as reflected in then-prevailing State-Department policy).

and list of the sources used in compiling the volume, a list of abbreviations used in the volume, and a list of persons referred to in the volume's materials. The tables of contents are of limited utility; they refer only to the pages on which general subject matter divisions begin. The individual items of diplomatic correspondence and other materials making up the volume are not catalogued or listed in the table of contents or at any other point in the volume. Each volume does contain a comprehensive subject index.

The primary use for *The Foreign Relations of the United States* is probably for those working in the field of political foreign relations. However, for a researcher of international law who happens to be working on a subject covered by one of its volumes, the series can be immensely valuable as well. As noted above, the diplomatic correspondence can contain indications of state practice, but also especially indications of what states view to be required by international law. A researcher seeking to determine whether *opinio juris* might exist for a potential rule of customary international law should in many cases consider whether the issues being researched could be covered in one or more of the volumes of *The Foreign Relations of the United States*.

B. *The Public Papers of the Presidents of the United States*

Since the presidency of Herbert Hoover, the Government Printing Office has published detailed volumes of the publicly available official papers pertaining to each presidential administration. Each president is usually accorded between three and twelve volumes, depending upon his length of service and the quantity of documents included. The documents are arranged in chronological order, but there is a very useful subject index at the end of each volume. In addition, a set of cumulative indexes has been published, separately bound for each president, as far as William J. Clinton. There are also helpful appendices in most volumes, including separate lists of press releases, reports, and proclamations.

If a researcher of international law is interested in the U.S. view of the permissibility of a certain act under international law, this series could be an excellent source for the official U.S. position. Many of the documents are issued by the Secretary of State, or senior officers at the State Department. Their statements could often be viewed as authoritative.

C. *Satow's Diplomatic Practice*

This is a single-volume treatise that can provide helpful background for many diplomatic issues. It may also be useful for general legal questions, as much as for discerning customary international law. For example, it has a detailed discussion of ratifications of, and reservations for, treaties and conventions. A current citation would be:

    Satow's Diplomatic Practice (Sir Ivor Roberts ed., 6th ed. 2009).

The *Satow* volume is also useful for any issues that arise concerning diplomatic or consular powers or immunities.

V. Digests

A "digest" is a form of research tool that can still be useful today, but was very important in the years before searchable electronic databases. Digests can still be used in domestic legal research, although for many researchers they can be eclipsed by electronic methods. In the practice of international law in the United States, the availability of current digests has varied from period to period. For about the last twenty years, the U.S. State Department has been maintaining an international law digest, which will be discussed in more detail below. Complete research in an area of public international law can often require reference to this current digest, to the extent the yearly coverage corresponds to the topic being researched. However, international law sources and authorities often refer to earlier State Department digests as well. These are also briefly discussed below.

One useful and modern serial reporter, *International Law Reports*, already introduced in chapter 6, began publication in 1919 as the *Annual Digest of Public International Law Cases*. Publication began under its current title in 1950. It is kept current and retains some of the superficial features of a digest. But, as noted below, it is no longer a "true digest," and it functions more as a standard case reporter than a digest.[37]

First, a general review of what a "true digest" is. Domestic digests in common-law countries generally are devoted to case law. Those who prepare a digest for a particular common-law jurisdiction review all the cases issued by the courts of that jurisdiction on a continual basis. They create brief summaries ("squibs") of every analytical point covered in each case, and each squib closes

---

37. Certain other academic publications may also use the word "Digest" in their title, which are not true digests, but simply academic journals or law reviews of the usual style. The use of the word "Digest" in this context is a matter of journalistic license. *E.g., International Law Digest*, published at Hofstra University in 2002 and renamed the next year as the *Journal of International Business and Law*. Such publications can still be valuable, of course, but they are not true digests as that phrase is described above.

with a citation to the case and the place in the case where the analytical point being summarized in the squib is found. Then, at the end of every year, or tenth year (or other specified time period), all the squibs are compiled into a digest attributed to that time period. Naturally, at the end of every such time period, there are thousands of squibs, each relating to each analytical point made in each case in that jurisdiction during that period.

Each periodically issued digest begins with a subject-matter outline of the jurisprudence covered in the whole series. This outline, called a "digest analysis," breaks down all the subject-matter areas into "bite-size" elements, down to each analytical point found within each subject-matter area. Each analytical point is then assigned a successive section number, according to its position in the digest analysis. Then the bulk of the digest follows: the thousands of squibs accumulated for that period are reproduced in the order of the section numbers attributable to them in the digest analysis.

A researcher in any jurisdiction can review the digest analysis at the beginning of the digest series, go the subject area in the digest analysis that is of interest, find the section number that corresponds to the analytical point he or she wants to investigate, and then go to the volume in the digest that sets out the squibs relating to that section number's analytical point for whatever time period is of interest. The researcher reads the squibs dealing with that point in the digest volume for that period, and then finds the case and citation at the end of each squib. The researcher can also consult the original cases as well.

From the late nineteenth century, the U.S. State Department has sponsored successive versions of an international law digest. Some of the earlier digest series were designed to be complete, while the later series are intended to serve as updates, to be used in conjunction with previously issued series. The earlier series were named for the primary editors engaged by the State Department to oversee their creation. The three earliest major digests completed for the State Department were:

1887	*A Digest of the International Law of the United States (2d ed.)*	(3 volumes)	Francis Wharton
1906	*A Digest of International Law*	(8 volumes)	John Bassett Moore
1940–1944	*Digest of International Law*	(8 volumes)	Green Haywood Hackworth

As is clearly seen, there were substantial time gaps between the coverage periods of these digests. However, in spite of these gaps and in spite of their age, sources and authorities sometimes still reference them. Each of these digests is generally cited and referenced in discussion according to the last name of its editor. (A conversational reference to the last of these digests, for example, would generally be to the "Hackworth Digest.")

In more recent years, the State Department Office of the Legal Advisor has again been publishing digests. For the most part, these bear the title, *Digest of United States Practice in International Law*. Publication details for these newer series are as follows:

1963–1973	*Digest of International Law*	(15 volumes)	Marjorie M. Whiteman
1973–1980	*Digest of United States Practice in International Law*	(8 volumes)	Arthur W. Rovine Eleanor C. McDowell John A. Boyd & Marian Nash
1981–1988	*Cumulative Digest of United States Practice in International Law*	(3 volumes)	Marian Nash
1989–most recent	*Digest of United States Practice in International Law*	(at least 16 volumes)	[various editors]

These more recent digests contain case summaries, but they also contain summations and excerpts of U.S.-government oriented secondary materials. For example, they contain statements made by U.S. representatives to international organizations, U.S. government press releases regarding U.S. government activities and positions touching on international law, reports relevant to international law issues made by U.S. government agencies (especially the State Department) to the U.S. Congress, summations of U.S. court cases with international law aspects, and other similar materials.

These more modern digests can be useful for establishing state practice or *opinio juris* for customary international law, as well as possible authority for general principles of law. The earlier digests can also be useful in the same ways, if their materials are relevant and one wants to establish patterns over long periods of time. Most academic law libraries (and some municipal law libraries) would carry all or most of these digests. The volumes covering 1989 to the present are available on the State Department website.

As we saw at the beginning of this part V, the serial publication, *International Law Reports* (or "ILR"), began as a true digest in 1919, incorporating a formalized digest analysis and section numbers for analytical points. Subsequent volumes initially arranged the cases and other material according to the digest analysis and its section numbers. However, in 1987 (at volume 75), the ILR abandoned its character as a true digest. It stopped using the digest analysis and its section numbers. Instead, each volume of the ILR now contains merely an introductory one-page "List of Main Headings," followed by a list of the cases contained in the volume, catalogued according to the "Main Heading" under which it falls. Although the ILR is a valuable resource, this does not provide the same level of detail as would a true digest. This feature, combined with its annual rather than decennial publication, would make it very cumbersome to use the ILR as one could use a true digest.

In the international context, the 19th edition of the *Bluebook* provides guidance for citations to digests in rule 21.15. Note that the prescribed form can vary according to which time-period series is being referenced.

VI. Academic Journals and Law Reviews; Yearbooks

The largest source of academic commentary on international law is the huge reservoir of academic law journals and law reviews. Many academic law journals and law reviews publish articles on international law, and a large number of them even specialize on international law in general. For example, not only do students at the Harvard Law School publish the *Harvard Law Review*, but they also publish the *Harvard International Law Journal*. Similarly, student editors at the University of Chicago Law School publish both the *University of Chicago Law Review* and the *Chicago Journal of International Law*. Similar publications are produced at many other schools and by many other bodies.

Some academic journals or law reviews specialize on particular areas of international law. For example, currently being published are the *International Trade and Business Law Review*[38] and the *Northwestern Journal of International Law and Business*.[39] At least as a general proposition, articles and essays in journals and law reviews such as these can qualify as source material under Article 38(1)(d) of the ICJ Statute. As long as the content is relevant to the subject being addressed, it should not matter whether the publication itself is reserved for international topics or a single international subject area.

---

38. It is currently edited at the Murdoch University School of Law in Perth, Australia, and (unlike most U.S. academic law reviews) is faculty-edited and juried. It began, under the name of "*International Trade and Business Law Journal*," in 1995 as a publication of the Australian Institute of Foreign and Comparative Law.

39. This journal began publication in 1979.

A. Qualifications to Keep in Mind

Recall that Article 38(1)(d) of the ICJ Statute specifically covers the teachings of only "the most highly qualified publicists of the various nations." This can impose some significant qualifications, depending upon the type of work one is doing.

Traditionally, discussions of international law could be thought of as being either related to *lex lata* or *lex ferenda*. The phrase "*lex lata*" refers to the law that is factually in force in a particular context.[40] The phrase "*lex ferenda*" refers to a proposed law that would be the most desirable to adopt in a particular context.[41] Legal discussions can take either form; some are discussions of *lex lata*, and some are discussions in the nature of *lex ferenda*.

The qualifying language in Article 38(1)(d) specifying "the most highly qualified" publicists, and publicists "of the various nations," should be fairly read strictly for purposes of a *lex lata* discussion. In this context, the more prominent and more accomplished the authors and publications are, the more persuasive any references will be (other things being equal), since the ICJ Statute specifies "the most highly qualified" publicists. Also in the *lex lata* context, a set of several journal and law review articles coming from more than one area of the world should be more persuasive than a set of journal and law review articles all coming from the same country (other things being equal), since the ICJ Statute refers to publicists "of the various nations."

When making an argument in the nature of *lex ferenda*, however, the qualifying language in Article 38(1)(d) should not be read as strictly. When the argument is about what should be, rather than what is, reasonable and persuasive evidence and assertions can come from a broad variety of sources. In this context, one can legitimately feel less constrained in the choice of articles from journals and law reviews.[42]

Additionally, in both the *lex lata* and *lex ferenda* context, a counter-qualification is in order. The intrinsic quality and relevance of an academic article or essay are also very important. So on occasion, even for a *lex lata*

---

40. *E.g.*, Fox, *supra* note 1, at 198 (defining "*lex lata*" as "the law that is in force or applicable to the jurisdiction or situation").

41. *E.g., id.* (defining "*lex ferenda*" as "the law which would be the most desirable to establish").

42. Regarding the distinction between *lex lata* and *lex ferenda* in the context of academic writing on international law, *see* Anthony Aust, *Handbook of International Law* 9 (2d ed. 2010).

claim, it is appropriate to rely on an academic article or essay, if especially proficient and relevant, even if its origin is not as prominent as it might be.

While paying due regard to these considerations, a researcher will have a relatively broad array of articles and essays from academic journals and law reviews from which to choose. The same electronic and hard-copy techniques used for domestic research in these materials can be used for international research.

B. Yearbooks

In view of the qualifications in Article 38(1)(d), and in view of the character of academic authority as a "subsidiary means" for the determination of international law, we will briefly discuss yearbooks, an internationally common type of academic journal. Yearbooks (as the name implies) are published annually, and the most prestigious are published by renowned multilateral bodies.

Most yearbooks contain academic articles and essays of the type normally found in academic journals and law reviews. The subject matter in a given annual issue of a yearbook can sometimes be included for general interest, and need not always pertain to events solely within that annual period. A yearbook published by, or affiliated with, a major international institution may also contain archival or other reference material related to the institution involved. Yearbooks published by, or affiliated with, major international institutions can seem to fulfill the expectation of Article 38(1)(d) that publicists be among those "most highly qualified." In addition, there is the minor inference that a yearbook, which is only published once a year, could contain more selectively accumulated material than journals that publish several times a year.

Here are some examples of prominent yearbooks with institutional affiliations:

Yearbook of the United Nations (1946–present)

Yearbook of the European Convention on Human Rights (1958–present)

Yearbook on Human Rights (1944–1988; published by UN Secretariat)

Yearbook of the International Court of Justice (1946–present)

Yearbook of the International Law Commission (1949–present)

Yearbook of the United Nations Commission on International Trade Law (1968–2009)

Max Planck Yearbook of United Nations Law (1997–present)

At various periods academic groups or institutions outside the United States have produced yearbooks covering international law, attributing the nationality of the group or institution to the yearbook in its title. Some of these are no longer published, but can remain the source of useful material. As with all these publications, the name "yearbook" may or may not appear in the title. Among these "national" yearbooks are:

Australian Year Book of International Law (1965–2008)

British Yearbook of International Law (1920–1973); (2005–present)

Chinese Journal of International Law (2002–present)[43]

German Yearbook of International Law (1948–present)

The suggestion that these yearbooks present a national compendium, in some sense, could be thought to address the Article 38(1)(d) expectation for work of "the most highly qualified publicists," although this suggestion is of course highly subjective. Again, if articles and essays are of high intrinsic quality and especially relevant to the point at issue, they can be valuable even if they do not appear in especially prominent sources.

Finally, there are many other yearbooks published by particular academic institutions, and many yearbooks related to particular subject areas within international law. Examples would include:

Yearbook Commercial Arbitration (1976–present)

Yearbook of International Environmental Law (1990–present)

Yearbook of International, Financial and Economic Law (1996–2007)

Yearbook of International Humanitarian Law (1998–present)

Yearbook of Women's Rights (2001-present)

C. Use of Yearbooks

As a general rule, yearbooks would be used as repositories of information, rather than tools for initial investigation. That is, one would refer to material in them upon coming across a citation to such material, rather than going to them as an initial matter. The exception would be institutional yearbooks, such as the *Yearbook of the United Nations*, or the *Yearbook of the European Convention on Human Rights*, which contain archival and institutional material. If one had a clear idea of what was being sought, including its date of origin, initial recourse to these yearbooks could be productive.

The 19th edition of the *Bluebook* provides guidance for citations to yearbooks in rules 21.7.8 and 21.14.

---

43. A forerunning *Chinese Yearbook of International Law and Affairs* was published in 1981.

VII. Chapter Summary

Article 38(1)(d) of the ICJ Statute directs the court to apply "the teachings of the most highly qualified publicists of the various nations, as subsidiary means for the determination of rules of law." These phrases mostly contemplate treatises published by established commentators on international law. However, the phrases also contemplate other reference works, codifications, academic periodicals, and other materials discussed in this chapter.

On the one hand, these phrases in Article 38(1)(d) encompass a large variety of material, as the coverage of this chapter helps to show. We broadly refer to these different types of materials as "academic, professional, and diplomatic sources." On the other hand, the phrases in Article 38(1)(d) also suggest limitations. First, the language encompasses only works of "the most highly qualified" writers. Second, the language warns that this material is to be used as a "subsidiary means" for determining international law rules. While due regard needs to be paid to these limitations, when particular source material is especially helpful to an advocate's cause, we think it is fair for an advocate to use them. Advocates should be aware that opponents or decision-makers may minimize, to a degree, the weight of these materials. However, some of these materials can also be used as possible sources of state practice and *opinio juris* to show rules of customary international law, and as sources for general principles of law.

Academic treatises originally formed the basis for the historical law of nations. The classic treatises are sometimes still cited today, but contemporary works are more useful. The most helpful, such as those listed in this chapter, are encyclopedic in character, comprehensive, authored by prominent academic writers, generally available, reasonably recent, general in scope, and reasonably succinct.

Academic and professional organizations also produce works that qualify within this category of sources. For example, the American Law Institute (the "ALI") has produced its *Restatement of the Law (Third): The Foreign Relations Law of the United States*. This is the most helpful source published by the ALI specifically regarding public international law. The *Third Restatement* often carries authoritative weight because of the prestige and background of the ALI and its members, who are chiefly academics, judges, and prominent practitioners. References to the *Third Restatement* may be more frequent in discussions within and by legal institutions in the United States. However, it will sometimes receive some recognition outside the United States.

Another example of an academic organization is the *Institut de droit international* (the "IDI," or "International Law Institute"). It is a private membership organization consisting of international law specialists from around the world.

It works in small-group "commissions" preparing draft resolutions designed to promote the progressive development of international law. The IDI's resolutions are issued in the form of deliberative resolutions, such as a debating society might produce.

Still another academic organization is The Hague Academy of International Law, which organizes advanced courses in international law every summer. The speakers for these courses produce monographs memorializing their lectures, and the monographs are published in an influential periodical known mostly by its French name, the *Recueil des cours* (translatable as "Collected Courses").

UNIDROIT (the International Institute for the Unification of Private Law) is a multilateral international organization, currently composed of sixty-three states parties. It issues draft international conventions for adoption by states, and also sometimes "principles" that are not meant to be binding international agreements, but rather to be general guides to behavior. A prominent example is the UNIDROIT Principles of International Commercial Contracts. UNIDROIT is exclusively concerned with private international law.

The American Society of International Law is a private membership organization headquartered in Washington D.C. Two of its most prominent periodicals are *International Legal Materials* and the *American Journal of International Law*. At its website, it maintains helpful electronic resources, such as the Electronic Information System for International Law, the Electronic Resource Guide for international law, and the i-LEX database for case-law and other authority based in U.S. sources.

The International Law Commission is a subsidiary body of the UN General Assembly, discussed in chapters 5, 8, and 9 of this book. It prepares draft treaties that can function both toward the progressive development of international law and the codification of customary international law. It also sometimes produces written "principles" or "articles" of international law that can have a constructive effect for development and codification.

The International Committee of the Red Cross (the "ICRC") plays a very substantial role in the monitoring, development, and codification of modern international humanitarian law. While the Swiss government is technically the depositary for the four 1949 Geneva Conventions, the ICRC maintains on its website a detailed database pertaining to them and many other treaties and documents regarding international humanitarian law. Studies and interpretations by the ICRC should certainly qualify as sources for most purposes under Article 38(1)(d).

Diplomatic sources can be useful for establishing either state practice or *opinio juris* for rules of customary international law. A detailed source of U.S. diplomatic correspondence is *The Foreign Relations of the United States*. It provides comprehensive documentation of major foreign policy decisions of the U.S. government.

There is also a published series of *The Public Papers of the Presidents of the United States*, beginning with Herbert Hoover. These can be useful for establishing official U.S. positions on questions of international law. Finally, the single-volume *Satow's Diplomatic Practice* provides helpful background for issues of diplomatic and consular immunities.

Digests can be a potentially useful source for deriving state practice or *opinio juris* for customary international law rules, and also for discerning general principles of law. There have been several digest series published by U.S. authorities since the nineteenth century. Although there have been gaps in coverage over the years, some of the older digests are still sometimes cited by authorities and advocates. There is a current digest series, published by the U.S. State Department's Office of the Legal Advisor, which started in 1989 and has continued through the present.

The largest quantity of sources of academic commentary on international law is found in academic law journals and law reviews. Some journals and law reviews focus specifically on international law, while still others focus even more narrowly on specific sub-areas within international law. However, even the general-interest journals and law reviews often contain high-quality articles on international law.

For making assertions regarding "*lex lata*," or international law as it exists, the more prominent and more influential the authors and publications are, the more persuasive the reference to journal and law review articles will be. For making assertions regarding "*lex ferenda*," or the law that would be most desirable, the concern for prominence and influence could be somewhat less.

Yearbooks can also be a good source of academic commentary. They are published by international organizations, legal practice groups or publishers in other countries, and particular academic institutions.

VIII. Chapter Review Questions

1. Article 38(1)(d) of the ICJ Statute refers to "the teachings of the most highly qualified publicists of the various nations, as subsidiary means for the determination of rules of law." What types of materials are mostly contemplated by these phrases?

2. The language in the ICJ Statute referencing the use these materials suggests certain limitations on their use. What are some of these limitations?

3. What are some of the characteristics to look for to determine which academic treatises are most helpful sources?

4. What is a helpful source, for research in public international law, produced by the American Law Institute (or "ALI")?

5. When the IDI (the *Institut de droit international*, or International Law Institute) publishes a resolution, in what form is the resolution issued?

6. The Hague Academy of International Law publishes a multi-volume periodical called the *Recueil des cours* (or "Collected Courses"). What do the volumes in this periodical contain?

7. With what particular subject area is UNIDROIT exclusively concerned?

8. What are two periodicals published by the American Society of International Law?

9. The International Law Commission (or "ILC") prepares draft treaties. It also sometimes produces other written materials that can have a constructive effect for development and codification. What are general descriptive terms for two kinds of these other written materials?

10. When the International Committee of the Red Cross produces studies and interpretations, what would be significant about them under Article 38(1)(d) of the ICJ Statute?

11. What types of documents are contained in *The Foreign Relations of the United States*?

12. What governmental body in the United States publishes the most recent digest series?

13. In what type of publication is found the largest quantity of academic commentary on international law?

14. What is the difference between "*lex lata*" and "*lex ferenda*," and how might it influence research in sources described in this chapter?

15. What are several types of entities that publish "yearbooks" that would be of use to research in international law?

IX. Additional Resources and General Bibliographic References

Anthony Aust, *Handbook of International Law* (2d ed., Cambridge University Press 2010).

Robert J. Beck, "International Law and International Relations Scholarship," in *Routledge Handbook of International Law* 13–43 (David Armstrong ed., New York: Routledge 2009).

Morris L. Cohen, "International Law Treatises in Early America," in *Essays in Honor of Jan Stepan on the Occasion of his Eightieth Birthday* 321 (Jarmila Bednarikova, Frank Chapman eds., Zurich: Schulthess Polygraphischer Verlag 1994). This source is also commonly referenced by its German title: *Festschrift fur Jan Stepan zum 80. Geburtstag.*

Peter Hippold, *What Role for Academic Writers in Interpreting International Law?*, 8 Chinese J. Int'l L. 291 (2009).

Robert Jennings & Arthur Watts, *Oppenheim's International Law* (9th ed., London: Longman's 1992).

Charlotte Ku & Paul F. Diehl, *International Law: Classic and Contemporary Readings* (3d ed., Boulder, Colo.: Lynne Rienner Publishers 2009).

Peter Macalister-Smith & Joachim Schwietzke, *Bibliography of the Textbooks and Comprehensive Treatises on Positive International Law of the 19th Century*, 3 J. Hist. Int'l L. 75–142 (2001).

Jan Paulsson, "Scholarship as Law," in *Looking to the Future: Essays on International Law in Honor of W. Michael Reisman* 183 (Mahnoush H. Arsanjani, Jacob K. Cogan, Robert D. Sloane & Siegfried Wiessner eds., Leiden: Martinus Nijhoff 2010).

See generally Classics of International Law (a series of 22 titles published in 40 books by the Publications of the Carnegie Endowment for International Peace, originally produced from 1911 to 1916 and edited by James Brown Scott, reprinted by William S. Hein & Co. in 1995). Each title in the series is generally devoted to the work of a single classical author on international law.

See generally United Nations Audiovisual Library, *Scholarly Writings in International Law* (HeinOnline), http://heinonlinebackup.com/HOLtest/UNLAV (last visited April 17, 2013).

About the Authors

Anthony S. Winer is a Professor of Law at William Mitchell College of Law in Saint Paul, Minnesota. He teaches courses in U.S. constitutional law, public international law, and related subjects. With Mary Ann Archer, he devised the public international law research curriculum used at William Mitchell. He received his A.B. degree from the University of California at Berkeley, his J.D. from the University of Chicago Law School, and his LL.M. from the New York University School of Law. Prior to entering teaching, Professor Winer practiced law with a prominent agency of the U.S. government in Washington, D.C., and also worked in private practice for law firms in New York City, Paris, and Athens. He has lectured throughout the United States, and also in Mexico, France, the United Kingdom, and Turkey. He also has substantial experience with legal academic work in the South Caucasus region, including service as a Fulbright Scholar in Baku for the 2008–2009 academic year.

Mary Ann E. Archer served for ten years as the Associate Director for Public Services of the Warren E. Burger Law Library at William Mitchell College of Law. During the closing portion of that period, she also served as Interim Director of the Library. With Professor Winer, she helped develop the public international law research curriculum used at William Mitchell. She received her J.D. from William Mitchell and her M.S. in Library and Information Science from the State University of New York, Geneseo. Since retirement from William Mitchell in 2010, she has undertaken several ongoing bibliographic projects. Primarily among these is a historical compilation of bibliographic data, covering 1947 to the present, on U.S. violations of the UN Charter's prohibition of armed intervention.

Lyonette Louis-Jacques is the Foreign and International Law Librarian at the D'Angelo Law Library, University of Chicago Law School. She has written and presented on researching human rights law, international trade law, sources on careers in international law, finding legal resources on the Internet, use of new and emerging technologies in law libraries, and digital collections of foreign, comparative, and international law. She is co-founder (with Mila Rush) of INT-LAW, an electronic conference for the discussion of issues related to foreign, comparative, and international legal (FCIL) resources. She is a "Legal Information" columnist for the Slaw.ca blog.

Index

A

academic and professional organizations, 242–51

academic writings
  journals and law reviews, 257
  qualifications regarding *lex lata vs. lex ferenda,* 258–59
  for researching reservations, 119
  as sources of law, 74–75, 239–42
  treatises, 241–42

acceptance of consent to be bound by conventions, 89

accessions to conventions, 89

African Court on Human and People's Rights, 130

agreements, executive, 85–86

Alabama Claims arbitration of 1874, 45, 138

ambassadors. *See* Diplomatic affairs; Diplomatic immunity

American International Law Cases (American ILC), 140

American Journal of International Law, 247

American Law Institute (ALI), 242–43

American Society of International Law (ASIL), 111, 113–14, 247

ancient Greece. *See* Classical Greek law

annexes of UN resolutions, 152–54, 169–70

Annual Digest of International Law, The. See International Law Reports (ILR)

approval of consent to be bound by conventions, 89

Aquinas, St. Thomas, 27–28

arbitrations, 137–39
  definition of, 137
  League of Nations and, 55
  during Middle Ages, 25
  during nineteenth century, 45
  research of, 144–45

Article II treaties, 85–88. *See also* Treaties

Asakura v. City of Seattle, 129n

Asylum case (Colombia v. Peru), 177, 181

Augustine, St., 27

Australian Treaty Series, 111

authorities. *See* International law, sources of

Avalon Project website, 115

B

Bahrain, Qatar v. See Maritime Delimitation and Territorial Questions

269

S

sales publications, UN, 234
Satow's Diplomatic Practice, 253–54
Sawyer, Youngstown Sheet & Tube Co. v., 86*n*
scholarly articles. *See* Academic writings
Seattle, City of, Asakura v., 129*n*
Secretary-General, UN. *See* UN Secretary-General
secularism, 30–34
Security Council, UN. *See* UN Security Council
session law volumes, 106
signatory states, 91
signature dates of conventions, 91, 92
signatures of convention, 88
Sixth Committee of UN General Assembly, 160–61
social contract, 36
soft law, 84–85, 199–201
sole (presidential) executive agreements, 85–86
sovereignty, 30
squibs, 254–55
stare decisis, 133
state
    contracting, 90–91
    definitions of, 3*n*, 8*n*
    depositary, 93*n*, 118–19
state of nature, 36–37
state practice, 177–79, 183–84
state sovereignty, 30
states parties, 91
Status of Treaties database, 109
statutes, 12, 14*n*
Statutes at Large, 106
Suárez, Francisco, 29–30
Switzerland, Belilos v., 96*n*, 99*n*

T

Temple of Preah Vihear (Cambodia v. Thailand), 136*n*
Thailand, Cambodia v. See *Temple of Preah Vihear*
Third Restatement, 242–43
Thirty Years' War, 34
TIAS series, 107
TIF. *See Treaties in Force* (TIF)
Timberland Lumber Co. v. Bank of America, 7–8, 7*n*
treaties. *See also* Reservations
    bilateral, 82, 91–92, 94
    citations for, 119–20
    conventions *vs.,* 83
    definition of, 81
    executive agreements *vs.* Article II, 85–86
    historical development of, 42–44
    labels for, 86–87
    multilateral, 82, 91–92
    nature of, 79–82
    non-binding agreements *vs.,* 84–85
    ratification of, 87–92
    research of
        electronic searches, 104
        international organizations' collections, 113
        other English-language collections, 113–14
        tools, 103–4
        treaties prior to 1945, 114–15
        treaties to which U.S. is a party, 104–8
        United Nations Treaty collections, 109–10
        websites, 110–12
    statute- *vs.* contract-like nature of, 79–80